TONY DEMEO'S

TRIPLE GUN OFFENSE:

AN EVOLUTION OF OPTION FOOTBALL

BY TONY DEMEO

Want to Watch the Video?

Go to the Appendix in the back of the book to find scannable QR codes for over 100 plays discussed in this book.

ABOUT THIS BOOK

Introduction to this Book

This book is basically my journey through option football and how the Option Offense has evolved over the years. I let you know where my ideas about option football came from and the coaches that influenced my offensive thinking over the 40 years I spent coaching college football.

The Option Offense in College Football has been a transformational offense. By that I mean that every breakthrough in the use of the option has transformed the team that made the breakthrough but also the rest of college football was changed forever. This makes the Option unique among every other offensive system. Whether it is The Wing T, The Air Raid Offense, The Run and Shoot none have made the impact on College Football like the Option.

What I am trying to do in this book is to show how the system of Option Football evolved over the years and how a young football coach grew with it and combined it with various threads of different systems to develop his own system of offensive football and then completely redo it a second time!

The book is divided into two parts. The first part is about under center option football and those concepts are relevant today. Also, I cover the under-center pass game which included early RPOs. I explain how my two week visit with Darrell Royal and his staff at The University of Texas was my launching pad into option football. So, if you're a Flex-bone guy or another under center coach, you would get some ideas on the under-center option and how to add a simple passing game to it. Chapter Two is a great chapter for under-center option guys, especially the section on "Opening Up the Bone". There are some unique things we did that you could incorporate into your offense.

I also try to give the reasons for some of the changes we made in our approach to Option football. The "Why" is a very important ingredient to putting together an offensive strategy. If you are an under-center option guy with no desire to go to the Gun, I guarantee you'll pick up some ideas to add to your under-center attack.

The second part of the book is the evolution from the under-center option (The Multi-Bone Offense) to The Triple Gun Offense. The Triple Gun Offense is an entire offense based on "Strategic Flexibility" where one play can morph into another play based on defensive reaction. It's football Jazz. It's freedom within structure. Every run contains a pass, and every pass contains a run.

In this section, we will teach you the plays of The Triple Gun Offense, how to teach them and how to game plan them. But this book is unique because every play has an accompanying video so you can see it run during a game. It is an Interactive Book! So, you can read about the play then see a video on the play right in the book.

How to Use this Interactive Book to Win Games

The Evolution of Option Football is a completely interactive book with videos as part of the book that you can go to while reading about the actual play. So the temptation is going to be that you just watch video. You can do that and be entertained and not really get all this book provides. Here's my advice:

1. Read the book first to understand the concepts. I give the source of each play and how I incorporated it into one offense. Once you get the concept of "Strategic Flexibility" everything will fall into place. Bruce Lee said you should attack like water, always adapting to your opponent.

2. Study the section on Meaningful Stats. Reflect on your own experiences. How do your wins and losses fit in with The Meaningful Stat Matrix?

3. Next, go through the book to study each play. Know the "Why of the play" see how it fits in with the core plays. Study the diagrams especially the blocking schemes. Every play in your offensive package should be there for a specific reason or answer a defensive tactic.

4. Then watch the video to actually see the play executed. Look at both the wide Copy and End Zone copy. Review the video any time that play comes up.

5. Get a sense of the Tactics of The Triple Gun Offense. Get a handle on Clock Control. Learn how to put the clock on your side.

6. Go through the Game Planning Chapter and match it up with your opponent's defenses. See exactly what your mode of attack vs all the standard defenses

This process will help you get the most out of this interactive Evolution of the Option because you'll understand the "Why" of every aspect of the offense. Once you understand the offense conceptually it will be easy to adapt to your style.

Foreword

I've known Tony DeMeo for 20 years, and in that time, I've observed him as not only an innovator, but an excellent teacher of the game. This book is a holistic overview of option football from the Wishbone, to the Flexbone, to the Triple Gun. Tony not only shares his ideas but explains where they originated from and who's influenced his thinking.

"Tony DeMeo's Triple Gun Offense: An Evolution of Option Football" book gives you the fundamental keys necessary to follow the evolution of this offense over time. Coach's innovative approach combined the passing game with the option, making his offense especially difficult to defend. The interactive approach of this book will allow readers to see the diagram of a play while simultaneously watching a video clip that complements the text. Whether you're looking to implement an option offense, defend against one, or just gain a better understanding of the game there's something in this book for everyone.

James Franklin

Head Football Coach

Penn State University

Chapter 1
Learning Option Football: The Beginning
How I Fell in Love with Option Football

So how did a guy from New York get involved with Option Football? It started when I was in grammar school watching Bud Wilkinson's Split T on a New Year's Day Bowl Game beat their opponent. I thought this must be the magic of winning football games.

Of course, running back Prentis Gautt may have had a little to do with it. He was the 1959 Orange Bowl MVP. Bud Wilkinson was considered by many to be the #1 College Football coach in the country in the 1950s. He had an unbelievable 47 game winning streak which is still a record to this day. He finished his career with a 145 – 29 – 4 record and 3 National Championships.

The offense Coach Wilkinson ran was The Split T which featured a Dive Option with a lead blocker and was the father of The Wishbone and Split Back Veer Offenses. I learned later that Wilkinson borrowed The Split T from Don Faurot, the Head Coach at The University of Missouri where he developed The Split T in 1941. The early option was a Double Option, pitch or keep, there was not a dive read. The Dive was a separate play.

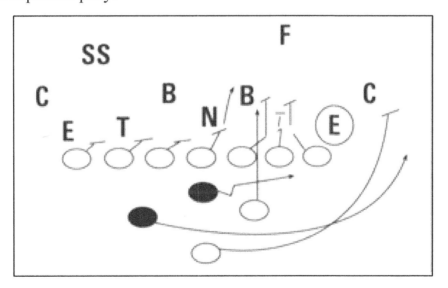

I forgot about the option for a while because my high school ran The Delaware Wing T & I played a Wing. There was no hint of any option football. In college we ran

The I formation with no options either, but I was becoming interested in coaching, so I started to pay more attention to what was trending in the college game.

I realized that an Option Offense is a "Transformative Offense" – The Split T at Oklahoma under Head Coach Bud Wilkinson became unbeatable. The Sooners had a 47 Game Win Streak and OU had never experienced that kind of success before.

The Split Back Veer

Bill Yeoman is generally considered the inventor of The Split Back Veer Offense at the University of Houston. The Coogs were coming off a 2-6-1 season in 1964 and managed to score barely 100 points and Coach Yeoman's seat was heating up. This the third disappointing season for Yeomen. Then with speedster Warren McVea joining the Varsity, Yeomen tweaked the Split T and told the O-line "to get out of the way" and the Triple Option was born in the spring of 1965.

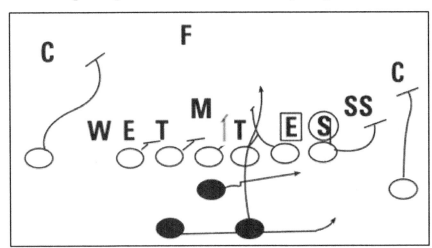

So Yeoman's Split Back Veer took a Double Option and made it a Triple Option and this was the next major development in Option Football. It transformed The Houston Cougars from a cupcake to an Offensive juggernaut.

The Coogs started out in 1965 1-4 and scored only 40 points. Yeoman felt his offensive line could not handle the defenses they faced so he went exclusively to his new Veer. His career and College Football changed forever the day Houston upset Ole Miss with a 17-3 victory running the Split Back Veer. The next week UH upset #8 Kentucky 38-21. They ended the season with a 4-5-1 record. In 1966. UH finished 8-2, and as they say the rest is history.

Bill Yeoman went on to a Hall of Fame career & changed football forever. His final record with UH was 160 – 108 – 8. The success of UH got me interested in the Veer as I was starting to think seriously about coaching football. Later in my career I had the pleasure of speaking on Option Football at one of Coach Yeoman's clinics in Atlanta in 1990 & then spent the entire afternoon using up all the napkins in Atlanta talking ball with The Father of The Veer.

The Wishbone

The next Option Offense to explode on the scene also came from The Lone Star State. It was called The Wishbone.

The Wishbone added a lead blocker to either side by having 3 backs in the backfield. This really created problems for defenses playing "The Monster Defense" - a 5-2 front with the Strong Safety rolled up to the field.

There's a lot of discussion on the inventor of The Wishbone. Was it Texas Head Coach Darrell Royal or his Offensive Coordinator Emory Bellard? My guess it was a combination of both.

How did it come about? In 1968 Texas had come off 3 subpar seasons and despite having great athletes, were not scoring points. In 1967 they averaged only 18 points per game. So in the spring of 1968, Coach Royal installed The Wishbone Offense which featured 2 Halfbacks and a Fullback in the Backfield. After starting out the 1968 season 0-1-1 The Longhorns went on a 30 game winning streak, a National Championship and 6 straight Southwest Conference Championships! I would say The Wishbone transformed Texas from mediocrity back to National prominence.

The Wishbone also transformed Alabama's football team under legendary coach Bear Bryant. After 2 very mediocre seasons losing 10 games Bear switched to the Wishbone and from 1971 to 1982 won Three National Championships and Nine SEC Championships!

The Wishbone also transformed The Oklahoma Sooners again in 1971. The Sooners had been mired in mediocrity since Bud Wilkinson's retirement but in 1971, the Sooners offensive coordinator, Barry Switzer, installed The Bone with Jack Mildren at Quarterback and speedsters Joe Wylie and Greg Pruit at Halfbacks and they went 11-1! Switzer became the Head Coach in 1973 and he rode the Wishbone to 3 National Championships and 12 Big 8 Championships. His final record at OU was 157- 29–4.

As an aspiring, young football coach, I was really intrigued with this offense because it seemed so simple and it seemed like Texas always had the ball. I played in college for a coach, Ben Bedini, who preached ball control and clock control with the zeal of an evangelist. "If we have the ball, they can't score" We didn't run the option but controlled the clock with the I formation. But it seemed to me that The Wishbone was the formation to take ball control to the next level. I would be investigating the Wishbone after graduation.

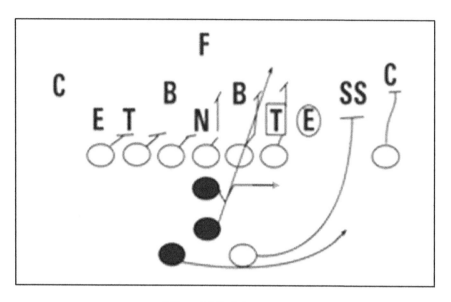

The Wishbone

The Eyes of Texas upon Me

After graduating from Iona College, I wanted to pursue a career of coaching football but how do I get started? So I went back to my high school coach, Augie Auteri for advice. He suggested that I help him out, which I did. After the season, he told me that he wanted to run The Wishbone. So I wrote a letter to Darrell Royal for advice. Coach Royal invited me down to their spring practice and down I went.

Coach Royal could not have been more welcoming. He introduced me to his staff and they were just as welcoming. They opened their meetings, film room and all their practice sessions to me. I took 9 legal pads of notes in the 2 weeks I was there. It was like going to graduate school for football. Knowing the plays of the Wishbone was merely scratching the surface of this offense (or any offense). At Texas I learned HOW to do it and HOW to teach it. I learned that the difference is in the DETAILS. The value of maximum reps was hammered home to me. I also figured out that the fewer the plays you ran, the more reps each play could be given. What an experience for a guy just starting his coaching career. I was sold on The Wishbone. I was all set to implement The Wishbone when fate intervened.

My Option Sabbatical

When I returned from my trip to Texas, I had two job offers to be an assistant coach. One was from Fordham University and the other from Pace University. I knew both Head Coaches well and couldn't go wrong with either. Neither program ran the option, but The New York Giants trained at Pace University and that was the deciding factor. By going to Pace, I could study Coach Bill Arnsparger and learn from the Giants program as well as from the Pace staff. So for the next 2 years I shadowed Bill Arnsparger.

In the meantime, I turned to coaching books to further my option knowledge. The first was Jake Gaither's Split Line T. Gaither's Florida A & M teams were rolling up big scores and I was curious how. That was my first introduction to using line splits to enhance your offense and make the offensive line more productive.

The second book I absorbed was Homer Rice's book: Homer Rice On Option Football. This book was extremely important to me because it was the first time I had ever heard about combining the option and the passing game. This was revolutionary! The 1968 University of Cincinnati Bearcats went 5-4-1 led by dual threat Quarterback Greg Cook who threw for an amazing 554 yards in one game while running the Split Back Veer! This book opened my imagination. Coach Rice ran the Split Back Veer with 3 wide Receivers which really opened up the pass game. A defense could not stop both the pass and the option. The QB could check to a pass vs a loaded box or to a run vs covered up Wide Receivers. Years later I met and talked option football with Coach Rice who graciously sent me a signed copy of this book. So, Homer Rice ran an Option Offense that was really a pass first, option second offense.

The third book that was a big influence in forming my early philosophy of football was: Installing the Wishbone T Attack by Pepper Rodgers and Homer Smith. Pepper was the Head Coach at UCLA & Homer Smith was his Offensive Coordinator. This book was an outstanding text on The Wishbone. I got to know Homer Smith when he was the Head Coach at Army and learned a lot about run/pass balance. This book is the most detailed football book I ever read. Homer Smith was a great teacher of the game.

Miles Davis and Strategic Flexibility

As I was studying the game of football and pouring over all the notes I had accumulated, I asked myself why certain offenses are more effective than others. What caused an offense to be productive? Obviously the number one reason was the players. With good players, offenses will move the ball – simple. But wait a minute, Bill Yeomen had the same players prior to going to the Split Back Veer and went 2-6-1 before breaking loose. Darrell Royal had a stellar backfield in 1967 and averaged only 18 points per game prior to his record-breaking run with the Wishbone.

And finally, Vince Lombardi took the 1-10-1 Green Bay Packers to a winning season in one season and to an 89-29-4 record and he did not run the option. What was the commonality in these programs' turnaround? What did Lombardi's Offense have in common with the Triple Option Teams?

The answer is the Green Bay Sweep, the Packers core play, changes AFTER the snap of the ball. Vince Lombardi coined the "Run to Daylight" which is the reason the Sweep made such an impact. The Sweep could go around the end, off tackle or up the middle based on the way the defense is blocked. As long as the O. Line keeps a hat on a hat the play will grind out first downs. Lombardi also added the Halfback Pass off the Sweep to further threaten the defense. Watching Paul Hornung run the Lombardi Sweep was a thing of beauty. Hornung improvised on every sweep based on the defensive reaction.

The Triple Option from either The Split Back Veer or The Wishbone also changes AFTER the snap based on the defense. But instead of the Halfback running to daylight, the play changes based on the Quarterback's reads. He can give the ball to the dive back, keep it on the edge or pitch it to a trailing Halfback. The Split Back Veer guys also added a Dump Pass where the QB reads the SS & either pitches or passes to a wide Receiver. Sounds like RPO.

The other way to adjust the play is a "Check with me system" where the Quarterback has a package of plays that he can pick from based on the defensive alignment. This changes the play BEFORE the snap which is not as effective.

I likened the plays that change AFTER the snap as structured improvisation like Miles Davis playing jazz trumpet. You know the song, but he never plays it the same way – freedom within structure. I call it: Strategic Flexibility. This became the principle behind all my offensive thinking the principle behind all my offensive thinking.

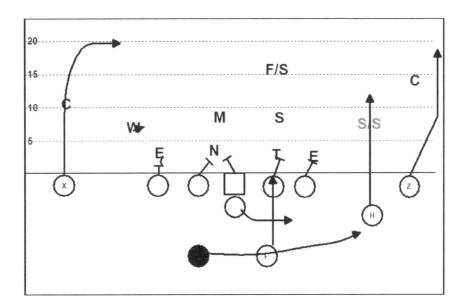

Running the Wishbone

After 2 years coaching at Pace University for Head Coach George Maier & being a student of the game, fate dropped a big bombshell in my lap. My alma mater, Iona College was searching for a Head Coach after coming off the worst season in the school's history (3-6). After being turned by legitimate candidates, Iona contacted me and I became the youngest Head College Football Coach in the nation!

Now I was going to turn all the offensive knowledge I accumulated loose on Iona's opponents. There was only one tiny problem – there was no Quarterback on the team! This severely limited what we could do offensively. The answer was: The Wishbone.

Now I had to think like a Head Coach and not an assistant. Being so young, I knew it was important to have early success so I'd be around a second year and build our talent pool. Without an experienced quarterback, we were not going to win many shoot outs, so we had to play great defense and control the clock on offense. We put a Free Safety at QB, Pat Garvey, who was smart and could read the Triple.

THE WISHBONE

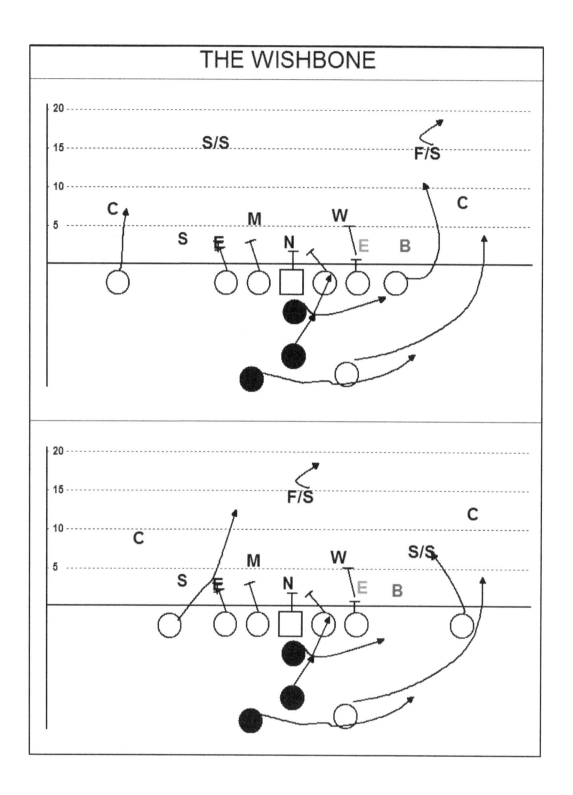

The idea was to keep it simple: The Triple Option, The Belly and the fullback cutback. A couple of Play Action Passes and no turnovers.

Wishbone Belly

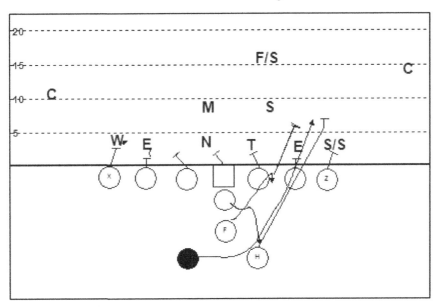

Belly Pass

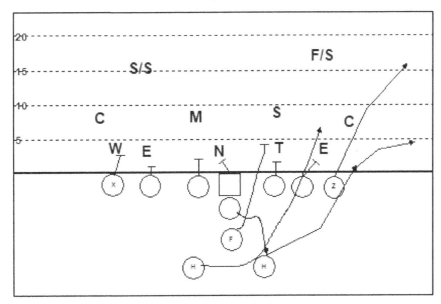

The league picked us dead last, but we actually finished tied for second and played for the Championship in the ninth game of the season. We didn't score many points but we were on the field wearing out the grass the majority of the time and killing the clock. I learned a lot that year and most of it from an unlikely source.

Hello Jimmy V

When I got the job at Iona, I was given a cubicle next to the new Head Basketball Coach. He was a young, gregarious Italian and we hit it off immediately (I wonder why). His name was Jim Valvano but he liked to be called "V" and he was a great source of advice whether I wanted it or not. He taught me some of the most valuable lessons on winning that stuck with me my whole career and were responsible for many wins. Here is a list of The Valvano Principles:

1. Every game whether Basketball, Football or Parcheesi has a formula for winning and as head coach, you are responsible for finding it.
2. He who controls the pace wins the race. If you are facing a more talented team, you have to slow the game down and shorten the game. Play 4 corners. Reduce the amount of time you actually play. Use the clock, it's your friend. This was a critical principle that really helped me in my first year at Iona. We slowed the game to a crawl. As a lover of offensive football, I had to put my ego on a shelf and keep the game low scoring.
3. The only lead that matters is the one at the end of the game. This one also was a big help over the years but especially that first year at Iona. We conditioned the team very hard and I coined the mantra "The Fourth Quarter is ours" so basically if we were at least within striking distance we could pull the game out in the fourth quarter. If a team is a big favorite and you're still close in the 4th Quarter, they tend to panic. That first year we won 4 games in the last 2 minutes of the game
4. If you have a superior team, accelerate the pace – make the play! That happened in my later years at Iona.

Jim Valvano knew how to win and he was a big help teaching me how to approach a game and the importance of **The Clock**.

As he was well known for saying, "He who controls the pace wins the race."

Breaking the Bone and Other Changes

After running The Wishbone for a year and having great success in turning the program around, I realized some weaknesses in The Wishbone I was running. The biggest ones were:

1. We couldn't handle long yardage situations. 3rd & 7+ were disasters.
2. Though we could shorten the game, we could not lengthen it. Comeback situations were very difficult.
3. We had a non-effective two-minute offense
4. Very difficult to pass with 3 Backs in the backfield.
5. I wanted the best athlete at Quarterback not just the best reader, so we had to simplify reading the mesh.
6. Defenses were loading the box to stop the run. We had to have a more threatening pass attack.

I got to know Homer Smith the author of one of my sabbatical books and considered him to be an offensive genius. He had left UCLA and was now the Head Coach at Army. I got to know him attending press luncheons and he was friendly and helpful at all times. So I told him my thoughts about passing more from The Wishbone. He told me to eliminate the triple option and use double options and pass. But you can't throw and run the triple. It would take too much practice time. Now at this time, holding was illegal. You couldn't pass protect using your hands. So pass protection was much more difficult.

After getting Coach Smith's advice, I knew we could run the Triple Option AND throw the ball IF:

1. We simplified the Triple Option and made it easier to execute.
2. We reduced the number of runs in the offense.
3. We installed a simple pass game.
4. We had to use more formations that employ 3 Wide Receivers but substituting a Wide Receiver for a HB, we could reduce the number of things the HBs had to learn.
5. Regardless of the formation, we had to be able to run The Triple Option from it.
6. We had to learn more about extending the game and how to finish the game when we had a lead.

So we had a plan to adapt the base Wishbone into a more flexible Multi-Bone that would best fit our move toward a more balanced offensive attack. This would keep defenses from zeroing in on a one-dimensional offense.

Multiple Formations. The first step in the Wishbone transformation was to add formations because this is the easiest of the steps. You don't have to execute a formation. You just have to line up.

The first variation was subbing a Tight End for a Split End. This was called Tight. This formation was used in short yardage situations to add a gap to the defensive front. We liked to use The Belly Series from this set and The Toad Triple (TE Load) where the TE blocks the end man on the line of scrimmage.

The second formation added was a Split End subbing for a TE which we called Wide. This set was used to throw the Double Post Route vs a 3 Deep Defense. Of course you could still run the Triple from this set as well.

Wishbone Double Post

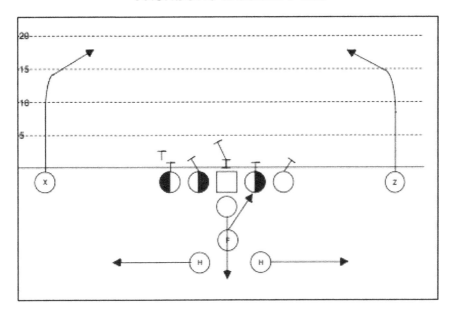

Next, we subbed a Wide Receiver for a Halfback to come up with Twins. This is the base set of the Split Back Veer teams. This set added a lot to the Multi-Bone because it created problems for 8 man front teams that we were seeing a lot. The Dump Concept stolen from The Split Back Veer was tough on a Strong Safety. The O. Line base blocked the Front and the QB faked the dive the read the SS. If the SS covered the WR, the QB pitched it but if the SS played run the QB threw to the WR. The WR showed block to the SS to lure him up then released by him and looked for the ball. An RPO before RPOs existed.

Homer Rice Influence

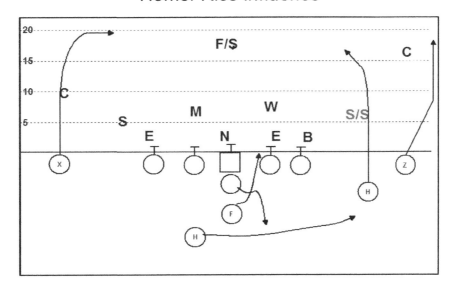

If we were in a long yardage situation or obvious pass situation, we added a third Wide Receiver and called Wide Twins. From this set we could run a little more of Homer Rice's pass game. Adding the word Heavy put the HB to the same side as the Twins and gave us the set to Sprint Out from.

The new formations made us more flexible but we always had the capability of running The Triple Option to either side. We never moved the Fullback because we wanted the mesh to be constant. Our passing game would grow exponentially just by getting a third receiver on the line of scrimmage. But Homer Smith's warning about practice time called for simplification.

Simplify Quarterback Play. To simplify the Triple Option, the position to focus on was The Quarterback. The rest of the positions are already simple they just have to be mastered.

The Footwork. Changing the first step by the Quarterback was very important to simplification process. Most option teams teach the QB to step back at a 45-degree angle so the QB could give the dive back a good ride. However, by doing this, the QB's eyes came off the read key. So, we had him step back but he had to have his toes pointing to the sidelines. Basically, a parallel step. This way his eyes never left the read key. The result - more accurate reads.

Thought Process. "I'm giving the ball every time *unless* the Hand Off Key comes down flat and hard on the Dive" The Hand Off Key's Head has to come in FRONT of the Fullback for it to be a pull read. We wanted the read to be a Quick Read made on the QB's first step. NEVER RIDE AND DECIDE. BETTER WRONG THAN LONG. This was sacrilegious at the time so why change this.

1. The longer the read, the more time for the defense to pursue.
2. The longer the indecision, the more likely for the ball to be on the ground.
3. The longer the ride, the less effective the Fullback is as either a runner or a blocker.
4. The long ride fools no one on defense, every defense plays assignment football vs The Triple Option.
5. The longer the ride, the harder it is to handle edge pressure from a level one Pitch Key

The Handoff Key Blocked Rule. The Hand off Key Blocked Rule is one of the best things we did to make our Quarterback more effective. It's simple but had a major effect on taking the risk out of running the Triple Option. The Rule is: If the Hand off key (HOK) is blocked by the Tackle (Or by the Tight End in unbalanced) its an automatic PULL read. So if the HOK pinches inside the Tackle, the Tackle will wash him down and the QB keeps the ball to the Pitch Key. If the HOK lines up inside the Tackle in a 4I it's a PULL read. As soon as the QB sees the HOK being blocked or lined up inside the Tackle in a 4I technique, he aborts the mesh and snaps the ball to his heart & is ready to attack the Pitch Key. If the HOK lines up in a 4I but slants outside, the QB ducks up inside behind the Fullback and it becomes Quarterback ISO

When the Fullback sees the Quarterback abort the mesh, he gets width and blocks Linebacker to Safety. He doesn't have to chase them because the QB will be on his outside hip, so the defenders will have to come through the fullback to get to the QB.

This simple adjustment greatly reduced the risk in running The Triple Option.

HOK Blocked Rule

Adjusting Line Splits. This is another way we made the Quarterback Reads simpler. This idea was hatched from Jake Gaither's book The Split Line T. This was also the forerunner of "Smart Splits" which became a huge part of The Gun Triple. Our basic line splits had the Guards at two and a half feet. These splits stayed constant because they provided an aiming point for the Fullback. The Tackles base split was 3 feet BUT if the guard was uncovered, the Tackle could take as big a split as he wanted as long as he could protect his inside gap. So typically, the Tackle would widen to a 4 foot split and sometimes a little more. By widening the tackle, the QB had an easier read on the HOK The wider split made it very difficult for the HOK to take the dive unless he got in a 4I, in which case see the HOK Blocked rule above.

Load and Toad Blocking. Another adjustment we made to simplify the Quarterback's reads on the Triple Option was to block the defender responsible for QB. We employed this tactic against level one option keys.

Load

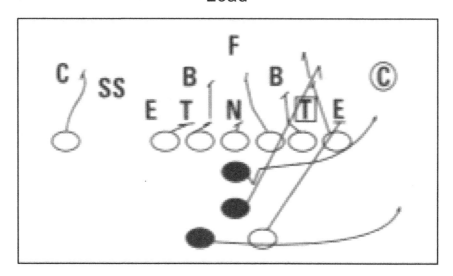

The first blocking adjustment was Load Blocking. We liked it the Tight End side so the TE could set up the HB's block. However, this was a tough block for the HB, so we went to TOAD Blocking, (Tight End Load) this worked much better because our TE could handle a OLB better than our HB. Now our HB read the TE's block and sealed the LB and this was a great short yardage play & great on the goal line.

Toad

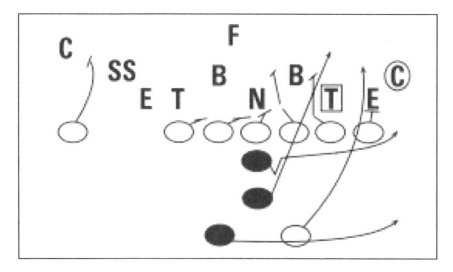

These simple adjustments completely jet propelled our Triple Option and in a roundabout way followed Homer Smith's advice. We made The Triple Option as simple as Double Option.

Adding Some Other Elements. To be a little more diverse we added a couple of simple runs that would take pressure off the Quarterback. These runs gave us a way to run the ball without depending on the Quarterback's reads.

The Belly Series. By simplifying The Triple Option, it opened some practice time to add a few supplemental runs. In year number one we ran the Belly or Drive series popularized by Bobby Dodd at Georgia Tech in the 50s. The Quarterback faked the dive to the Fullback and the handed the ball to the second man through with a lead blocker. This was a very productive short yardage play and the Play Action Pass was super.

The Fullback Cutback. Our second supplemental run was a misdirection play to the Fullback. The popular Defense of the day was The 34 with the Nose trying to beat the center. Some teams even stood the Nose up in a 2 point stance and he blitzed the A gap in the direction of the play. So the Fullback cutback was a valuable answer play.

Fullback Cutback

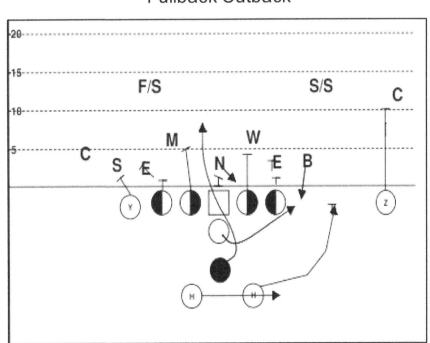

The Counter Call. The Wing T was a very productive offensive system that was built on deception and misdirection. So we decided to send the Fullback in the opposite direction of the play call. If the Line heard the word "Counter" they just blocked base. So Belly Right Counter looked like Army's Counter ISO that Greg Gregory perfected and it was great vs defenses that were keying on our FB. The great part there was zero new teaching!

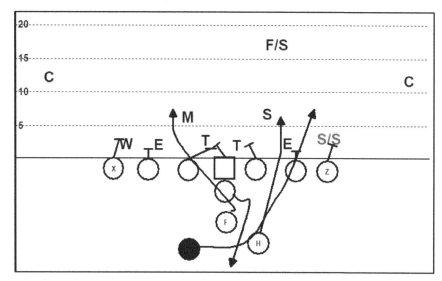

The Counter Dive. The Counter Dive was stolen from The Split Back Veer Guys. We liked it from a Broken Bone like Twins but it could be run from any set. The QB faked the dive to the FB one way the pivoted and handed the ball to the Halfback driving over the backside Guard. We got fancy and folded the backside Tackle if the DT was inside the OT.

Counter Dive Option

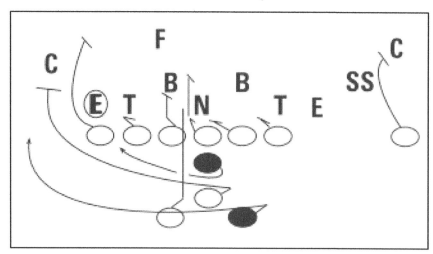

Creating a Simple Passing Game

The next step in bringing balance to the Multi-Bone Offense was to create an effective pass game. That was the basic purpose of "Breaking the 'Bone". The Wishbone is a good passing formation in a non-passing situation but not when everyone in the stadium knows you gotta throw it. Also, at this time, the rules were very strict and there was no holding allowed. The rules changed in the 80s and passing became easier.

Basic Wishbone Passes. Our first year at Iona, we had a successful season with a Free Safety at Quarterback. But in the first year of the Multi-Bone we had a record breaking QB taking the helm and the FS was back at FS. The first pass we used was a Post Route to exploit a Free Safety filling on the option. This was a feast or famine throw. It was a good shot on a run down. The second pass that was our best pass was The Belly Pass. The Quarterback faked the Belly Play and then looked for the Tight End on a Corner Route or the lead Halfback in the flat. We also added a "Throwback" call to throw to the Split End on a backside Post.

Expanding the Play Action Pass. Using the Twins Formation put an 8 man front SS in a bind. We liked The Curl/Flat Combo off the Triple Option fake. We blocked basically Big on Big frontside and turnback backside. The Fullback was responsible for the playside Linebacker. We kept the TE in unless no defender came off the edge, then he released on a Drag. The QB read the SS Curl to Flat. Now if we saw the Cornerback jumping the Curl, we would call Curl/Wheel. The Slot Receiver would start his Flat Route, look for the ball and turn upfield and go deep. The QB still threw Curl first, the Wheel if he saw the CB converge on the Curl. If we saw the FS try to rob the Curl, the call was Post/Wheel. The QB read it Post to Wheel, he always threw the Post UNLESS the FS stayed deep. We also had the ability to tag the Pattern Throwback Curl or Post.

Twins Play Action Curl/Flat

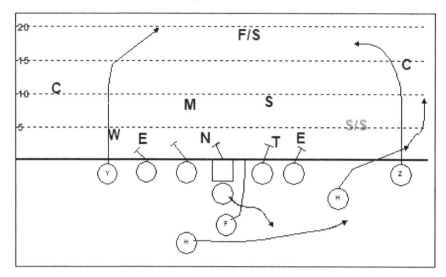

Play Action Post/Wheel

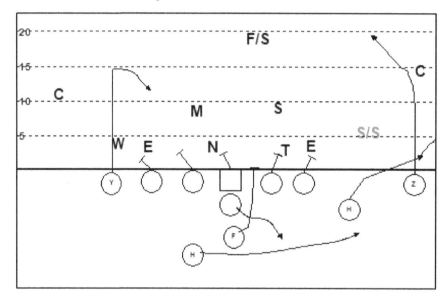

Adding The Split Back Veer Dump Pass. One of my favorite aspects of The Split Back Veer was The Dump Pass. The Dump Pass was an RPO before anybody ever heard the clever term. A problem going to the Twins Formation was a Wide Receiver blocking the Strong Safety. That's a tough block. So the Dump Pass was the answer. The Line blocked the same as Play Action Pass, Big on Big and turnback. The Fullback was responsible for the LB. The Halfback ran his pitch path and looked for the pitch. The Slot Receiver attacked the SS like he was going to block him, released by him. The Quarterback's read was simple: Throw the Dump every time UNLESS the SS ran with the Slot, then pitch it to the Halfback.

Home Rice Influence

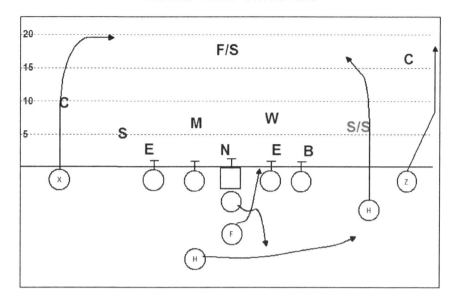

Passing In Passing Situations. Okay so breaking the Bone certainly helped our Play Action Passing but what about Passing in Passing situations? My original Plan was to install a Dropback Pass Attack similar to Homer Rice or some Dropback passes I picked up from observing the NY Giants. But Homer Smith was on target: with the blocking rules not allowing blockers to use their hands, there wasn't enough time in the day to master Dropback Pass Protection.

Adding the Sprint Out Pass and the Half Sprint. The sprint out pass protection is very similar to our Play action Protection but it was all Turnback with 2 running backs leading the QB on the edge.

The Quarterback had the opportunity to run if the routes were covered and option QBs are good runners. The QB opened up at a 45 degree angle, get 7 yards deep behind our Tackle, flipped his hips, got square to the target & made his throw moving to the target. If he was in doubt, he ran. If he was forced to pull up, he had the Tight End on a Drag.

And the beauty of the whole thing is we used the same patterns for the Sprint Pass we did for the Play Action Passes! The only difference is that we used The Strong Twins Formation. We also tagged the backside route for either the Tight End or The Split End like backside Post or Curl.

The Sprint Out Pass added a key element to The Multi-Bone Offense and we actually became one of the best passing teams in our conference. In 1977, our QB finished 2nd in the Met 7 in passing.

Strong Twins Sprint Pass

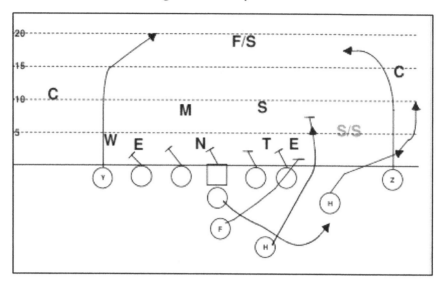

The Hot Draw. The Hot Draw was an RPO before they existed. This was basically a gadget that was the forerunner of Triple gun Dragon Package. We ran it from a Pro Bone Set. The SE and Flanker just did Go routes. The Line blocked Play Action Protection. The Tight took an outside release away from the Inside Linebacker and looked for the ball. The Quarterback took a quick drop and read the LB. His rule:" If he comes, I throw, if he drops, I go". Very simple.

Pro Bone Hot Draw

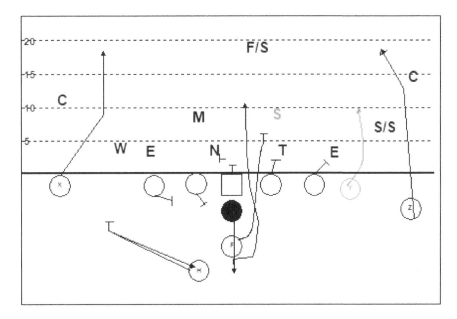

Opening up The Wishbone into the Multi-Bone was a very successful experiment. All four years I was Head Coach at Iona, we beat the toughest team on our schedule. We had an undefeated season and broke all of Iona's offensive records. Our last 3 years (after switching to the Multi-Bone) we were 15-3-1 in our conference.

Chapter 2
The Evolution of the Multi-Bone
Taking a Gamble at Penn

After 4 great years at Iona and our successful experiment creating The Multi-Bone Offense, I left to join Harry Gamble's staff at The University of Pennsylvania. I loved my time at Iona College, but Iona was run by the Irish Christian Brothers who wanted me to take a vow of poverty, so it was time to move on.

Football was evolving into a more wide-open game. The coming of Astro-Turf reduced the number of quagmire games and increased "the need for speed". The legalization of holding was one of the biggest boosts to offensive football probably in the history of the game. So as the game was evolving, I felt the need to evolve as well. Fortunately for me, I had a great mentor in Harry Gamble.

Penn was running its own version of a Multiple Wishbone Offense. Penn had a successful run in the early 70s running the Split Back Veer and then went to the Wishbone in the late 70s. Now, they were trying to incorporate both. (Sound familiar) The only difference was instead of using a Half Bone like we did at Iona, Penn got in the I formation.

A couple of things I picked up at Penn was running The Wide Veer from both the Wishbone and The I Formation. This was Coach Gamble's favorite play.

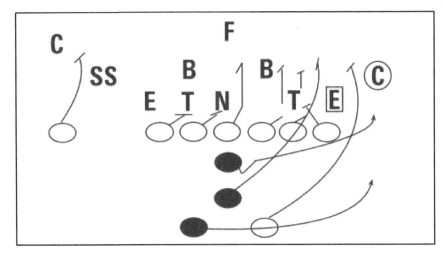

Wide Veer from the Bone

The second thing I picked up was the use of unbalanced sets like Bone Over or I Twins Over. We used Bone-Over to run the Veer and Twins Over for the Sprint Pass. I used unbalanced sets from this point on in my career.

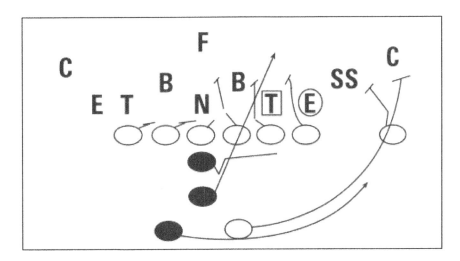

Unbalanced Bone Triple Option

Coach Gamble also instructed me, his play caller prior to every game to "Do not lose the game at the end of the half" – very sound advice. In other words, don't take risks at the end of the half trying to get a quick score and turn the ball over and let your opponent get a quick score. I followed this advice and always passed it along. The Kansas City Chiefs cost themselves a chance at a second straight Super Bowl championship by losing it at halftime. Trailing The Bucs 14-6 and the Bucs with the ball at midfield and a 3rd and 4 situation, The Chiefs called Time Out! Giving Tom Brady the ball at the end of the half is suicidal. The Bucs capitalized immediately, and KC went into the locker room down 21-6 instead of 14-6.

The Joe Restic Influence. Joe Restic was the Head Football Coach at Harvard while I was at Penn and Coach Gamble considered him an offensive genius. So I rounded up all the Harvard Films I could and spent an hour everyday studying Joe Restic's Multi-Flex Offense. It was a defensive coordinator's nightmare. He used a trillion different formations, and it was near impossible for the defense to determine which receivers were eligible and which were ineligible prior to the snap of the ball. As a result, there were receivers wide open because someone didn't think he was eligible. To tell you the truth, I don't think the refs knew who was eligible on some plays. Add to the confusion were shifts and motion and every DC in the Ivy League packed a bottle of "Pepto" and a package of Tums when they played Harvard.

After hours of study, I decided, Coach Restic basically ran the Wing T, Buck Sweep Series: Sweep, Trap and Waggle Pass. But with all the formation recognition issues those were the only plays he needed. For example, he ran Wingover Waggle with the TE being ineligible then came back with Tackles Over with the TE being backside and eligible and then used 4 offensive linemen and 2 TEs but one was eligible and one wasn't.

I decided I was going to add weird formations to the Multi-Bone. The only difference instead of the Buck Sweep Series, we would feature the Triple Option. This was the forerunner of The Exotic Sets we featured in the 80s and from then on.

Conclusion on My Penn Experience Though I only spent 2 years at Penn, I learned a ton. Coach Gamble was very patient with his brash young assistant and often reminded me "Tony, you're not the only genius in the Ivy League, those guys have chalk too". Coach Gamble and his staff really gave me the opportunity to grow as a professional. Harry Gamble left Penn and became The CEO, President and General Manager of The Philadelphia Eagles. I always say, before Penn, I knew *how* to coach but Harry Gamble taught me how to *be* a coach.

Back to the Future

My next challenge was to start a Division III program from scratch at a small Catholic college in Erie. PA. Mercyhurst College was founded by the Sisters of Mercy during the Depression. It was an all-girls school until the late 1970s. In 1981 I was hired to start a football program, build male enrollment and give the school a less feminine image. I was hired on March 11th and our first game was the following September 5th – 6 months to put together a team and play a varsity schedule in 5 months!

We recruited all freshmen except for 3 transfers. So things were going to be simple to see the least. We had to have a plan that would give us a chance to win or at least be in every game. Just to add to the difficulty, the administration scheduled a Division II team for Homecoming!

The Multi-Bone scaled down. So a lot of the great ideas I put together at The University of Pennsylvania had to be put on a shelf and we had to put together a plan that would win at a first year program. Similar to the Iona Plan, we built up the defense first. We had the speed & quickness to play a 50 Defense. On offense; we had good athletes but no Quarterback. (Sounds like Iona Deja vu all over again). So we put our best athlete at Quarterback and used an Iona style offense.

The NCAA rules committee decided to allow use of the hands to block so the passing game was going to open up but not until we could actually throw the ball with some consistency.

Multi-Bone Formations. Because lining up is simpler than executing, we started with formations. Our Base set was The Wishbone, but we added to it by using The Over-Bone like we did at Penn and the added a Jumbo Set with 6 offensive linemen, a Tight End and a Wishbone backfield. The Belly Play was a great short yardage play and enhanced with this set. Picking up 1st Downs to control the clock and scoring on the goal line were critical to this fledgling program. When we broke the Bone, we used the I formation not the Half Bone. This was the same thinking Coach Gamble had at Penn. I Twins and I Twins Over were our most frequently used 2 Back Sets.

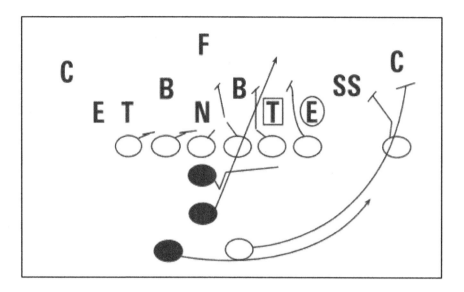

Unbalanced Bone Over Triple Option using a third OT

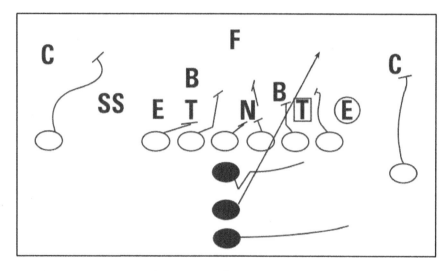

I Pro Option

The Multi-Bone Run Game. The run game was just a few basic plays that we could execute. We started to use Seal Blocking vs a 44 Defense or an Eagle look. The onside Slot would SEAL the onside or Stacked LB. The Quarterback still read the Handoff Key, but now pitched off the SS or OLB. This reduced the back-to-back pressure on an inexperienced QB. This was the single biggest addition to The Multi-Bone Triple Option. The only other was The I Lead Draw which was a handoff to our I Tailback with ISO Blocking up front. Our Tailback was a gifted runner and we had to get him more touches. Again, I had to put philosophy on hold and do what it took to get some wins.

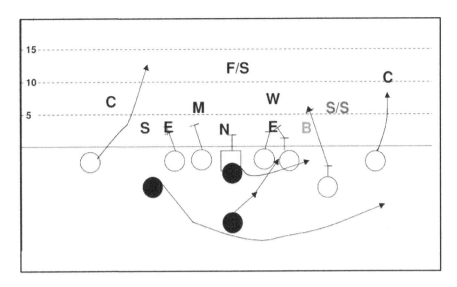

Shoot Triple Seal

The Multi-Bone Pass Game. The pass game was reduced to giving us just enough to get through the year. We ran the I Twins Sprint Attack that we used at Penn and we threw Play Action out of the Bone. We also used Play Action off the Lead Draw but the routes were the same as Sprint Out. This was another year my desire for a balanced option attack had to be put on hold because of my greater desire to WIN! We used more I Formation to get our best running back the ball more times. We used him both as an I Tailback and as a Flanker.

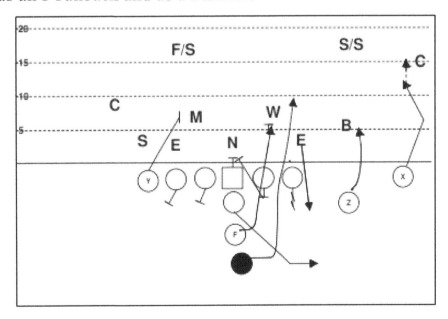

I Twins Lead Draw

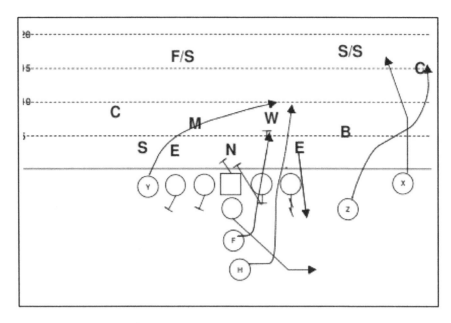

I Twins Lead Draw Pass

Blocking the Run and the pass the same way simplified this I formation series.

Valvano Redux. Though the Xs and Os were important, the lessons learned from Jimmy V were even more essential to fielding a winning team at Mercyhurst College. We slowed the game to a crawl and shortened the game to as fewest snaps as possible. "He who controls the pace, wins the race" Jim my V. We also prepped the team to win the game in the 4th Quarter by making our motto "The 4th Quarter is Ours", following The Valvano Doctrine that the only lead that matters is the one at the end of the game. We could not win a shootout so we had to drag teams into the alley and win ugly.

The Plan was In Place. The next step was how to implement it. I spent the entire summer working on every practice schedule for the year so we could maximize our practice time. We had to teach work ethic on *how to practice.*

Practice is Always Sacred

The easiest way to improve any team is to improve practice. The more productive your practices are the better your team will play and the greater chance of your team reaching it's potential. The most important role a head coach has is to make sure practice is productive and that the team gets as many quality repetitions as possible.

When you put your offensive scheme together it's important you have a detailed plan on how to practice it. A great play is useless if it can't be practiced. Remember when it comes to plays less is best. The more plays in the playbook, the more techniques there are to master. So your offense must have as many crossover techniques as possible. This is the secret to a simple offense that appears complex. Another secret is to use Strategic Flexibility as a "Core Principle"

Strategic Flexibility is the ability of a play to change after the snap of the ball. So you don't need answer plays because the answer play is built into the core play. When The Gun Triple is mastered, you have almost a complete run offense in one play. Plus the supplemental runs all use the same techniques as the Gun Triple. This philosophy reduces practice time while maximizing repetitions.

Once the play menu is developed, the next step is to put together a technique chart to ensure that all techniques by every position will be repped in every practice. This is usually a good time to slim down the playbook. If you can't practice your entire offense every day, you're doing too much and will be mediocre at many things and good at none. Remember, it's better to run a lousy play great, than a great play lousy.

We divide our practice into 24 five minute periods. The first 6 periods involve stretching, conditioning and special teams. Our offensive line is not involved in Special Teams so they get right into their block progression. QBs use this time to do arm warm drills. Then the rest of the periods look like on a Tuesday and Wednesday. (Monday is a short practice focusing on special teams and Clutch Offense & Thursday is a team practice focusing on situational practice)

Starting on period 7

Periods 7 & 8

- QBs & WRs do routes on air, the Backs do a block progression as does the offensive line.

Periods 9 & 10

- QBs & RBs do routes on air, The WRs stalk block and Line continues block progression

Periods 11 & 12

- QBs & RBs work on Play Cycles repping the Jet Sweep, and other supplemental runs. The WRs work on ball drills and release drills. The line works pass progression

Periods 13, 14, 15, & 16

- Read Drill involving the whole working off a master script so we see every front every day.

Period 17

- Play Action Pass Review. 2 groups at a time. O. Line Pass Protect

Period 18

- WRs vs DBs 1 on 1 – O. Line & RBs vs Defense Blitz Pick Up.

Period 19 & 20

- Team vs Scouts – 3rd & 4 and 3rd & 5

Period 21 & 22

- Team vs Scouts – 3 & 6+

Period 23 & 24

- Team vs Scouts 3rd & 3 and 3rd & 2 plus Goal line on Weds.

Note: We will do 7 on 7 on Mon. & Weds. For 2 periods.

Some Practice Tips. These are some practice tips that help make practice more productive.

1. Always be on the practice field waiting for your players.
2. Hustle to set the example
3. Enthusiasm is caught not taught.
4. You get what you demand not what you wish for.
5. Stick to the schedule don't improvise.
6. No on field clinics or oratory. Repletion's are the best teacher. Keep drills moving and never have players standing around.
7. Correction is important but so is encouragement.
8. Never skimp on water, make sure your group is well hydrated.
9. Always praise effort and hustle.
10. Deal in the details of discipline. Discipline leads to consistency
11. When your group is competing against another group, make sure you praise players in the other group if they make a good play.
12. Teach players *how* to practice. There is no excuse for a bad practice.
13. Every coach is responsible for the enthusiasm of his group.
14. Reward the behavior you want and punish the behavior you don't want
15. Never let a mistake go uncorrected.
16. Always visit the locker room after practice. If you've been hard on a guy during practice, make sure you see him after practice.
17. Always end practice on a positive note.
18. Review practice the next day in pre-practice meetings. Always use walk-troughs as part of your meeting time.
19. Practice must make techniques intuitive.
20. There is no status quo, every day that you don't get better, you get worse.

Practices must be planned to the minute, wasting the players' time is a morale killer. Make sure you have every possible scenario covered. Improve practice and improve performance.

"Teams that practice hard get better, teams that don't, get worse".

Chuck Daly – Head Coach of the NBA Detroit Pistons and the original U.S.

The Foundation for Success

We had a very successful first year and finished 4-2-1 playing a varsity schedule including a 14-7 win over Division II Glenville St. on the 1st Homecoming in Mercyhurst College history. It was a typical ball control, clock killing style that helped secure this huge upset. We blocked 2 punts in the last 3 minutes that was the difference. Despite our success playing "Stall Ball" we knew we had to grow the offense.

Growing the Team. The next 2 years, we increased our talent pool with heavy duty recruiting and by instituting a strength and conditioning program that made our guys stronger. We brought in two good, fast young Quarterbacks that showed that we would develop into a balanced offense. Our first year Quarterback became a record setting Wide Receiver.

Second Huge Upset. In the second year of the program, we upset the number 6 ranked Division III team in the country, Gettysburg College at Gettysburg 21-20. This really showed we were on the right path. To get a win on the road against a quality program like Gettysburg with only Freshmen and Sophomores was really noteworthy.

Time to Re-assess. After the first 3 years of the Mercyhurst Football program, our record stood at 13-9-2. Respectable but not where we wanted to be. In 1984 we were scheduled to play Division III power, Widener University, led by their Hall of Fame Coach, Bill Manlove. Who in their right mind would schedule such a mismatch? That would be me. My first year at the Hurst Widener Won the D III National Championship and I wanted to be able to play the best and Widener, along with The University of Dayton, led by their Hall of Fame coach, Mike Kelly were the best. So we were scheduled to play Widener at Widener in 1984 and Dayton at Dayton in 1985. Harry Gamble, my mentor, and my trusted advisor, was good friends with Coach Manlove. So when I called and let him know that I had just scheduled Widener, Coach Gamble paused and then gave his total support by saying "You're in trouble". So I knew we had to make some major changes to play these teams. We had to increase our ability to put points on the board while still being able to control the clock.

Opening Up the Multi-Bone Offense

The Mercyhurst College Schedule really got difficult in 1984, the addition of perennial power Widener University, Alfred University, Canisius College and Frostburg State was a quantum leap in our schedule. So, we had to be both more efficient on offense and more explosive while still being simple.

Using More Formations. The first step was to dig into my Joe Restic Multi-Flex notes and add some new formations. You don't have to execute a formation but you can create recognition problems for the defense. The first thing was to use more One Back sets. The main one was a Double Slot Formation called "Shoot". This set gave us 4 quick receivers on the Line of Scrimmage and gave us a great set to run our 3 Step Pass Game that we were installing.

The next set was Wingover which was stolen directly from the Joe Restic Multi-Flex Offense. We Used the Tackle over formation as well.

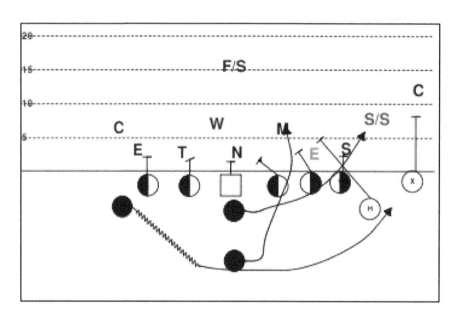

Wingover Toad Triple

The Exotics: Then we added 3 more sets we called "Exotics" and they all were about both Wide Receivers to the same side of the formation with different people being eligible and ineligible. The base formation was Ends with the inside Wide

Receiver being ineligible. The next 2 formations were either shifted to or lined up in on the first play of a series or after a Sudden Change. The second set was Receivers with both Wide Receivers being eligible but the onside Slot was ineligible The last set was Friends in which everyone was eligible but the backside Slot was on the line of scrimmage Later we added Pals which was the same as Friends but with 3 Wide Receivers in the game. We used the Pals formation as our pass attack grew.

Our Goal was to add formations that would, in the words of Stonewall Jackson "Mystify, Mislead and Confuse." Who was eligible? This was a question the Defense had to ask on every play and **then** had to play defense. My thought is in football "If you think you stink."

The Exotics:

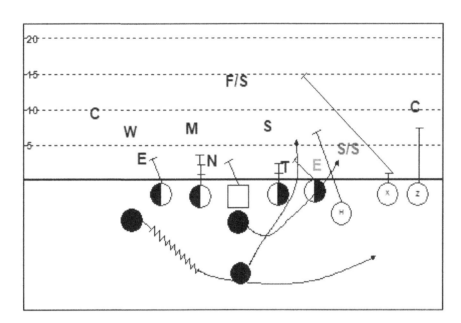

Ends Triple

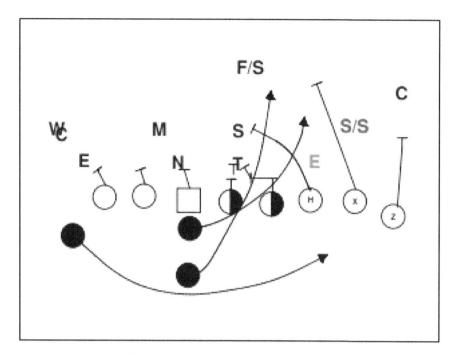

Receivers - Unbalanced

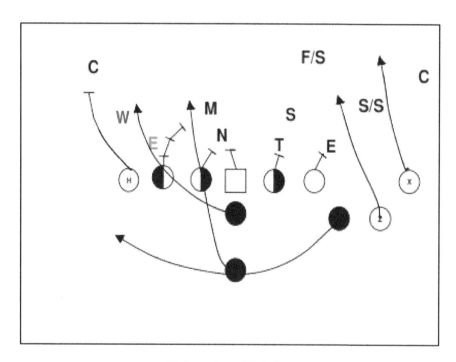

Friends - Triple

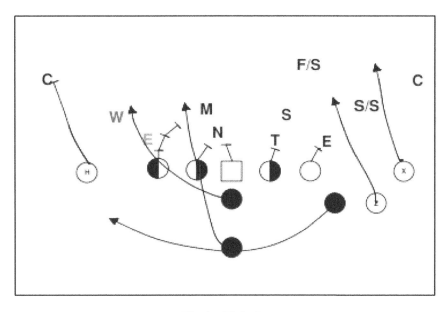

Pals Triple

Expanding the Pass Game. As our Quarterbacks ability to pass improved and the pass protection rules relaxed, it was time to create that explosive, balanced offense I was in search for. It was clear to be a National Power in Division III, we were going to have to have the capability to score more points. And we had the athletes to do it. The goal as always was to emphasize **simplicity.** So we had to reduce the run game so we have the practice time to develop the pass game. We couldn't beat teams like Widener just running the ball.

 The Quick Game. The Quick Game was an important supplement to The Triple Option because we could attack a 44 Defense and stop defenses from taking their Outside Linebackers and bringing them into the box. The 3 step Hitch gave us a perfect answer to the boundary and the Slant/Flat Combo gave us a great pass to the field. The Double Slot formation was the perfect set for The Triple Option and Quick Game Package. The Rule was: "8 between the Slots throw Quicks and Hots".

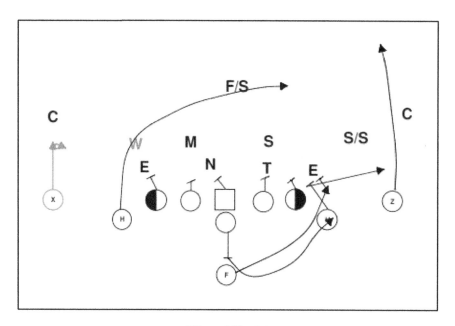

The Hitch

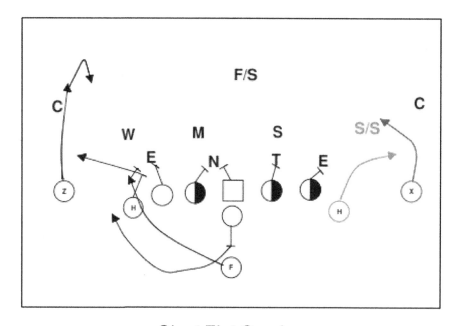

Slant Flat Combo

The success of the Quick Game was, as in any play, lying in the details.

The protection was Slide Protection away from the call with the Fullback responsible for the man outside the onside Tackles block. The Offside Slot was responsible for any defender outside offside Tackles block. If the Center called "Solid" the blocking was man on

The Routes were also very simple. The Hitch was drive down 6 yards stick your outside foot in the ground, get your numbers to the QB and look for the ball. The key was to take an outside release and sell the fade route. The Slant Route was also simple. The Wide Out takes an outside release, drives hard for 6 yards, plants and slants inside looking for the curl/flat defender (usually a SS). When he clears that defender, he gears down, puts his numbers to the QB & looks for the ball. The Slot's Flat route has a key coaching point. When he releases on his Flat Route, he turns his upfield shoulder to the QB to give him an easier throw.

Adding a Boot to the Quick Game. The one thing we had trouble with the Quick game was against Press Cover II. The Hitch was supposed to convert to the Fade which was great on paper but low percentage on the field. We wanted to be able to throw the Hitch on 1st down but if they were in Press II, now it was 2nd & 10. Not good for an option team. Then totally by accident, we discovered the answer and it became a huge part of our offense ever since.

In a scrimmage, our QB saw the converted Hitch blanketed, so he took off and sprinted in the opposite direction for a huge gain. Eureka! So we put rules to it and called the "Scramble Rules" (Later we just taught it as part of the pass). So, the Play started out as a Quick Pass one way but ended up in a Sprint Pass the other. Strategic Flexibility! The onside Slot ran an Over route getting 12 to 14 yards deep. The backside Slot blocked for 2 counts and released in the Flat, we called this a "Slam & Slide" route. The Backside Wide Receiver ran a clear route (Fade vs Press CB or a Skinny Post vs a loose CB) his objective was to take 2 – make both the CB and the Safety cover him. The QB looked at the Hitch if it was open, throw it on your 3rd step. But ii was covered, he booted away, getting 7 yards deep behind the opposite Tackle (Just like Sprint Out) and throw Slam & Slide to Over Route. If they were covered – run. This was a radical innovation in 1982.

Upgrading the Play Action Pass Game. We kept our basic Play Action Passes that we had been using and were very effective but with the new formations, there were many more opportunities for big plays. The "Exotic Formations" created the recognition problem of eligibility first before deciphering run or pass.

Lining up in Ends and running The Triple Option sets up the Post/Wheel Pattern from Receivers Formation. It also set up The Dump Pass RPO.

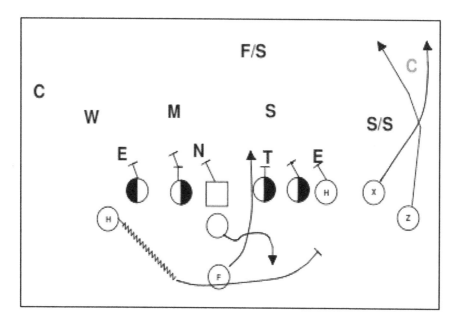

Receivers Play Action Post Wheel

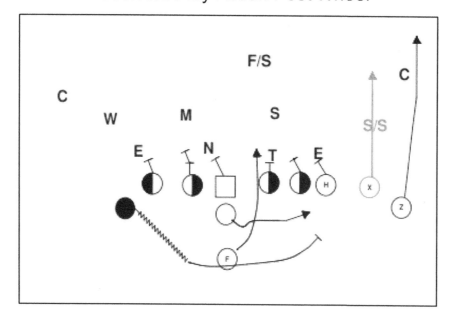

Receivers Dump Pass - RPO

Running The Triple Option away from Ends set up our most productive Play Action Pass from Friends - the Throwback Pass, which matched up our fastest Wide Receiver on their SS. This pass produced the most 20 yard plus gains.

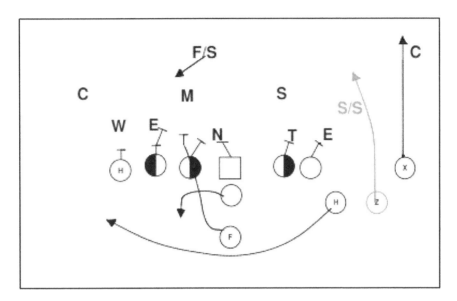

Friends Throwback Pass

The Play Action from Wingover was also very effective The Post Corner gave the illusion of a Crack on the Safety and an Arc block by The Wing. This lured the Free Safety to fill and the Corner to take on the Arc Block leaving the Wide Receiver wide open. A great short yardage pass.

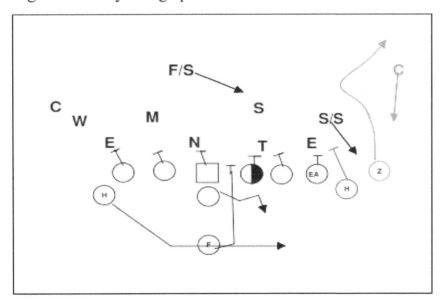

Wingover Play Action Crack Corner

A New Look for the Sprint Pass. The new formations upgraded our Sprint game. We had still been using the I Twins Over formation but now we turned to our new sets. Wingover gave us a great formation to get the edge but also the Slot's motion gave the illusion of a Triple Option.

We really liked The Curl/Flat Combo from this set. The Wide Receiver ran a 14-yard Curl and Wing ran a Flat route getting no deeper than 6 yards. If covered, the QB tucked it away and ran.

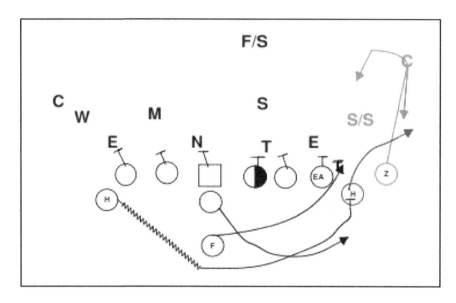

Wingover Sprint Out Curl/Flat

From our "Exotic Package" we used Receivers and Friends to Sprint Out. We ran a new Pattern called a Seam/Out.

The Inside Receiver did a Seam Route and his rule was to clear the SS. Once he cleared the SS, he looked for the ball. He went deep if the SS ran with him. The Outside Receiver did a 14 yard out unless Press Coverage, then he converted to the Fade. The Quarterback read the SS, if he ran with the Inside Receiver, he looked for the Outside on either an Out or Fade. If he didn't like that throw, he ran. The Blocking was Turnback. Another simple and effective package.

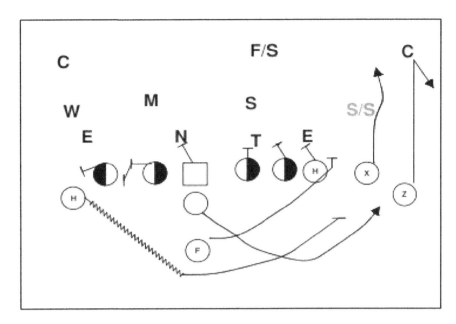

Receivers Sprint Pass Seam/Out

We ran the Sprint Game from Shoot as well, focusing on the Curl/Flat Combo. We did this with the idea of hitting the backside Wide Receiver on a Throwback Post if the FS tried to fill.

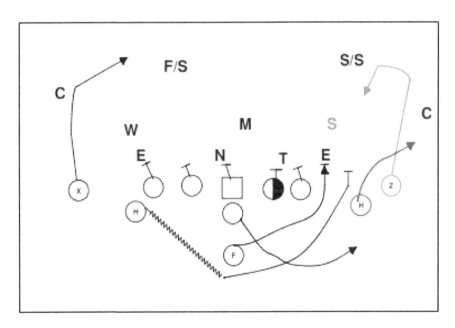

Shoot Sprint Curl/Flat

Updating the Run Game. We did not add any new runs, but the new formations added new life to the old runs. We really started to use Seal Blocking from the Slot against 8 man fronts. This was a huge step in the running the Triple Option. So we really became a predominantly Triple Option team. The Wingover set also provided a great Triple Option formation as did the "Exotic" sets. These sets enabled us to control the Free Safety and run the ball vs a loaded box.

Another Defensive Adjustment to the Triple Option was playing 2 Deep with Hard Corners that were difficult to Stalk Block. So we used the Dump Pass (RPO) into the boundary from Shoot Formation. We ran either our Load Scheme; so the QB read the Dive or our Play Action Scheme where we blocked the HOK with our OT. The Slot blocked the first man outside the Tackles Block. The Wide Receiver ran his Dump Route. The QB read the CB, he threw the Dump in the hole every time UNLESS the CB ran with the Dump then he pitched it.

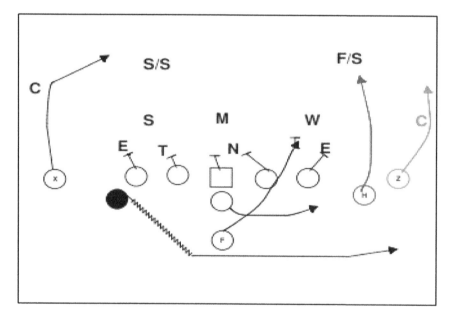

Shoot Dump Pass - RPO

The Quest for Balance. Having a balanced offense is essential to scoring points against good defenses. You have to keep the defense off balance and not zero in on your offense. These new additions of formations to where I wanted to be offensively and give us the firepower to play with the best in the country.

Studying a Tiger

In 1965, a high school coach from Ohio wrote a book about how he took a moribund High School football team and turned into a football power. That coach's name was Tiger Ellison, and his innovative offense was called "The Run and Shoot". Tiger's offense was flourishing in the 80s, popularized by Mouse Davis, John Jenkins, and Jack Pardee. It was a faced paced, wide open, high scoring, pass first offense that was fun to watch. So, what brought me to study The Run and Shoot Offense?

Widener University and the Run and Shoot. Well it just so happens that our best opponent in the school's brief history had been running Bill Manlove's version of the Run & Shoot Offense. So the first thing I did was buy Tiger's book and find out what it was about. I really liked some of the concepts and felt Tiger's ideas fit in with my philosophy of Strategic Flexibility. I also looked into the other coaches that were running and shooting at the same time.

How to Defend the Run and Shoot. The best way I found to defend the Run and Shoot was to keep it on the sidelines. We had to control the clock on offense and play scorched earth on defense. The other thing I noticed was that we could pressure their 6-man protection with our 50 Defense IF they didn't know which 6 were rushing. Plus, we had D.E.s that were very fast. (One was a legit 4.6 in the 40 at 240 lbs.). Our Defense worked perfectly! Widener went 88 yards on their 1st drive to take a 7-0 lead. Fortunately, we did slow things down and with the score knotted at 7-7 going into the 4th Quarter, we got into the 2 Tight End Wishbone and had the ball for 11 minutes to pull out a 17-7 upset.

I got a note from one of my mentors, Jimmy V congratulating me on the "W" little did he know how much he played a part in it. By the way in 1983, Jimmy V had taken underdogs North Carolina St. to the National Championship over The University of Houston 54-52 with a buzzer-beater by Lorenzo Charles. ("The only lead that matters is the one at end of the game" Jimmy V)

Adding Some Run and Shoot Ideas to The Multi-Bone. We felt we could add some ideas to our existing Quick Game and Sprint Game. I did not want to add more protections. We did add 2 semi-new formations, Twins which we had used but now we were going to use 3 Wide Receivers and only one back in the backfield and Trips which was the same formation except the Slot would SHIFT to Trips this would tip us off on how the defense was going to adjust to a Trips set. Also, we could run The Triple back away from the shift or throw the Quick Game

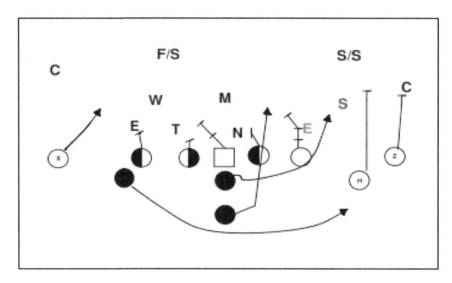

Twins – Triple Option

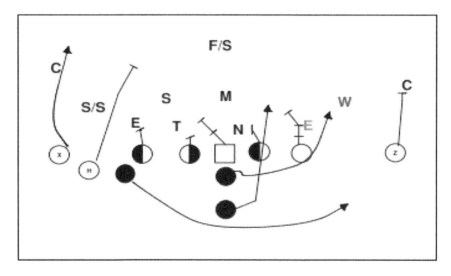

Trips – Triple Option

The next Run and Shoot idea we stole from The Run and Shoot was long Motion. Out of our basic Shoot formation we could send our backside slot in motion and get into a Trips set and we would signal if we wanted the Hitch to convert to a Fade or Slant. If the Quarterback booted, he would have a 3-level read. We also used Long motion to help our Sprint Game

Adding a little Run and Shoot to the Multi-Bone, gave us a side benefit of being able to give our defense a good look in their preparation for the powerhouse Widener football team.

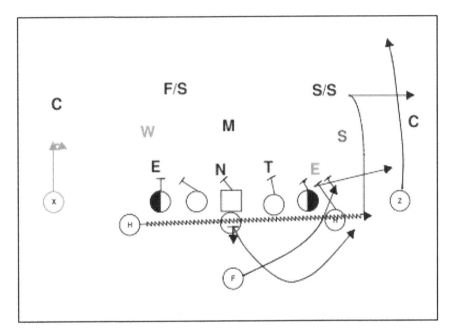

Motion to Trips

A Simple RPO Combining Joe Restic's Multi-Flex and Tiger's Run and Shoot

One little wrinkle we put in that used Wingover with long motion. The thing that Joe Restic did to a defense was add recognition issues for the defense to figure out before playing defense. Adding formations didn't take any execution.

This play was a simple addition which put the playside LB in conflict. The Wing took a wide release and looked for the ball, If the Linebacker was there, he blocked him. The motion took a flat course and kicked out the Cornerback. The Wide Receiver cracked the Strong Safety creating an alley. The Line blocked Triple Option except for the Tight End who blocks man on. The Fullback is the Pitchman. He takes a drop step and runs his pitch path expecting the pitch. The Quarterback takes a quick one step drop and looks for the Wing, if he is open, he throws him the ball, if not he pitches to the Fullback. Did I hear RPO?

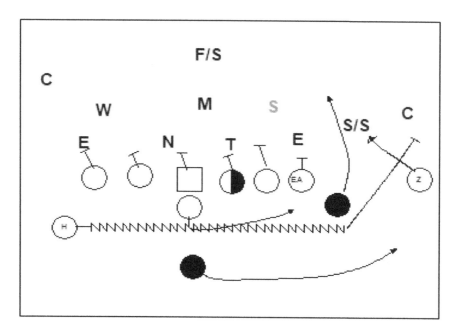

Wingover Long Mo Speed Pop

These simple additions created more defensive difficulties without creating any execution issues because we didn't add new plays, we just put a new dress on the same pig. We had a great 7 years at Mercyhurst College finishing with a 41-21-2 record. Combining the Option and the passing game was unique in the 1980s and it was transformative.

In my first 3 seasons at Mercyhurst using a conservative approach we were 13 – 10 – 2, a 54% winning percentage but after opening things up in 1984 our record my last four years with a wide-open approach our record was 28 – 11 a 72% winning percentage. We successfully created a balanced and explosive offense by combining the Option and the Pass.

Tempo is a Tool not a Way of Life

"He who sets the pace wins the race" Jim Valvano. This was the first bit of wisdom Jimmy V shared with me and I used it ever since. But usually, it was to slow the game down. But by 1984, Mercyhurst College had lots of speed, lots of playmakers and lots of depth. We had 2 complete backfields that were pretty equal in their ability. So now was the time to ramp up the pace and make teams play ball.

No Huddle Laker Ball. The first thing we did was to practice the entire pre-season without a huddle at a very fast pace. This was a great conditioner and increased the number of reps we got in practice. We went the entire first game running high speed no-huddle offense. But in the 4th Quarter up 35-0 we still used no huddle but I signaled the play in late so we could slow the tempo and kill the clock. So we used our Tempo to fit the situation and it worked beautifully. The other take-away was when we went No Huddle but waited, we could see the defense and choose a better play. We liked to get a lead with high tempo, throwing the ball and going high speed but in the fourth quarter we would still be no huddle but would pound the ball and finish them off.

When we played a dangerous team like Widener, we wanted to slow the game in the 4th quarter so when we had the lead we could keep it. So now we had the ability to play very fast or very slow. Simple but I don't recall other any other teams doing this in 1984.

Another advantage of using the clock as a weapon was it helped our defense. Once we bolted out in front and then started to stall in the 4th quarter, it made our opponents offense one dimensional because they knew they had to throw.

The Need for Multiple Launch Points

As the Multi-Bone evolved into a more balanced offense, we had to help our pass protection. One of Bill Walsh's principles was every pass must start with protection. So the more launch points, the more difficult it is for the defense to zero in their pass rush to one spot. If an offense was only a dropback team, the defense could pin their ears back and come after the Quarterback. To be effective passing the ball and have greater balance in our attack, we had to establish more launch points and further blur the line between run and pass.

The Quick Game: Multiple Launch Points on the Same Play. The Quick was a great weapon vs the pass rush. First, rushing the Quick game is difficult by itself because the ball is out of the Quarterback's hands so quickly. This is the reason Bill Walsh used the Quick Game to turn around the Cincinnati Bengals using a very average QB, Virgil Carter. He later did the same thing with The 49ers and Hall of Fame QB, Joe Montana. Now The Multi-Bone added another element: The Boot off the Quick Game. Every defensive coordinator in the world will tell you, they defend the Quick Game by telling their D. Line to get their hands up. Now have them chase the QB on the perimeter with their hands in the air. So the Quick Game was a critical cog in our passing strategy.

Enhancing the Sprint Pass. The Sprint Pass had been very effective out of both our base Shoot Formation (Double Slot) and our Unbalanced Sets (Unbalanced & Receivers) We also used Motion and Trips Sets. These were all discussed earlier in the book. Now we needed a Sprint Draw and some complementary routes.

A Sprint Draw Named Sally. The Sprint Draw came Compliments of Tubby Raymond and his staff. This will be discussed later in the book in the section "When Tony met Sally". But we used Tubby's Power of Sequence to add two Sally Passes.

The Sally Pass. The first Sally Pass is a full sprint after the Sally Fake. The QB has two lead blockers, the Fullback and the Motion Slot. The Offensive Line just blocks Sally. The Onside Wide Receiver runs a 14 yard Curl or Pivot Out Route unless the Route is tagged to be something else. The backside route is a 12 yard Over Route. The Quarterback is thinking Run first unless a Secondary defender plays run, then he looks for the Out. If he's forced to pull up he has the Over Route.

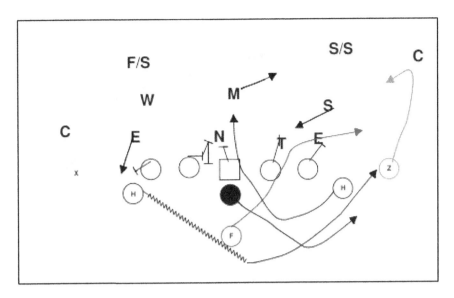

Sally Keep Pass

The Whirley Sally Pass. The second Sally Pass was a true Play Action Pass. The Quarterback did not attack the perimeter but instead dropped back afire the Sally fake. The blocking was Play Action Blocking. This motion slot used "Whirley Motion and ran a Flare unless tagged. The backside ran a 14 yard Curl Route unless tagged. The field Wide Receiver has an In route at 14 yards. The QB reads Curl unless the Outside Linebacker is under it, then he dumps it to the Flare. We tagged this pass "Switch" and the Split End did a Post and the Whirley Slot did a Wheel Route. The QB like on any Post/Wheel Combo reads inside/out Post to Wheel.

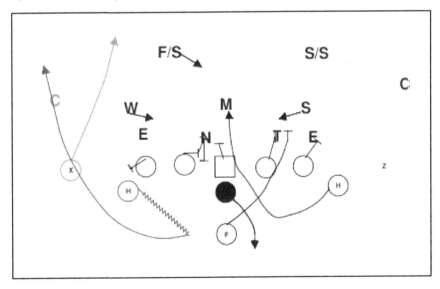

Whirley Sally Pass Switch

Sally Meets The Run and Shoot. Using Trips or long motion was also very effective in our hybrid Run and Shoot phase of the Multi-Bone. The blocking was the same but the long motion gave it a different look. The obvious complement was the Play Action Pass.

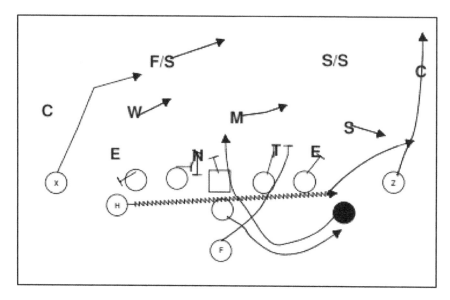

Shoot Liz Sally

Using the Delaware Sally Play as a Sprint Draw and adding Play Action off it really helped our passing game and kept defenses off balanced.

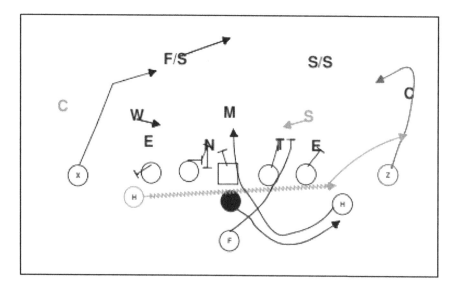

Shoot Liz Sally Curl/Flat

Larry Smith Helps Me Cross Up the Defense. In the mid-90s, I was put on the NCAA rules committee. (Someone said it was like Jesse James a sheriff). While I was serving on The Committee, I met Larry Smith who was the head Coach of The Missouri Tigers at the time. Coach Smith had been a very successful coach and in 24 seasons as a Head College Football Coach had a 143-126-7 record. Coach showed me his favorite Play Action Pass which I really liked and adapted it to the Multi-Bone as part of The Sprint Package. (We later used it as a Play Action in The Triple Gun)

The Protection was Sprint Protection with the Slot blocking 2 counts before releasing on a 6 yard Drag Route. The #2 Receiver did an Over Route and the #1 Receiver did a Post. The Backside Single Receiver did a Skinny Post, never crossing the Hash mark. The Quarterback sells Sprint, pulls up and reads the backside Post – "I'm throwing the Post every time unless the FS is deep. If the FS is deep I'm throwing to the Drag and the to the Over Route". We could run it from Trips or with long Motion.

This was a valuable addition to our Sprint Game and gave us a great way to combat teams using their scrape Linebackers to stop our Sprint Pass.

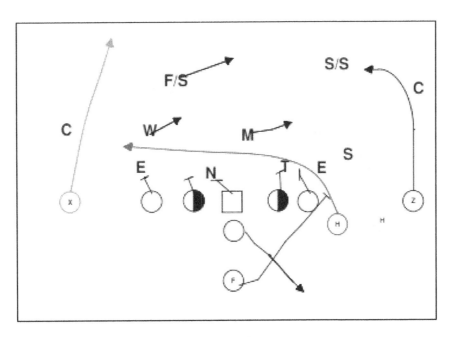

Trips Sprint Crossers

63

Zen and the Art of Quarterbacking

How does Zen help anyone play Quarterback? Where does the connection come? How does an ancient Eastern religion affect a modern western sport?

The answer is simple. As the offense started use more and more of a "Strategic Flexibility" approach, the Quarterback had to master his emotions and make "no fear" decisions. I wanted our Quarterbacks to react, not deliberate. I wanted them to be more like Bruce Lee than Bobby Fisher. I wanted them to be able to improvise within the structure of the offense. I wanted their play to be intuitive not robotic. In other words I wanted them to master the offense.

To be a master at anything requires a combination of mind, body and spirit. No one achieves excellence, let alone mastery without this combination. It is only through the process of mastery that sport becomes an art.

The key to mastery of sport is the control of the spirit. Everyone knows basically the physical skills required but what separates the master from the rest is his control of his spirit. Regardless of whether its Joe Montana or Muhammad Ali; they have control of their spirit.

This is even more important when directing the Triple Gun Offense, because the Offense revolves around the Quarterback's decision making. He is not only responsible for his own mechanics but he must distribute the ball and put our team in position to be successful. This increases the stress level for the Triple Gun Quarterback above the level for most quarterbacks. So using Zen and relaxation techniques increases the performance level of the Triple Gun quarterback. It relaxes the mind and enables the Triple gun quarterback to make better decisions.

The single biggest destroyer of performance is fear of failure. Thinking about what you are afraid *might* happen, can become a self-fulfilling prophecy. Negative thinking leads to stress which leads to tension which leads to mistakes which circle back to more negative thinking. Before you know it your Quarterback is on a downward spiral to a poor performance.

Superstars have figured out that you can't be winner if you are afraid to lose. Great players hate to lose but never fear losing. Masters know that no one is perfect and that an error is part of the game. If you make an error – get over it and get on with it. You can't change the play that just happened so you must focus on the next play.

Freedom from the fear of failure liberates a quarterback to get into a state of "flow" or "the zone".   The following are some tips for getting into a state of relaxed concentration:

1. Have a pre-game ritual. Listening to certain music on your IPOD or using some deep breathing or whatever relaxes you prior to the game.
2. Always give yourself positive encouragement through your self-talk. Have some positive affirmations that prepare you for the game.
3. Prepare a positive reaction to any setback that occurs in the game. Poise over panic. Masters never get lured into the "I gotta" mode. They maintain a positive mental attitude.
4. The great ones never lose; time just runs out.

Some characteristics of top performers are:

1. They react to the challenge not the menace.
2. They expect success. They have the realistic belief that they will succeed.
3. They set goals for the future but only focus on the task at hand. They forget about future goals during the game and focus only on the present play.
4. They always focus on the process and not the result. The Masters' scoreboard is internal.
5. They savor the moment. They love the battle for the sake of the battle. They never tie their self-worth to an outcome.

Zen controls the spirit by letting go of the spirit. You gain control by losing control. You achieve the greatest results when you completely forget about results. By using the principles of Zen you can free yourself from the prison of results and get on the path to mastery. Only by removing your ego from the contest will you reach your optimum level of performance. Zen extols intuitive action which is the critical component of mastery. By eliminating the fear of failure you open the door to a higher level of performance that comes from your intuitive ability. The basic principles of Zen in regards to football are:

1. Intuition is more important that intellect.
2. Intuitive skills are developed through quality repetitions.
3. Intuition is gained by letting go of self and by learning from experience.
4. Mastery is a process that is ongoing not a product.

5. Always perform in the present. You can't change the past nor can you predict the future. Enjoy the day.
6. Focus on the NOW.
7. Conquer haste. Patience is power.
8. Even a tornado has an inner calm. Always maintain an inner sense of peace.
9. Only improve yourself, never compare yourself or concern yourself with your opponent.
10. Be unshakable. Poise is a part of mastery. It's always your choice how react to a circumstance. You are in control of your response.
11. The greatest warriors are patient and wait for their moment. They are poised and ready like a coiled snake and strike quickly.
12. Let go and let flow. Trust your training.
13. That which is flexible will triumph over that which is rigid. Old trees snap off during strong winds while flexible trees sway with the wind.
14. Take your ego out of the contest. Your self-worth is not at stake. No ego helps intuition flow.
15. Training replaces intellect with intuition. The less thought the greater the performance. It's not what you know; it's how fast you process information and respond. Be intuitive, instinctive and immediate.
16. A focused relaxed mind has no limit.
17. Open your mind to learning by quieting your ego.
18. Anticipate fulfillment.

These are some ideas I picked from a study of Zen. Using Zen to quiet your mind is a great way to create a relaxed state to bring your performance to a higher level. I always want my Quarterback to be in a state of relaxed focus so he could play fast and loose free from fear.

Chapter 3
Tutored By Geniuses

Bringing the Triple Option to the Wing T

In 1989 I was approached by Tubby Raymond to add the Triple Option to the Delaware Wing T Offense. Considering that Tubby Raymond was the Godfather of the Wing T; it was an offer I couldn't refuse.

Coach Raymond along with David Nelson created the Wing T. Tubby modernized The Wing T by adding more passing and using detached receivers. His success at The University of Delaware was legendary. He retired with a 300-119-3 record and 3 National Championships. He was a true football genius who understood all phases of the game and how to teach it.

He had a great staff around him and his offensive coordinator, Ted Kempski was almost as well-versed in the Wing T as Tubby. So it was a great experience coaching with guys like this.

I did not know anything about the Wing T despite playing Wingback in it in high school (we went undefeated my senior year). But my job was to teach the Triple Option to the Blue Hens.

Why add the Triple Option to the Wing T? When Tubby explained to me why he wanted to add the Triple Option it made perfect sense:

1. He wanted a play that changed after the snap of the ball. The Wing T had answers to a defensive tactic but involved another play. For example: If the defense closed down on the Trap, you answered with the Buck Sweep which looked like the Trap. But it was on the next play so you were *guessing* that the Defense was going to squeeze down on the Trap. Tubby wanted "Strategic Flexibility"
2. The Trap Play wasn't as effective because defenses were "wrong-arming' the Trap causing it to bend east/west. Tubby felt that the dive phase of the Triple Option would be a more effective B Gap Play.
3. Tubby wanted to make better use of his running Quarterbacks.
4. Tubby didn't think the transition would be too difficult because the playside techniques used in running Trap were almost the same as Veer Blocking.

Ironing Out Some Differences. Despite the similarities, there were also some critical differences. The first was the Quarterback seating the ball. In the Delaware Wing T, the Quarterback pulls the ball into his belly upon receiving the snap from center but when running the Triple Option, he had to extend the ball out so the fullback could run over the ball. The second difference was that The Wing T was based on deception but in the Multi-Bone, the Fullback was a runner or a blocker not a faker. Creating wider splits also was against Wing T dogma. Tubby finally bought in to the changes but declared me a Bolshevik.

Changing the Down Option. The Down and the Down Option were a pair of complimentary plays that were designed to look exactly alike. However, the Down Option was called when the Defense closed down on the Down. Another guessing game. But you could tweak the Down Option to be good vs everything and no guessing. The idea was for the QB to only flash fake the Fullback rather than ride him into the line to allow him to be a lead blocker. If the DE was logged by the guard, he led around the guard's block and blocked Linebacker to Safety, The Slot sealed the LB and the QB took it outside. But if the DE widened and the Guard kicked out the DE, the FB took it inside on the LB & the QB followed him inside. The Slot went up on the FS. This play was a great play to the Tight End and a great play to Wingover.

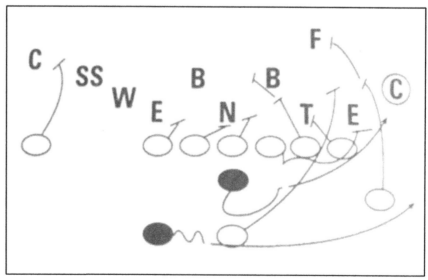

The Down Option

Introducing UD to the Exotic Sets. The Exotic sets Ends, Receivers, and Friends fit in perfectly with the Wing style of deception. They enhanced both the Triple Option and the Play Action Passes

Learning from a Master of the Game. I may have added some things to the Wing T but I picked up a lot more from Tubby Raymond, a Master of the Game. There wasn't much in pure Xs and Os that I picked up from The Wing T, The Down Option was one play I adapted and there was another that I'll talk about later. I learned more about overall strategy and tactics from the Delaware staff. Here are some of them:

1. *The Power of Sequence.* A play that is part of a sequence of plays is far more effective that a stand-alone play. For example, the trap is more effective when part of The Buck Sweep and Waggle Pass then just by itself. The effectiveness of The Buck Sweep and Waggle are also more productive when part of the group. Each play of the sequence should look alike and create a defensive conflict. So if a defense squeezes the Trap, the Buck Sweep kills it. And if the secondary rolls to stop the Buck Sweep, The Waggle is deadly. So I always made sure that every play in the offense, always had complimentary plays the created a sequence.

2. *How to add plays.* Your offensive system should have all the answers you'll need to handle any defense at the start of preseason camp.
   Therefore there should be no need to add plays. But if you want to add a play in pre-season here's the test. If you have to add a new blocking scheme or even a new technique the forget it. The cost is too great in practice time. "Every idea is great until you have to practice it" Tubby Raymond.

3. *The Value of Misdirection.* Misdirection makes a defense think and not react. It freezes the defense and slows pursuit. The faster the flow of a play the greater the need for misdirection. Boots and Waggles are great misdirection passes, not only are they play action they attack the opposite perimeter.

4. *You Can't Scheme a Scheme.* A defense can't create a special defense for your system because they only have a few days to practice it and you practice your scheme all year. So even it's a good defense for your scheme, your guys will out execute it because of how many repetitions they have had running it. Execution always beats Xs and Os. Have patience, and your guys will prevail.

5. ***Think in Terms of First Downs***. First downs control the clock. If you take a shot on first down and it's incomplete, second down should pick up half the yardage needed for a 1st down. So on 2nd & 10, you should get 5 yards setting up 3rd & 5. Or if you get 8 on first down, second down could be a "take a shot" down.

6. ***Always look for an Exposed Flank***. Tubby's idea was to use Wingbacks to secure the edge, anytime a Wing had leverage on the end man on the line of scrimmage, you had that flank because the Wingback had a great angle to block him. So in the Wingover Formation, there was an exposed Flank to either side but numbers favor going to the Nub or short side (D I later used this principle to run Stud Option, a double option in which the Wing and Tackle double team EMOL, (The End Man on the Line)

7. ***"Winning is a by-product of doing things right"*** *Tubby Raymond*. Just stay the course and the wins will come.

When Tony Met Sally. I couldn't add many Wing T plays to the Multi-Bone but I fell in love with the Sally Play and it became a big part of the offense until we went to the Gun and even then we used the exchange principle on almost every run or pass. We called it a "Smoke Call" I'm not going to attempt the explanation of the name of the play, suffice to say it had to do with a Red Light District in Baltimore.

The Sally Play was a counter play Delaware ran off the Down play and involved no pulling linemen. I used the play off the Sprint Out Pass more like a Sprint Draw like I previously explained earlier in the book. The playside Slot got deep and received an inside handoff from the QB the got North and South running to daylight, The Smoke call was made by the backside Tackle if he couldn't cut off the DE. Then the Guard would explode on the DE and the Tackle would look for anyone off the edge.

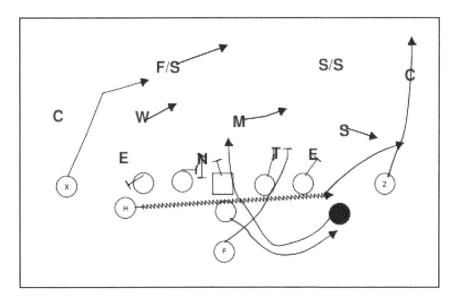

Shoot Liz Sally

I had a wonderful experience at The University of Delaware, Tubby Raymond and his staff treated me great and I'm forever grateful that a legendary coach would give me this opportunity.

Coaching Tips from a West Coast Genius

In the winter of 1998 I had the unbelievable opportunity to have dinner with the late but certainly great Bill Walsh. This was every coach's dream. We talked for four hours about everything from his Italian wife to Rommel to boxing and oh yeah - football. He was easy to talk to and had a great sense of humor. Though he was brilliant; he was far more down to earth than I expected a genius to be. He was just a guy who happened to know more about the game of football than almost anyone on this planet. It was a great night. He questioned me on my thoughts on offensive football. He asked me how I taught the triple option, and also asked me if we threw the quick game. When I told him about my use of "unless rules" – he smiled and said he taught the passing game the same way.

I shuddered when he asked me about the quick game. This was like Einstein asking a junior high teacher about math. And my anxiety was magnified by the fact that we had our Quarterback boot if the initial pattern was covered. Should I lie and give a conventional answer or tell the truth and risk the end of the conversation and leave Bill Walsh thinking I was a lunatic. Anyone who knows me knows what I did – I asked the waiter to bring more bread. I bought myself time hoping to change the subject but Coach Walsh wanted an answer so I told him. He stared at me for what seemed like an hour and a half and said "that's brilliant, where did you get it?" I explained how I took what my quarterback at Mercyhurst College (Eddie Ricci) did on his own and put some rules to it and there it was. He liked it and the conversation flowed freely about football from then on.

I had the opportunity to spend more time later that winter with Coach Walsh, Sam Rutigliano, and Brian Billick talking football in Ft. Worth. They were all great and I took a ton of notes. The result was a spike in our pass game efficiency that was phenomenal. I always believed in combining the option with the dropback pass but now I knew how to do it more effectively.

So what did this not so young grasshopper learn from the master? **How did Bill Walsh's West Coast Offense become part of an option attack?**

Here are some of the key coaching points from Bill Walsh:

1. Everything must start with protection. It doesn't matter what pattern you're installing it must start with how you are going to protect it. He was a strong believer in 7 man protection unless the defense was in nickel then 6 man protection was OK. So I followed his advice and stressed protection and taught the quarterback to direct the protection to match up with their rushers. This really helped us against Zone Blitzes.

2. Coach Walsh did not like throwing "hot" because he said your quarterback is going to get hit if you throw hot and that hit could put him out of the game. So is a 6 yard gain worth losing Joe Montana?

3. Always have a contingency plan if the routes are covered. The famous catch that Dwight Clark made was an example of the contingency plan. I think this is why Coach Walsh liked the boot off the quick game because it gave the Quarterback a contingency when the routes are covered. I also added a contingency plan to our dropback and play action passes. If all were covered it's QB Draw.

4. You beat Zone Defenses with your Running Backs and Tight Ends and you beat Man coverage with your Wide Receivers. Against Man Coverage expect the blitz so it's OK to "max protect" and let your Wide Outs use double moves to beat the corner.

5. A Quarterback's ability to run with the ball destroys Two Deep Man Coverage (which is the toughest coverage to throw against). A Quarterback that can be a run threat also puts a pressure on a defense that drops eight men into

coverage. The advantage of having an option QB involved in the passing game is obvious. Steve Young was a Wishbone Quarterback in high school.

6. Every route has a rhythm and timing. So when you put routes together into a pattern; the routes should open in a timed sequence so you can't have an "all hitch" pattern because the hitches will open at the same time and the quarterback won't be able to throw to his second hitch look without being late on the throw. So if you want to throw an all hitch pattern; the hitches must be at different depths. The same is true with all curls etc.

7. Details are everything. If you can't rep your offense with detail cut your play list down. You are doing too much. You don't need a lot of routes and patterns to have an effective passing attack. You just need to be able to execute the routes you do have.

8. Speed at receiver can be used either down the field or across the field. Coach Walsh was a master at getting the ball to Jerry Rice on those shallow drags and crossing routes. We tried to do the same with our wide receivers.

9. Using Play Action Pass on a run down or normal down and distance is the best way to throw the ball downfield. The run fake not only affects the secondary but also gives the linebackers conflicting reads. Coach Walsh loved the pressure the option put on a defense because the secondary had to be involved in run support but he did not think coaches that ran the option took advantage of that. I made the run/pass balance a priority and in 2009 our team led the nation in pass efficiency.

10. When evaluating a Quarterback there are two simple questions: Can he run the team? And can he carry the club? If he can do those things, then as a coach you have to live within your quarterback's limitations and capacities. The key is for the Quarterback to know the system and make good decisions and use good judgments.

These are ten coaching tips I got from a great coaching legend, Bill Walsh. I have other tips he gave me that I'll pass on in the future.

Sam Rutigliano was a great mentor to me when I was trying to learn the passing game.

Chapter 4
Developing a Philosophy
Building a Philosophy of Winning Football

After being a head football coach at two different schools and being exposed to some of the greatest football coaches in the game, I started to develop a philosophy of how to maximize the ability of your players. That's the secret, the scheme you use should maximize your players ability. So here are a few things I weaved together into my philosophy.

Strategic Flexibility. The use of audibles made offenses more effective because they put the offense in a better play against the defense's alignment. This was a big innovation. But this was *before* the ball was snapped. The next level of the audible was for the play to change because of the defense *after* the ball was snapped. This is huge. Plays that change after the snap bring offensive football to new level. However, these plays require reps to be able to execute, so your play list must be carefully crafted to minimize the number of plays you have in the playbook. The fewer the plays, the more repetitions each play will get and the better the play will be executed.

The Jazz Factor. If you ever heard a jazz artist like Miles Davis or Ray Charles, then you can understand improvisation in offensive football. You may recognize the song but you have never heard it played that way. Its advanced Strategic Flexibility. I wanted there to be an element of Jazz or improvisation in the offense. Patrick Mahomes is a good example.

The Clock. Jim Valvano taught me the value of owning the clock my first year as a head coach at Iona College. This idea was a huge part of my 25 years as a Head College Football Coach. It was a great lesson. The Atlanta Falcons had a 28-3 lead over the Tom Brady led Patriots in the second half of the Super Bowl and did not drain the clock, the result a huge Patriot win and legend status for Tom Brady. Clock control is a must and the ability to either shorten or extending the game is critical to success.

Banked Reps. Fitting you offense is paramount to success BUT it must be within the framework of your system. So if you're an option team and one year get a great passer, you can't just become an Air Raid team because your team will have zero reps at The Air Raid. Their "banked reps" are running the option. So, what's the answer? The answer is to have a flexible, diverse play list so both the running quarterback and the great passer are running the same system. But with the passer you're just using the passing game more. This way the other 10 positions are not learning a whole new system. Instead, they are making use of their "banked reps" from their previous years.

Practice The Whole Offense Every Day. As a head Coach, I wanted the entire offense to be simple enough that the entire offense could be repped in every practice. I don't mean practicing every play with every possible formation. We practiced every play and every formation. The offense should also be simple enough that a freshman can play.

Score on the Best on Your Schedule Without Turning the Ball Over. The teams I usually took over as a head coach were not defending champs. They were usually struggling. And usually struggling teams do not have great offensive lines. So, to move the ball against the powerhouses in your conference, you must run the option so the quarterback can eliminate defenders by reading them instead of us trying to block them. Also, the pass game must include screens and the quick pass. The second part of this is that you must move the ball without turning the ball over, it must be low risk.

The Universal Truths of Offense and the Three Laws are also explained in detail in this chapter.

Universal Truths of Offensive Football

Regardless of the offensive scheme you run there are certain "Universal Truths" that if followed will produce points.

1. Put Speed in Space – the more you do the more points you'll score.

2. Make Cover Guys Tackle & Tackle Guys Cover – create mismatches.

3. Balance is Essential – option, power, & counter – dropback, sprint, & play action

4. Better to Run a Lousy Play Great then a Great Play Lousy

5. Get a Head Start - use the threat of a counter to keep the defense still while the offense is moving.

6. Stretch & Pierce - a ball carrier going north & south while linebackers are going east & west will always gain yards.

7. Attack Complexity with Simplicity & Simplicity With Complexity

8. You Are Only Limited by Your Ability to Teach & Organize

9. Details Are the Difference – minimize techniques & maximize their use. The fewer the techniques, the more practice time you have to master them.

10. Attack a Powerful Defense with Finesse & a Finesse Defense with Power.

11. Attack a Speedy Defense with counters & a Slow Defense with Speed

12. Prepare for the Blitz or It Will Give You Fits. Have multiple answers built into your system. Don't rely on just "hot" reads or "max" protection. Always protect your protection.

13. Maximize by Surprise & Disguise – a play that is part of a sequence or a package is far more effective than one that stands alone.

14. Repetition is the Greatest Teacher If the Reps Are Done with Awareness. Repetition is the Greatest Teacher If the Reps Are Done with Awareness Repetition is the greatest Teacher. If the Reps Are Done with Awareness.

15. Too Many Answers to a Problem = No Answer & One Problem – one great answer is better than ten mediocre ones. Do what you do.

16. The Only Tendency That Is Valid is Your Tendency to Score.

17. Your Scheme Must Magnify the Talent of Your Offense. A good scheme is flexible to adapt to the strength of your personnel, your opponent, the score, field zones, weather without panic. Create a broad-based menu from which to choose your weapon as long as your basic principles remain consistent,

18. The Most Important *Ability* Is Depend*ability*. Never depend on an undependable.

19. Never Fight Today's Battles with Yesterday's Weapons.

20. Talent Is Only Talent If It Fits Your System.

21. A great play caller is more concerned with being effective than being clever.

22. "He who controls the pace wins the race" Jim Valvano. Control the tempo of the game to give your team the best chance to win. Know when to milk the clock & when to go into a hurt up mode.

23. Use the entire field – make the defense defend the entire waterfront. Throw deep & get the ball on the perimeter.

24. When in doubt go back to fundamentals – there are no "magic bullets" The plays that work best are the plays that are taught the best.

25. Points after a turnover are a more important stat than just turnovers. You must capitalize on turnovers and red zone opportunities.

26. Time of possession is only important to an exorcist. It's an ESPN stat.

27. Limit the plays maximize the ways. Lining up in a new formation doesn't require much execution but a new play call for a lot of work.

28. Use it or lose it. If you practice it use it. You'll only get good at something if you use it in a game. The exception is a specific answer or contingency play.

29. Stick to your knitting – this is something Ralph Isernia, our former OC reminded me of if started to stray away from the Gun Triple.

30. The main thing is to keep the main thing the main thing. The object is to win – total offense, rush yards, pass yards nothing is as important as the" W".

These 30 Universal Truths are never outdated. They will always be current & relevant regardless of the scheme you use. One thing I've learned over the years is it is imperative that above all your team must play **FAST,** if they have to think, they stink. Football isn't chess, there is no place for deciding. Football is about **REACTION.** It doesn't matter what you know or what your players know; it's about how fast they can process information.

The Law of Balance

One of the most over-used misunderstood terms in college football is "Balance". Other than "there's the Wildcat" every time a quarterback runs the ball or there's an RPO, the ESPN crowd love to talk about balance. To them, balance is throwing & running for the same yardage or equal attempts. But I think of balance in multi-dimensional views.

Sun Tzu the author of <u>The Art of War</u> said deception is everything in warfare. Never let the enemy know when where or how you are going to attack. *"If he must defend everything he will defend nothing"* Sun Tzu also said the best attack is where there is no defense. A formless attack should flow like water adjusting as it goes, completely flexible. How does this "ying/yang" stuff apply to balance?

Tubby Raymond's Wing T Attack used the "Power of Sequence" to achieve balance. Tubby and Ted Kempski always had a counter and play action pass to go along with their base play. For example their Buck Sweep sequence was the sweep, the Trap and the Waggle that all looked the same. So the enemy had to defend 3 plays at the snap of the ball. Tubby always said that the effectiveness of a play improves dramatically if it's part of a sequence that creates defensive conflicts.

Unbalance is another way to create balance. Paul Johnson's Spread Option Attack is so potent on the ground that it makes the Pass game easy to execute. To stop Johnson's running game you have to commit so many defenders that you have to play his wide outs 1 0n 1. So Paul achieves balance by forcing defenses to be unsound against the pass and thus easy to exploit with big plays. The Triple Option also forces the defense to view *every* back a threat. Mike Leach and Hal Mumme also created balance from the opposite direction. Their passing game was so good that defenses must commit so many defenders to defending the pass that they have a simple and effective running game. They always have a 1000 yard running back. By being <u>so</u> good at one phase of offense creates balance because the defense must commit an unsound number of defenders to combat your strength. The key is execution.

The Triple Gun came into existence for the sake of balance. The Shotgun made it easier to protect the QB – it's that simple. We got in the Gun to improve our pass protection and then developed the Gun Triple to go along with it. Originally the Gun was a part of our package that included a complete under center package, but as we got better with the Gun Triple, the under center package disappeared.

The style of creating balance may differ but old Sun Tzu was right; "attack where they can't defend". Strength vs. weakness gives you an edge. But the key is this: "A weakness is only a weakness *if* you can exploit it" That is a BIG *if.* That is what makes Paul Johnson a great coach – he can exploit weaknesses as could Tubby or Leach. Coaches that struggle are those that don't get great at executing their answers. If your answer to a Safety fill is the Post, you better be able to hit it often.

The Triple Gun gives us great balance for a variety of reasons.

1. We can run from a pass set (even Empty) and throw from a run set.
2. We can throw on run downs and run on pass downs.
3. We are equally effective in two minute offense or kill the clock offense. (We led the nation in time of possession).
4. We are effective in the Red Zone or in the middle of the field. (Our red zone scoring was 92% while scoring almost 40points/game).
5. Every back is a threat to carry the ball. (We had 3 rushers in the top 10 in the conference).
6. Every pass in The Triple Gun has a run built in to it as an escape and every run has a pass built in to it (Flash & Bubble).
7. The Gun Triple has a built in counter play because of the cutback possibilities.
8. The Gun Triple is such a great run that the defense must become unsound against the pass (like Paul Johnson's Triple Option)
9. The Triple Gun pass game is so effective (we led the nation in pass efficiency) the defense

How can you achieve this type of diverse offense? The key is to have a limited but inclusive menu and then get great at that menu. The Gun Triple is our base run, how a team defenses that signature play will set up the rest of our attack. We've been running the Triple Gun for so long that we know how teams will defend the Gun Triple, so we have a set of answers ready. The Gun Triple is so tough to defend that we don't need many other runs hence we can really get a lot of reps at the runs on the menu. And because we don't have many runs we can devote 60% of our practice time to the pass game. You become what you practice, the more you rep something the better you execute it. So the more you limit your menu, the more detailed you can be and the better you'll execute it. So have enough answers to handle every defense, but not over kill. So if your answer to a Free Safety fill is the Post route – rep the post so you can hit in your sleep. Every play in your offense should have a **specific** use and be an answer to a **specific** defensive scheme. Remember too many answers to the same defense equals NO answer. There are many great plays out there but unless a play has a specific spot on your call sheet – leave it out.

In conclusion The Triple Gun Offense is a balanced offense that is "formless" because we have the capability of instant adjustments even after the snap. The Gun Triple is such an effective run play, that we have the practice time to develop a simple but very effective pass game. Hence we can exploit a defensive weakness and "attack where there is no defense". The Triple Gun forces a defense to defend everything. The Gun Triple is such an effective play; the defense must commit too many defenders to stop it. But our Quick game is so good, that it forces a defense to stay out of the box as well and that makes the Triple Gun so effective. Stay simple with effective answers, run plays that complement each other and rep those plays. Sun Tzu will be proud of you.

The Law of Details

The single greatest lesson that I have learned in coaching is not how *many* plays you run but *how well you run those plays*. The secret to execution lies in teaching the *details* of a play. Details plus reps = *execution*. The more plays you have the less detailed you can be so keeping your play list lean. Make sure you choose plays that provide the most answers for your offense. But remember one good answer executed well is more effective than many answers executed poorly. This why I am so high on the Gun Triple – it's a running game by itself which allows you to focus on details & the Passing game which leads to offensive balance. Excellence lies in more details & more reps not in more plays.

1. "Greatness lies in the details"

2. The more detailed a play is practiced the better the execution.

3. The better the execution the more poise & confidence in clutch situations

4. Coaches that truly know their system don't have excess plays. Too many answers to problem is no answer.

5. Billick 20% Rule. – if you don't use more than 20% of your game plan, you have too much. Have specific answer plays. Practice checks & answer plays only vs. the defense they are in the plan to exploit.

6. Practice your plan – use packs & checks to limit your plays.

7. The more plays you have – the less detailed you can be – thus execution suffers. Reps are the key to detailed execution.

8. The fewer plays you have the more detailed you can be – then execution will improve. Fewer plays mean more reps per play & execution improves.

9. Limit the number of techniques you have for each position. The fewer the number of techniques the more individual time for each technique & execution will improve. Use the same techniques in as many plays as possible (cross-over techniques). Never add a new play that adds new techniques that must be drilled during the season.

10. A good system has "Cure-All Plays – those that are good vs. all defenses – this your core. Your system must have complimentary plays to protect your core. Also specific "Answer Play to take advantage of specific defense or for specific situations (Q.B. sneak in short yardage). Have few plays but run them in many ways.- disguise them. Limit the techniques - a critical criteria for adding a play to your core. When in doubt throw it out. Game plans are usually too big.

11. Never put in a play or plays that your star or stars struggle with. Better to have your playmakers comfortable than a coach being clever.

12. Prepare in detail – Detailed preparation leads to detailed execution & high performance, Poised & confident.

The Laws of Teaching

Coaching is above all teaching. The greatest coaches are the greatest teachers. The most important aspect of a play is how you teach it. There are no magic bullets; it's all about breaking a play down to the individual techniques used in a specific play & teaching the players those techniques until they are mastered. The following are some ideas I picked up along the way.

1. Preparation

    a. Know your subject matter

2. Organization of Presentation

    a. Have an organized manner of presenting your material

        1. Whole - Part – Whole method

        2. Teach concepts and the reason why

    b. It is not about how many plays you know, it's about how well

    they can be executed. Execution is the answer.

3. Variety of Presentation

    a. Use multiple venues of presenting material

        1. Video

        2. Chalk –just an overview, most OGs don't care about a pass route

        3. Playbook – mainly for coaches and Quarterbacks.

        4. Walk through – prefer walk throughs over meetings.

        5. Individual drills – it all starts with stance and starts

6. Partner drills – make each other better

7. Group drills – Read Drill must be done daily at full speed.

8. Team Scrimmage Situations – only scrimmage specific situations

b. Make the field your chalk board

4. Break down Skills into Drills

a. Have a drill progression for teaching each individual technique

b. Reps at game speed

5. Adhere to the Laws of Detail

a. Teach in small steps as well as the big picture

b. Details are the difference.

6. Encourage and Correct

a. Use video tape

b. Teach with enthusiasm, encourage learning

c. ALWAYS PRAISE EFFORT & push for improvement.

d. Challenge the players to do better – expect more.

e. Never criticize a mistake.

f. Mistakes are part of the learning process.

g. Only be critical of lack of effort.

7. Review and Repetitions

a. Reps are greatest teacher if done with awareness

b. Review with enthusiasm

c. Never let reps become boring

d. Use variety in review but always know:

    1) What the player saw & why he made his decision.

e. Reps lead to intuitive performance and mastery

    1. GAME SPEED IS A MUST

f. Two speeds: Teach specialized techniques & game speed

    1. Players must know the difference

g. Players learn more by doing than by listening

h. Don't fall in love with the sound of your voice.

When preparing for the season; remember the greatest coaches are the greatest teachers. Vince Lombardi and John Wooden both considered them above all teachers. John Wooden never spoke about winning to his team and yet he led them to ten National Championships in twelve seasons at UCLA. To be a more effective coach, you must work at being a more effective teacher.

Chapter 5
The Dropback Pass, Screens, and Boots

The Passing Game Incorporates the Dropback Pass

By the mid-90s the Multi-Bone had migrated to the Midwest to a small school named after Ichabod Washburn. Need I say more? Their nickname was naturally the Ichabods. To say this was a challenge maybe the understatement of all time, similar to calling Shaquille O'Neil tall. Washburn had won 3 games in their previous 3 years including a 0-10 record the year before our hero arrived. The 'Bods were competing in the toughest Division II conference in the country, the MIAA. Just to add to the fun Washburn had the fewest scholarships, the lowest budget and the worst facilities in the conference. My first spring we had 25 players on the roster.

But some of those guys were very good, especially a Quarterback (Joe Schartz who was inducted in the Washburn Hall of Fame and is a great High School coach at Manhattan HS in Kansas) and a Wide Receiver (Mike Dritlein who became the #1 receiver in WU history). So we had to take advantage of their talents against this super challenge. We also had to go back to "Stall Ball" to keep our defense off the field. We also had to find a way to protect our QB with a young, inexperienced offensive line against some of the best pass rush defenses in Division II football.

Putting Bill Walsh's Lessons to Good Use. Obviously the Quick Game and the Boot off it was going to be an important part of the puzzle. We could get rid of the ball before the pass rush could get to the Quarterback.

The one thing we could do is make our QB more effective. Here were points of emphasis:

1. Throw the ball on time. Every pass route has a rhythm that it must be thrown. In the Quick Game under center: The Hitch is 1, 2, 3 throw it. The Fade, the Slice and Flat are also 1, 2, 3, throw it. Take a big first step, a gather step and on the third step, point your toe where you want the ball to. If the primary route is cover go to the secondary route. The complimentary routes were 1, 2, 3, look and throw. So that would be the Stick with the Fade, the Slant with the Flat and the Corner route with the Slice. So the complimentary routes take a fraction of second longer to open. These rhythms are practiced every day in

"Routes on air" The QB must understand that the routes will open in a progression like venation blinds.

2. Throw away from defenders not at receivers. If the QB throws at the receiver, the defender can close the separation and knock the ball away. But if the QB throws away from the defender he actually forces the receiver to increase separation. It also cuts down on the possibility of an interception.

3. We always stress throwing a "Long Ball Long & a Short Ball Short" – in other words, if the QB is throwing a Post route or any Deep Route he wants to throw it ahead of the receiver so he has to really run to catch up to it. We never want to see a receiver turning back to catch a deep ball, the likelihood of a DB knocking it away increases greatly. On a short pass like an out or a curl we want the QB to throw that route short to make the receiver come back to the ball, again cutting down on a possible interception or a deflection.

4. This type of passing is "throwing the receiver open" When Tom Brady was with the Patriots, Tom Brady turned guys like Wes Welker & Julian Edelman into stars in the NFL by "throwing them open".

5. Our definition of "Open" is anytime the Receiver is between the ball and the Defender"

6. If all are covered use the "Quarterback escape" – Every pass has a built-in run or escape. The "Escape" for the Play Action Pass and the Dropback Pass is QB Draw. The "Escape" for The Quick Game is QB Boot and the "Escape" for any Perimeter Pass (Sprint or Boot) is QB Sweep.

OK so prepping our Quarterbacks on making their passing game more productive was a big help. Joe Schartz became the All Time Total Offense Leader in WU history. Now we had to do something to help our Offensive Line.

The Triple Screen Creates a Dropback Pass Game. The question we faced was how do you have a Dropback Passing Attack without blocking the Defensive Linemen? Well we run the ball without blocking all the D. Linemen by running the Triple Option. We knew we didn't have to block Defensive Linemen with a screen pass but how many times can you throw it in a game? Well you can give the Fullback the ball on the dive many times if it is the read in the Triple Option. That's the answer! Our base Screen Pass had to be a Triple Option Screen Pass, 3 Screens in one.

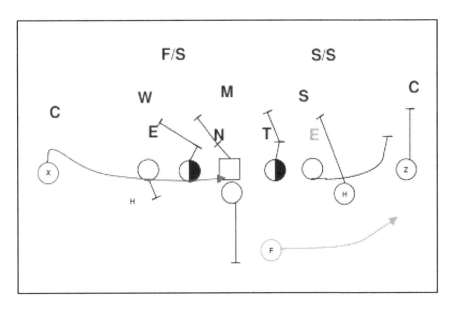

Shoot Triple Screen

The Screens had to time up like a pass progression. Screen #! Was a Quick Flare to the Fullback with 1 lead blocker; the Onside Tackle. This was a "Show and Go" Screen – fast. The Quarterback threw to the FB every time *unless* the End Man on the Line covered him. Our Fullbacks caught over 30 screens that first year. Their rule is "Drive for Five" – use the Tackle as a lead blocker like a sweep.

If the Flare Screen was covered, the QB retreat with his hips square yo the line of scrimmage and throw to Screen #2 – the Jailbreak or Tunnel Screen to the Wide Receiver lined up opposite to the Fullback. The Wide Receiver takes 2 Quick steps upfield and then comes back to the QB going behind the Line of Scrimmage. If he gets the ball he turns North and South and gets upfield. This Screen produced the biggest plays.

The third screen was the backside Flare. But this was a Slow Screen with the Halfback going in motion. The Motion HB's job was to read the Cornerback on the Wide Receiver. If he covered or trailed the WR, the HB yelled "Ball, Ball, Ball" which alerted the QB to flip his hips and throw to the motion HB. When the WR heard the Ball Call, he turned into a crack blocker.

The Blocking for the Triple Screen was simple and just had to be repped:

- Onside Wide Receiver stalk blocks man on (same as Option)
- The #2 Receiver (Slot, Tight End, Twin etc.) seals the first Linebacker inside

- The Onside Tackle shows Pass, the releases flat down the line of scrimmage and blocks the first defender he come to.
- The Onside Guard blocks the protection for 2 counts and the releases to block the MLB to Safety
- The Center blocks the protection for 2 counts and releases to the backside and blocks the MLB to Safety
- The Backside Guard blocks the protection for 2 counts and then releases to block the backside OLB.
- The Backside Tackle set and lures the end man on the line up field, then Butts and cuts.

The Triple Screen is formation friendly and is easily disguised which enables it to be called more frequently than a more conventional screen pass. Its' great from Pro & Twins .If we choose no motion, it becomes a double screen with the Halfback responsible for the "ball call" blocking the CB over the Wide Receiver

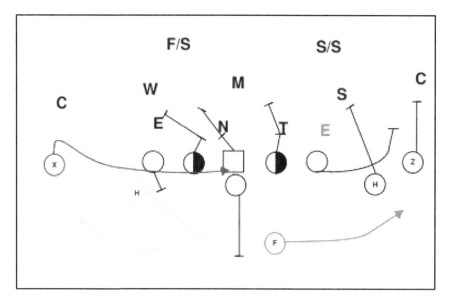

Twins Triple Screen

Adding the Dropback Stretch Pass. The Stretch Pass was stitched together in an attempt to come up with a "cure all" pattern that was simple for the Quarterback to read and that the routes adjusted based on the coverage. If we could develop this kind of pattern, we would only need one dropback pass. The key was route conversion and Strategic Flexibility. The other factor was that it looked similar to the Triple Screen. If they looked alike, it would slow down the pass rushers and help our pass protection.

The Stretch Pass Routes. The first rule was that there were field routes and boundary routes regardless of the play call. This was done so we could direct the protection in the direction of the rush. This was a major help in blocking zone blitzes. We also numbered the receivers to the field and boundary starting with the widest receiver being #1.

The Field Routes. The #1 (or widest receiver) does a fade every time unless the CB bails and gets depth, then the WR breaks his route off at 14 yards and does an In Route looking for a window with his numbers to the QB. He must force an outside release to "widen the window" The #2 Receiver does a Stretch Route to the middle of the goal post. Regardless of whether he lines up tight (Tight End or Slot) or wide (Twins) that's his landmark. The coaching point is if the receiver is tight he must get wide on his release. The #3 Receiver checks the Outside Linebacker, if he blitzes he blocks him. If the OLB drops into coverage, he runs a flare, like the Triple Screen.

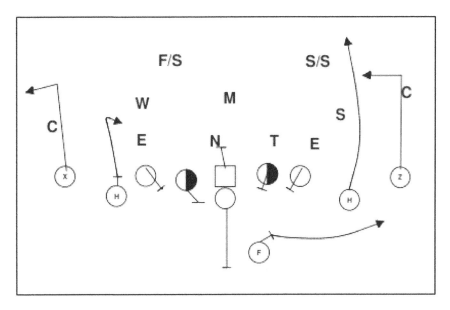

Dropback Stretch Pass

Coaching point: If we tagged the pass "Hot" the #3 receiver free releases to his flare and if the OLB Blitzes, he's the Hot Receiver.

The Boundary Routes. The #1 (or widest receiver) runs a fade every time unless the CB bails or gets depth. If the CB bails, #1 breaks his route off at 12 yards and runs an Out Route back to 10 yards. Coaching Point, the receiver must a 4-6 yard lane between him and the sidelines if he runs a fade route. The #2 Receiver (usually an RB) He check releases on the OLB to his side. If the OLB Blitzes, he blocks him.

But if he drops into coverage, he runs a 5 yard "Stop Route" and gets his numbers to the QB.

The Dropback Protection. The basic Dropback Protection is 7 man protection unless we free release one of the RBs or unless we add to the protection with a "Max" call which keeps all the RBs into block. The Protection is "Big on Big" with the Offensive Line responsible for the 4 Down Linemen and the Middle Linebacker. The HB & FB are responsible for the 2 Outside Linebackers.

Against a 34 Defense we start with a "Solid" call which has the guards help the Center unless the ILBs Blitz by using a Twins Formation the 34 is easier to decide who is rushing and we adjust by directing the protection to fit the rush. So if the Defense removes a linebacker, we use our normal Big on Big protection. However if they do not remove a LB and go to 3 Deep, we direct the protection to the field.

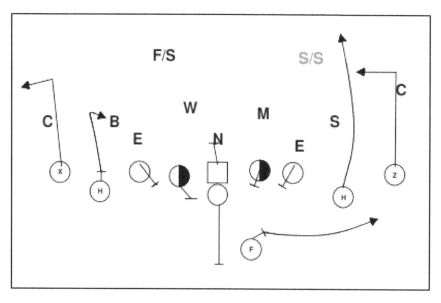

Dropback Stretch vs 34 – 4 Shell

If the Defense gives us 8 in the box, we use "Max" protection. In Max Protection all 3 RBs check release prior to releasing into their routes.

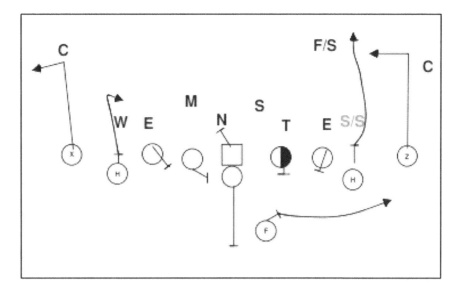

Dropback Stretch with Max vs 44

The threat of the Triple Screen really helped our protection but we did not use the dropback scheme as much as I liked until we developed into the Triple Gun.

The Quarterback Reads. The Quarterback reads are simple. We never want him to have to read the entire field, we divide the field in half based on the whether it's a 4 or 3 shell. If it's a 4 shell, he looks to the field and if it's a 3 shell, he goes to the boundary.

The Field Read. The thought process is: "I'm throwing the Stretch every time unless the Strong Safety Covers, the I'll look to the Z (Widest Receiver) and throw the "Fade/In" If I don't like that, I have the Flare or QB Draw. Remember Ball Security is the #1 priority.

The Boundary Read. The thought process is: "I'm throwing to X (The #1 Receiver) unless it's covered, then come down to the Stop Route (the #2 Receiver)"

The Quarterback Pre-Snap Thoughts. Prior to the snap on every pass, the Quarterback asks himself these questions:

1. What's my launch point?
2. What's my blitz control?
3. What's my key/read?
4. What's my escape?

Regardless of the pass, the Quarterback uses these 4 questions. Every pass has a built-in Blitz Control and Escape that the QB must remind himself of.

Route Conversion Made Simple. Some "experts" make route conversions a mystery but they are actually very logical. The best place to study route conversions is to watch a bunch of kids on the playground, they know hot convert routes.

Here's the way we simplified them. Start with the "unless rules". I'm running a Fade unless... Approaching the route in this manor, the receiver will explode off the ball and cause the CB to reveal the coverage. The receivers thought process is "If he's even, I'm leaving but if he's deep, I'll creep" in other words, if the DB is tight, I'm deep, but if he's deep, I'm short" Simple and effective. One other adage: "VS Zone stay but VS Man run away"

Conclusion. Our early dropback game was obviously, very limited, but it gave us a foundation to build on. It fit in with the Quick Game, Sprint Passes and Play Action Pass Attack.

Adding a Little "I" and Midline to the Multi-Bone

Tubby Raymond's advice led me to add one series to The Multi-Bone. I was still trying to develop a Play Action Boot and was failing miserably. We couldn't do it off The Triple because the Triple happened to fast. The Belly play had really diminished in the offense because it was really only effective in the full Wishbone which we weren't in very often. I also wanted to get our Slots the ball more. So we looked for a run play that could do all of that.

The Counter Isolation and Boot Series. We came up with a series that gave us all we were looking for:

1. It got our talented Slots the ball going North and South.
2. It set up a great Play Action Boot Pass.
3. It was a misdirection play so our Fullback didn't have to handle a filling Linebacker.
4. And it gave us a play that we could run on any down and distance.
5. The Boot Pass got the Quarterback on the perimeter and gave him the same reads as the Boot off the Quick Game.
6. The Offside or Bootside Slot used the same Slam & Slide Technique as The Quick Boot.
7. The Receivers ran the same Boot Rule except now the Split End did the Over Route.

The Counter Iso was an effective run play that looked like the I formation Lead Draw with motion BUT the Slot's motion would take him past the QB and FB. Then he would plant and go back. This made it difficult to distinguish which way the play was going. The Quarterback handed the Slot the ball behind him which further added to the deception.

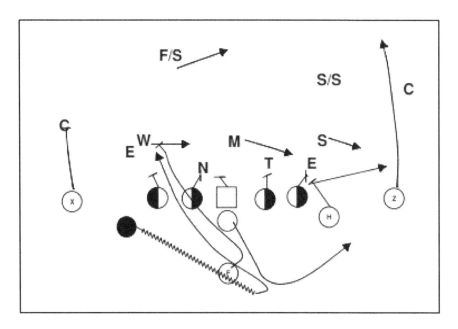

Shoot Li Iso Left

On the Boot Pass. The Quarterback looked for the Slam and Slide Route in the Flat but if the defense jumped the Slam and Slide, the Over Route was the next look. If all were covered – Run.

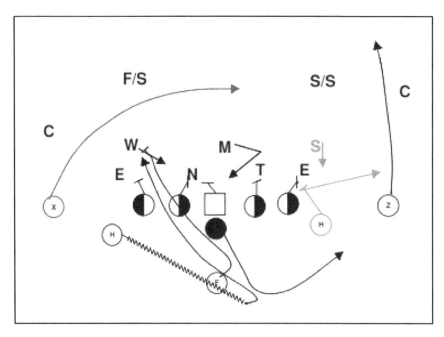

Shoot Li Iso Left Pass

So with very little cost we added a great little series that added a little more deception and launch points to the evolving Multi-Bone Attack.

We also added some Midline to the Run Game but because we were passing more, we ran it as a give or keep play with the Slots being lead blockers. This was to take advantage of an aggressive 3 Technique.

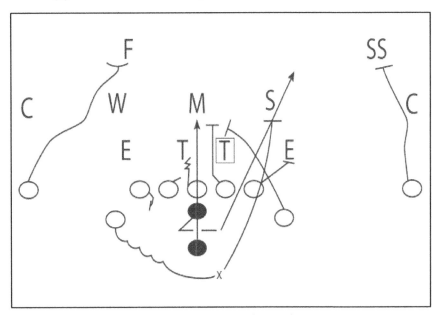

The Midline Lead

The Midline Lead could also be run with Long Motion to make it part of the Run and Shoot Package.

These little wrinkles really made The Multi-Bone more diverse, flexible and balanced.

Chapter 6
Putting The Triple Gun Together
Going to the Gun

The next phase in the evolution of Option Football was running the Option from the Shotgun Formation. This was another transformative development in offensive football caused by Option Football. It literally exploded on the scene and changed offensive football forever. This was like the coming of the Triple Option in the late sixties.

The Zone Read. The Zone Read was discovered by Rich Rodrigues while he was the Head Coach at Division II Glenville State University in West Virginia. He discovered that the Quarterback could read the End Man on the Line of Scrimmage (EMOL) and thus pick up an extra blocker. So, if DE did anything but chase the Running Back on the Zone, the Quarterback would give the ball to the Running Back. But if the DE chases the Running Back down the line of scrimmage, the Quarterback kept the ball. No one knew what Rodrigues was doing and he dominated his competition.

Coaches are the biggest copycats on this planet (Yours Truly Included). So, it wasn't long before the Zone Read spread throughout the world of College Football. Was it transformational? It was even more transformational than the Triple Option.

Rich Rodrigues left Glenville State to join Tommy Bowden at Tulane. Tulane was never known as a football power and Buddy Teevins, who Bowden replaced, had 11-45 record. Teevins, a good coach, had little success at Tulane. Bowden and Rodrigues hit The Big Easy armed with the Zone Read and posted a record of 18-4! The Zone Read was the biggest thing to come to New Orleans since Gumbo.

Northwestern, long the doormat of the Big Ten was mired in mediocrity under Head Coach Gary Barnett who had a 5-19 record for The Wildcats. Barnett hired Kevin Wilson as his offensive coordinator to run The Zone Read and bingo! Northwestern had a 15-1 record, a trip to the Rose Bowl and two Big Ten Titles.

So the Zone Read was very transformational just like the previous option innovations.

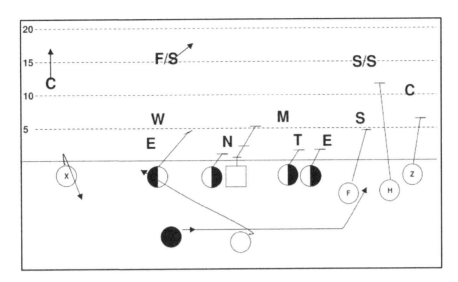

Trips Zone Read

The Need for the Gun. The updated, reconstructed Multi-Bone was working great. We became a balanced team that had become one of the top 3 passing teams in the conference. One of our Wide Receivers had set the schools receiving records and when I left Washburn 4 of the top 5 receivers in the school's history were Multi-Bone Receivers. Our Quarterbacks set numerous passing and total offense records as well. So why change?

The problem arose in 1998. The 44 Defense with a double A gap blitz completely limited our pass game because it limited our protection. Our only answer was the Quick Game with Gap Protection and our Fullback having to block the Defense's best pass rusher. Also, more sophisticated Zone Blitzes were also problematic. Though our offense was still effective, I saw a weakness. We were dependent on the pass game to provide answers to defensive adjustments and now that was in jeopardy.

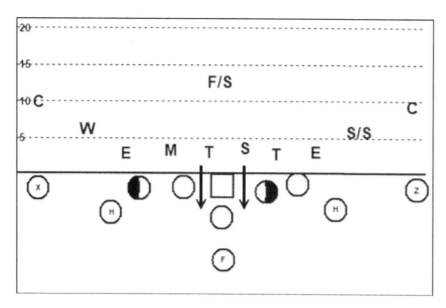

The 4-4 Defense

We went to the Gun in long yardage situations as a band aid answer for the rest of the season, but we had no significant run game from the Gun. So we were faced with a decision: become a Paul Johnson type of Flexbone (Run, Run & Run) or try to run the Option from the Gun. I investigated The Zone Read popularized by Rich Rodriguez & Kevin Wilson, but it looked at it as a glorified "Naked" play and not a downhill run. My Philosophy of Offensive Football was Balance and Flexibility, so it became evident that we would have to run the Multi-Bone from the Gun.

The Learning Process. The learning process for the transition from The Multi-Bone to the Gun was not an easy one. For one thing, I had no one to get advice from. As an under-center option guy, I could always call Greg Gregory (The OC at Army), Bob Noblit (The OC at Air Force), Gerry DiNardo or one of the many option guys in the country. But no one ran Triple Option from the Gun. And if there was a mistake to be made, I made it.

The first mistake was thinking all I had to do was move everyone back and run the triple just like under center – disaster. The offensive line's blocks happened too fast so by time the dive back got to the line of scrimmage, the defense was already off their blocks and tackled the ball carrier. So, we had to slow down the offensive line's blocks. Wow, that was crazy.

The second issue was by time the Quarterback caught the snap and turned to the Dive Back, the Hand Off Key was on the mesh and the ball was on the ground.

The third problem was the mesh was so late that even if the Quarterback did pull the ball cleanly, the Pitch Key was all over him.

The good news was adjusting the pass game was a piece of cake. The Quarterback's drops were easier and faster hence the ball was out of his hands faster. By putting the QB at 4 yards, his timing on the Quick Game was "catch, step, throw".

Fisher DeBerry (Air Force HC) – A true legend in Option Football

Putting the Offensive Line in Two Point Stances. This was a bold move for an option football team but remember we had to slow down the offensive line's blocks. We put them in a "Cocked" 2-point stance which was basically a 3 point stance with the down hand up. This stance allowed the line to come off the ball hard but not as fast as a 3-point stance.

Discovering Smart Splits. Since studying Jake Gaither's Split Line T Offense, I always played around with adjusting line splits. Big splits created big seams for the dive back. The problem was we would have to single block defensive linemen and with the running back getting to the line of scrimmage slower, this was a big problem. Especially at Center where he had to single block the nose while snapping the ball. So, we had to use Veer Blocking and Double the Nose. Problem: if the Guard took a big split or even a 2-foot split, a good nose would get penetration. I always study other coaches' offenses and I noticed in Manny Matsakis' Offense, he had some splits were wide and some tight. So we took Jake Gaither's big splits & Manny's accordion splits and combined them into "Smart Splits" the objective: Seams and Double Teams. Basically, tight splits on double teams otherwise wide splits.

Not only did Smart Splits make our line more effective, but it also made the Quarterback reads easier. But not easy enough.

Smart Splits

Changing the Dive Backs Aiming Point. The next adjustment was moving the running back further away from the Hand Off Key. The Smart Splits moved the Hand Off Key further from the mesh but now I wanted to move the mesh further from the Hand Off Key. So, we changed his aiming point to A Gap. This was almost a Midline Path. Now the Quarterback had an easier read than from under center. Plus changing the aiming point had a HUGE unintended consequence.

The Cutback Shows Up. Just as all the issues were being solved in a step-by-step approach, we had a huge breakthrough. Remember, we were learning this play as we went along in that first spring practice. I was driving our offensive staff insane. Then in a scrimmage, our very talented Tailback. Brandon Rainer got the hand off and cutback behind the Nose Guard for a long run. Then he did it again and again. I asked him what made him cutback and he said ''I just look at A gap & cut away from anything in there'' I've been teaching it that way ever since.

The other thing we changed based on the cutback was the offensive line getting vertical push on their double teams. In the past we wanted the line to create a crease and the dive back to stay on a track, now we wanted the line to create a *cavity* and let the back be a B gap to B gap runner. This was a big part of the success of the Gun Triple.

Basically, a New Play. The Gun Triple was a completely different play than the Under Center Triple. We created a new play. It was slower than the Under Center Triple, but it had a built-in counter. It was slower but had movement. It was like a Mariano Rivera cutter which is little slower than a fastball but much tougher to hit.

Constructing the Triple Gun

One of the major updates in The Triple Gun Offense is the expansion of our use of formations and motions. We not only increased the number of formations, we also kept the same personnel in the game to get into the formation. This limited defensive substitution and created mismatches. Moving the Tailback position into multiple spots made it very difficult for the defense to keep the ball out of his hands.

We also added "Compressed Sets" to create special flanks and to crack block the pitch key forcing the Corner to play pitch. (Make Cover Guys Tackle and Tackle Guys Cover).

Exotic Unbalanced Formations that were great in the Multi-Bone became another key weapon in the Triple Gun menu. We put both Split Ends to the same side and shifting to create a recognition and numbers problem for the defense. The same Exotic sets as under center but now in the Gun.

Using motion (Whirley) to create misdirection was another important development and evolution of the Triple Gun Offense. We also added "Jet" and "Tail" motion to run the sweep. The Jet Sweep Series was an outstanding complement to our option attack.

A couple of points should be made concerning the use of formations in the Triple Gun offense. Originally, we went under center and ran the triple, midline, and counters and threw the ball. Eventually we moved completely to the Gun. It took up too much practice time for the amount of time we went under center.

It should also be noted that this book does not use numbers to designate a specific play in an attempt to give coaches a system of communicating what particular play is called. Rather, coaches should determine for themselves how to denote the play within their own team's system.

In our program, formations are divided by following personnel groups:

- Normal formation: two wide receivers, two halfbacks, and a tailback . The Quarterback's toes are 4 yards from the ball and the Tailback is a yard and a half behind the QB.

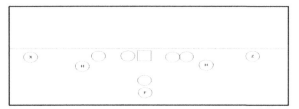
Gun Base Formation

- Pro formation: a tight end, a tailback, a halfback, and two wide receivers. A Tight End for a Slot

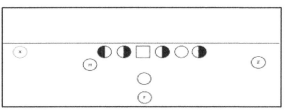
Pro Gun

- Twins/Slot formation: three wide receivers, a tailback, and a halfback . The Slot splits the difference between the Tackle and the Wide Receiver.

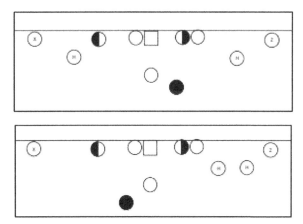
Slot and Backs Formations

An Evolution of Understanding

As I was explained earlier the primary reason we went to the shotgun was purely as a solution to pass-protection. Subsequently, however, as we developed into a shotgun team, because of the many other advantages of being in the gun including:

- It is much easier to develop the quarterback's drops in the shotgun.
- The quarterback sees better from the gun—especially a shorter quarterback.
- It is easier to avoid the rush because the quarterback already has a cushion between himself and the line of scrimmage.
- It is easier for the quarterback to find throwing lanes.
- The quarterback clearly has more time to throw.
- It is easier for the offensive line to pick up stunts and blitzes.
- Sight adjusts and hot throws are easier for the quarterback to execute.
- The alignment of the tailback makes it easier for him to get out on pass patterns.
- Quick screens and screens in general are more effective in the gun. For example, it's easier to combine a flash screen or bubble screen with a running play.
- Pass protection is more forgiving—room exists for the quarterback to escape a rusher.
- It's more difficult for the defense to "load the box."
- It's more difficult for defensive backs to distinguish between 3- or 5-step drops.
- It's more difficult for the defense to read play action pass. Offense line pad levels are the same on run and pass.

Shifts. The main use of shifts was in our "Exotic" package that we used in the Multi-Bone. With three wide outs, trips could be used as a pre-shift set. In that scenario, if we called twins, we would then shift to twins. Another way to shift is to call "shift open." In this method, we would align in any set other than the set called in that personnel group, and then shift to it

Motions. Another change in the Triple Gun Offense, is that unless motion is called the pitch back goes on the snap with **no** motion. Without motion the defense can't get any tip on the direction of the play.

We **call** Jump to get a "head start" or to create a counter situation. Using "Whirley Motion" is a great way to get a Counter Option look as is "Flip" Motion. Other possible motions calls include the following:

- "Jump" to motion the slot
- "Flip" to motion the Slot to be in position to be the Dive Back over the OG to his side.
- "Whirley" to motion of playside slot in 3 step motion and return in the direction of the play.
- "Jet" to motion the slot to run the Jet Sweep.
- "Web" to put the widest back to that side in motion from Backs or Bunch sets.

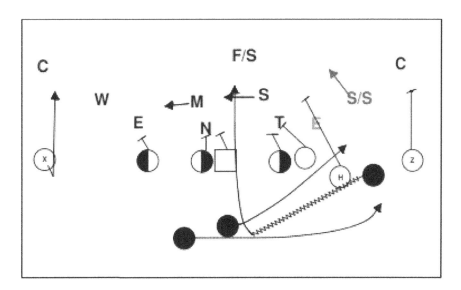

Backs Rt WEB Flip Rt

Using the Same Personnel for Many Formations. We not only increased the number of formations, we also kept the same personnel in the game to get into the formation. This limited defensive substitution and created mismatches. The less substitution the better. We could get into a three wide receiver set lie Trips or Twins by adjusting and widening the Slots.

Moving the Tailback position into multiple spots made it very difficult for the defense to keep the ball out of his hands. We off-set the Tailback when we detached a Slot unless we called "I" and we lined him up in Empty. The 2 Empty Formations we deployed became another very difficult adjustment for the defense.

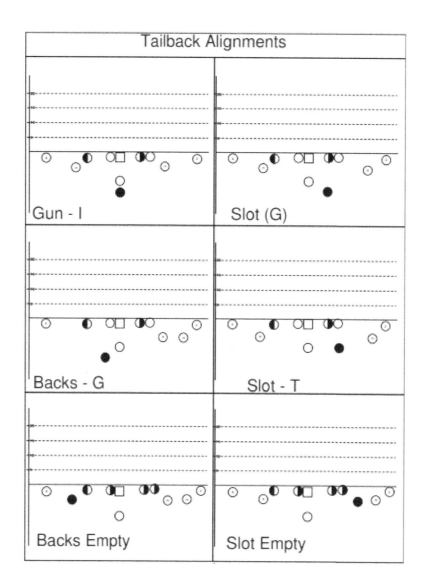

The Triple Gun Formations and Motions Just Window Dressing. This may seem complicated but The Triple Gun is *"A handful of plays run many ways"* remember you don't have to execute a formation. The "Smoke and Mirrors were designed to make the defense think and not react. Joe Restic, while at Harvard confused the Ivy League Defenses with his Multi-Flex Offense for years. The Triple Gun repeats *the same play but never the same way.*

Installing an Offense – Year One

Whenever a coach takes over a program or decides to change his offense, there is a question of how much to install. Most times a coach will try to do too much. It's always better to master a minimum amount of plays and concepts. I'd rather run a lousy play great than a great play lousy.

Self-adjusting plays are the basis of the Triple Gun Offense. Plays that adjust after the snap (Strategic Flexibility) eliminate the need for a fat playbook. The basis of the run game is the Gun Triple which adapts to the defense and even provides a built in counter play. The hub of the Pass Game is the Quick/Boot Package and the Play Action Pass that both\have a routes that convert based on coverage and a built in Quarterback run. The Triple Gun is completely flexible and can adapt to situations or talent. These self adjusting plays are "cure alls" because they are good vs. any defense.

The complimentary plays are "answer plays" because they are answers to a specific defense or blitz etc. These plays are more conventional plays and are only used as "answers" for very specific situations. We try to be limit these plays and make them part of a check with me package.

Another important principle in installing an offense is to minimize the number of techniques you're teaching & maximize the number of ways you use them. Also use the same patterns routes and reads for the QB in the passing game. Getting as many reps as possible is critical to execution, so by minimizing the skills that have to be learned you can maximize the amount of reps each skill gets. There are many great football plays but like cars you can't own all of them.

The following are some tips and guidelines that I've used the times I have taken over programs and had to install a new offense. The key is to always to keep it simple but have the answers you need to be effective.

1. **Goal** - Be simple enough to execute but diverse enough to be effective.
   a. Limit concepts but have enough variety for balance.
   b. Concepts must complement one another.
   c. Offense should be sequential
   d. Must be able to adapt to :
      1) Field Zones
      2) Time Management
      3) Talent Available – feature a great WR or TB – must get the ball to playmakers.
   e. Must be simple enough for talented frosh to master so they can contribute.
   f. Must have a "Jazz Element" – the ability to improvise.

2. **Pass Attack** – must revolve around protection & the assets of the QB
   a. Protection comes 1st – simplicity is a must. When in doubt – "Max "
   b. High % passes to control the clock.
   c. Must be able to pick up 3rd & long situations.
   d. Must have simple come from behind & Clutch Offense capabilities.
   e. Must compliment the run game. Create defensive conflicts produce big plays. Quick strike capability is a must.
   f. Must have pass/run threats for the QB
   g. Must be "blitz proof" – avoid sacks. Emphasis on "Ball Security".

3. **Run Game** – control the clock & be effective in run situations
   a. Feature the Option – put speed in space. Get your playmakers the ball.
   b. If QB is not a good runner use "Gun Speed Option"& Jet Sweep to get outside.
      1) Quick Screen & Bubble plays must be featured
   c. Every run must be part of a sequence. (Base Run, Counter & Play Action Passes)
   d. Package "Answer Plays" to best attack fronts & stay out of bad plays. (Simplifies Blocking Schemes). Only run & practice answer plays against the specific defense they are the answer for. For example only run a reverse against a defense not protecting the backside flank.
   e. Have Run Checks to exploit specific fronts (Simplifies Blocking Schemes)
   f. Must be able to run in run situations. (Goal line, Coming out, & Short yardage)

4. **Tempo Control** – clock management offense is a must..
   a. Clutch Offense, Victory Offense & Stall Ball.
   b. Limit contingency plays.

5. **Teach - detailed teaching in every technique**
   a. Build the foundation of system
   b. Limit techniques & maximize their use.
   c. Reps lead to mastery – the fewer the number of techniques the greater amount of reps for each. Use teaching & drill progressions to teach technique.
   d. Daily repetitions lead to good fundamentals. Law of Accumulation.

How to Use Meaningful Stats to Improve Your Program

I've spent a lot of time talking about "meaningful stats" and what stats are important and which stats are ESPN stats or meaningless. How many times have you heard an announcer proclaim that Joe Blow just threw for a school record of 500 yards and oh by the way his team is losing! Or how many times have you heard a coach on the short end of the score say "We outgained them by a hundred yards; they couldn't stop us" Those comments are a result of not understanding the difference between meaningful and meaningless stats.

I did an intense study of what stats were really meaningful. I looked at every game that I had been a head coach and some commonality of the wins and losses. My teams had a reputation of beating great teams, how did it happen? At Iona, the biggest wins were won when we held opponents to less than 16 points. At Mercyhurst, we beat Glenville 14-7, Gettysburg 21-20, Widener 17-7, and Dayton 19-6. And at that point we never lost a game when we scored 25+ points! When we started to throw more and became more dependent on the pass it increased the number of turnovers we had and decreased our ball control.

After studying my teams, I looked into all of college Football and the significant stats. Amazingly, the highest scoring teams were not necessarily the best. I made many other stat discoveries. For one thing though a stat might make a slight difference, like the team that rushes for the most yards wins 60% of the time is really not that significant. Here are some of my other discoveries.

Averages mean nothing. Every game has a unique dynamic that has little to do with previous games. Only the stats for each individual game matter. Because a team runs up scores on "cupcakes doesn't mean it has a good offense.

The Four Standard Meaningful Stats that decide wins and losses are:

1. **Score more than 25 points** in every game & against the best on your schedule. This is your baseline target. In every game you should have a game plan to score a minimum of 25 points which will win 88% of your games.

An example is the 2011 BCS Championship game between 2 very high scoring teams, Oregon (Avg. 50+ points/Game) and Auburn neither team could manage 25 points! Oregon was averaging double that amount all year, but we know averages are meaningless. Auburn held the Ducks to 19 and won the National Championship in 2010 by the score of 22-19.

In the Super Bowls only 6 times has the loser scored more than 25 points. In the 2017 Super Bowl, Atlanta wasn't satisfied with their 28 - 3 halftime lead and threw the ball more than in the first half. They not only didn't score, they lengthened the game and gave Tom Brady the time he needed to pull off the greatest comeback in Super Bowl history.

2. **Hold your opponent to 16 points or less**. This is my definition of playing great defense. If you can't score 25 points due to your opponent or the weather etc then hold your opponent to less than 16. If you hold your opponent to less than 16 points you'll win 92% of your games. If you can't score you must keep the ball away from your opponent and prevent them from scoring. The Jim Valvano Rule "He who controls the pace wins the race" Football is not like war, it has a time limit and the team with the most points at the end of the time limit wins.

3. **Score a non Offensive Touchdown and don't give up any**. If you score a non offensive TD it hurts your offensive stats but you win the game. If you give up a non offensive Touchdown, it *helps* your offensive stats but you lose the game! If you score a Non Offensive TD, you get no Total Offense Yards (Meaningless Stat) and no time of possession (Meaningless Stat). But you'll get 7 points & will win 90% of your games.

4. **Have a +2 or more turnover margin**. Ball security and getting takeaways is essential to securing wins. It's all about the ball and who possesses it. High Scoring teams that turn the ball over don't win championships. So it's imperative that you have an Offense that can score 25 points vs every team on your schedule WITHOUT turning the ball over. In 25 years as a head college football coach my teams were undefeated when we had a +2 Turnover Margin.

If you look at every college team it's about 98%. This is the greatest predictor of wins and by far the most Meaningful Stat.

If there are two other second tier elements that are important but fit into the four main stats. They are:

1. It is to score touchdowns in the Red Zone and force a Field goal attempt if your opponents are in your red zone.
2. Win the Sudden Change – stop your opponent from converting turnovers to points, conversely convert your opponents turnovers into points

So how do you build a team philosophy around these stats? In the book Moneyball by Michael Lewis he talks about how Billy Beane and the Oakland A's built their team around on base percentage. He tells how the A's built their roster with guys who could get on base. Typically these were not the highly sought after sexy sluggers that earned more money than small countries. They were instead guys who were very selective in their pitch selection and thus got on base often. We developed our Football Philosophy based on controlling the ball. We played guys who could hold on to the ball and guys who could get the ball. We also went with the quarterback who made plays and not turn the ball.

The first decision was to have an offensive system that could score 25 points against superior talent. Ken Hatfield said "you either have to be better or be different if you are going to win" – we had to be different. So we installed The Triple Gun Offense – which combined the elements of the service academies Flex-bone offense and the quick game of the West Coast Offense. Both schemes were developed for "have nots". The problem was: the Flex-bone was considered high risk. The goal was to score 25 against the best on our schedule and NOT turn the ball over. So we had to make The Triple gun Offense low risk. How?

1. Limit the number of run plays and maximize the reps to improve execution.
2. Minimize the plays, maximize the ways. Multiple Formations & motions.
3. Eliminate indecision by simplifying the thought process. (Unless rules) – "better wrong than long"
4. Make your plays have "Strategic Flexibility" – the ability to morph into another play after the snap. The Flash Screen is always part of any run

play, if there are 8 between the slots. The Quick pass becomes a boot if the route is covered. Protect the quarterback by always giving him an escape if the route is covered. For example he can run quarterback draw if the dropback pass is covered.

5. Always protect the mesh on the Triple Option.
6. Use "Smart Splits" and always look to get "speed in space"
7. Always create favorable mismatches (make tackle guys cover and make cover guys tackle)
8. Practice & emphasize Red Zone offense. Your system should be conducive to the red zone and goal line. You must always score touchdowns when you get the chance. The option is a great red zone weapon & is even more effective from the gun.

These are some of the ways to have a unique offense that is both highly productive and capable of scoring 25 points against the best you'll play.

The second Meaningful Stat is to hold opponent to 16 or less. To accomplish this you have to emphasize speed on defensive but you also use your ball control offense to limit the NUMBER of possessions in the game. Time of possession only matters to an exorcist. But how many possessions your opponent has matters a lot. Control the tempo on offense and score touchdowns on a greater number of possessions than your opponent. Play scorched earth defense, make them nickel and dime you down the field and then make them attempt a field goal if they get in the red zone. Keep the ball in front and inside. If your opponent keeps running the ball they are actually *helping* you shorten the game! The other thing you must do on defense is constantly look for takeaways by:

1. Putting DBs with good hands in the secondary.
2. Gang Tackle and strip the ball on every tackle once the tackle is secure. Touch the ball on defense on every play.
3. Have a turnover circuit every day in practice.
4. Be fundamentally sound, good tacklers and play fast. Speed is mandatory on defense.

The next meaningful stat is to score a Non Offensive Touchdown. This can be done either with a Punt Return or Punt Block, a kick Off Return, an Interception Return or a Fumble Returned for a touchdown. This means putting good return men in the lineup, good hands guys that can go coast to coast. Then practice your special teams

116

with great detail. The following are a few tips to give yours team a shot at a non Offensive touchdown:

1. Spend time coaching special teams, make them important. Put good hands and speed on your return teams. If you don't have a great returner, then develop great punt blocks.
2. Coach the cover teams hard so you don't give up a non offensive touchdown.
3. Be sure you teach ball security so you don't give up a pick six.
4. Practice scoring on defense: "scoop & score" drills and interception return drills.

The last Meaningful Stat is a +2 turnover margin. We've already talked about taking care of the football and making good decisions on offense and on defense emphasizing getting your hands on the ball. The more simple your offense, the more ball security your offense will have.

Our objective is to develop our offense that can score 25+ points vs the best on our schedule without turning the ball over and can control the clock with the run and the pass.

There is little doubt of the importance of these Meaningful Stats, however everything you do in your program should be directed at coming out on top of these Meaningful Stats. Remember, you get what you emphasize. Winning the meaningful stat battle may not excite Brent Musburger but you'll win a lot of games.

Ron Jaworski and Meaningful Stats

Ron "Jaws" Jaworski was one of my favorite NFL analysts. I especially enjoy his NFL Matchup Show on ESPN. Though he lost his mind for a while on Johnny Football, he is usually on target.

So when his book <u>The Games That Changed the Game</u> came out, I picked up a copy & read it. Not only was it very interesting, it gave tremendous testimony to the theory of "Meaningful Stats"

Jaws picked out seven games in NFL history that in his opinion changed the NFL. I personally would have included the NYG – Baltimore Colts sudden death game in 1958 & the Ice Bowl between the Cowboys & the Packers. But Jaws picked out these games where some key innovations changed the way football was played in the NFL.

What does this have to do with my theory of Meaningful Stats? Well in the seven games that Jaws picked that changed the game, the Meaningful Stats were very, meaningful.

1. No team that scored 25+ points lost
2. The four teams that scored more than 25 won.
3. Four teams held opponents to less than 16 points and they all won.
4. Four teams scored a non-offensive touchdown and three won.
5. Five teams had a +2 turnover margin and they all won.

That is a significant validation of "Meaningful Stats"

These are the seven games Jaws selected:

1. 1963 AFL Championship Game – Chargers 51 – Patriots 10

   Sid Gillman's vertical pass attack & the running of Keith Lincoln scorched the Pats' defense.

   Meaningful Stats: Chargers got 2 of 4. They scored 25+ (51) & gave up -16 (10)

2. 1974 AFC Championship Game – Steelers 24 – Raiders 13
   Bud Carson's Cover II Defense smothered the Raider's Offense & led to a 1978 rule change to help offenses against aggressive press corners. This was the start of what became Tony Dungy's Tampa 2.

The Meaningful Stat was The Steelers held the Raiders to -16 points (13). They missed the 25+ (24) but their defense was dominant. Neither team had any other meaningful stat.

3. Oakland Raiders vs San Diego Chargers 9/14/1980 & Don Coryell's "Roving Y" SD 30 – Oak. 24.

    Everyone knows Don Coryell's "Air Coryell Offense" which built upon Sid Gillman's Offense. However, few realize, it wasn't until Kellen Winslow emerged as a Tight End with Wide Receiver speed that Air Coryell really got off the ground.

    The Meaningful Stats scoreboard was:

    SD scored the 25+ (30) – the Raiders did not (24)

    The Raiders did score a Non-Offensive TD (Fumble Ret)

    But the really big one was San Diego had a +3 Turnover Margin.

4. NFC Divisional Championship Game 1/3/1982 – 49ERs 38 – NYG 24.

    The West Coast Offense was the most significant offensive development in the NFL since the Lombardi Sweep in my opinion because it gave less talented teams a chance. Bill Walsh was the mastermind behind the WCO but he also fused parts of Sid Gillman. Paul Brown & Tommy Prothro into his attack. In this game, Walsh adjusted his protection to stop Lawrence Taylor. The result was a huge 49ER win.

    The Meaningful Stat Scoreboard:

    The Niners got the 25+ (38) – NYG did not (24)

    The Niners got a Non-Offensive TD (Ronnie Lott pick 6)

    The Niners had a +3 Turnover Margin

5. Chicago Bears 44 – Dallas Cowboys 0 – 11/17/1985

    Buddy Ryan's 46 defense was at its peak in 1985, the year da Bears won the Super Bowl. Some people forget that Walter "Sweetness" Payton contributed a little to that season as well. But the 46 Defense was a dominant force. It was only the Miami Dolphins led by Dan Marino throwing the quick game that beat the Bears that year.

    The Meaningful Stat Scoreboard:

The Bears got the 25+ points (44)

The Bears held the Cowboys to -16 points (0)

The Bears got a Non-Offensive TD (Richardson's 36 yard pick 6)

The Bears had a +3 Turnover Margin.

The Bears got the Grand Slam – all 4 Meaningful Stats!

6. 1992 AFC Divisional Playoffs Buffalo Bills 24 – Steelers 3

Dick LeBeau's Zone Blitz Defense kept the Steelers in the game against the high-powered Bill's K-Gun Offense. The Zone Blitz was significant because teams could Blitz with reduced risk of giving up the Home Run. This caused offenses to be able to "direct the protection" to fit the rush. In this game The Bills went to the run game to get the "W"

Meaningful Stat Scoreboard:
    Neither team scored 25+ points but The Bills came close (24)
    The Bills held The Steelers to – 16 points (3)
    The Bills had a +3 Turnover Margin

Though Jaws was trumpeting Dick LeBeau's Zone Blitz, I thought Marv Levy the Bills' Head Coach, did a great job of adapting his offense to win the game. Some coach's try to prove a point (Mike Martz next game) but Levy went to the run game to pound out the "W" – Great Coaching!

7. Super Bowl XXXVI - 2/2/2002 – Pats 20 – Rams 17

This a great Meaningful Stat Game but also validation of the theory "Averages don't matter" Football is not like baseball where averages are important. Football is about matchups and the game THAT day. This is the theory behind Meaningful Stats. Can you score points vs the best on your schedule, or do you just run up scores on cupcakes?

Bill Belichick put it this way "Every week is its own challenge. Every game brings its own set of circumstances, adjustments, play style and matchups. We focus on what we want to do that week not what we did two weeks before or ten weeks before."

The Rams were heavily favored because of *averages* but those averages did not help vs the Pats. The Pats attacked Marshall Faulk and took him out of the game – the result – UPSET Pats!

The Meaningful Stat Scoreboard:

Neither team scored +25 Points

Neither team held the other to -16 but the Pats held the highest scoring Offense in the NFL to 17. Mike Martz would NOT run the ball vs a defense with 7 DBs.

The Pats scored a Non-Offensive TD (Ty Law's 47 yard pick 6)

The Pats had a +3 Turnover Margin

Ron Jaworski did a great job researching this book and gives plenty of food for thought which makes it a very worthwhile read.

Chapter 7

The Gun Triple

What Makes the Gun Triple So Special?

The Gun Triple is the heart and soul of the Triple Gun Offense. It's a play that is run 25 to 30 times per game. It literally guts a defense. And because it's such a great play, the defense must overcommit to stopping it and thus weakening the defense in other areas. Here are some of the things that make the Gun Triple a run game in itself:

It Wins the Meaningful Stat Game

- It is totally based on "Strategic Flexibility" and is completely based on defensive reaction.

- Moves the ball on the ground vs best on schedule and Controls the Clock.

- You have to be able to run the rock if you want to control the clock.

- Defenses can't defend it like the Flex-Bone because of the cutback and The Pass Game.

- The O. Line, in 2 point stances & using **"Smart Splits"** become more effective

- The cutback by TB is a built-in counter play that eliminates the need for a separate Inside Counter Play.

- The "Flash" screen to Wide Receiver on every snap (RPO) – "8 between the slots, throw quicks & hots" So there is a built-in pass on every play

- The secondary can't tell if run or pass which causes the secondary to react slower to support the run.

- The Quarterback is north/south runner that makes it difficult for the Pitch Key to use feather technique on the option phase of the play.

- The Gun Triple is good to both the one and the three technique thus no audible is needed.

- Because of the QB's depth, the OGs can't be pushed into QB by a great 2 technique.

- The depth of the Quarterback makes it easier to see and read the Hand Off Key. Making it easier to read leads to better ball security.

- The Gun Triple is formation friendly & can even be run from an Empty Formation

- Line blocking is a physical scheme that is based on double teams and vertical push creating a cavity not a crease which give the dive back the ability to run to daylight.

- The Gun Triple threatens the defense sideline to sideline from Flash to Pitch in one play.

Gun Triple vs a 4-3

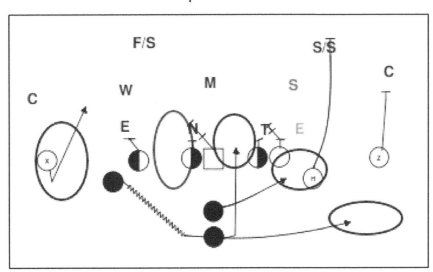

The funny thing is that we discovered most of these advantages *after* we had started installing it!

Offensive Line Play for the Gun Triple

The Triple Option makes the offensive line more effective because the Quarterback reads the Hand Off Key and options the pitch key so there are 2 less defenders to block. It's a great equalizer. The Gun Triple takes this principle to a whole new level. The Gun Triple's principles make it possible to use smaller more athletic offensive linemen that wouldn't be as effective in a conventional offense. So in the tradition of "Moneyball" we recruited some offensive linemen who were great in this offense but weren't attractive to conventional teams that were looking for baby elephants.

Before I progress, I have to give a shout out to B.D. Kennedy the first Triple Gun offensive line coach, who I drove crazy trying to develop the Gun Triple. B.D. went to Sweden to coach and became a bigger hero then Ingmar Johansson.

Ralph Isernia also gets a big shout out. Ralph was the Offensive Line and Offensive Coordinator at the University of Charleston and really refined the blocking principles and techniques. Ralph also helped take the Triple Gun to another level. Coach Isernia is now the Head Coach at Rensselaer Poly Institute and has turned RPI into a Division III power.

Blocking The Gun Triple:

Objectives: *Create seams & double teams. Create a cavity not a crease. Get vertical push.*

1. *Stance* – It starts with stance which is a **cocked** 2 point stance. The advantages of a 2 point stance are: It's easier to see a Linebacker and its better stance to pass protect. Must be able to EXPLODE from a 2 point stance. IT TAKES PRACTICE but it is worth the time.

2. *Smart Splits* –The biggest innovation in the Gun Triple was "Smart Splits" Using these splits created the weapon that made those smaller athletic linemen extremely effective. Smart Splits Rules: Start with basic 3 foot splits. If covered, widen a step. If uncovered, tighten a step. You can take as big a split you want as long as you can protect your inside gap. If the guard widens the tackle doesn't. If the Guard tightens, the Tackle widens.   Remember the objective: *Seams and Double Teams*

3. *Technique* – Double Team the down lineman but eyes on the LB. Only go to the LB when the LB comes to you. If he is running E/W – stay on the double

team & look for backside LB. If you are going to block the plug LB – *VAULT* to the LB & get a hat on a hat. Remember: the most important thing is to control the down lineman and to get movement at point of attack and never allow penetration. Double unless.

4. *Rip & Post Technique*. Inside offensive lineman is Rip guy and responsible for inside gap on the double team. The outside lineman is the post guy and responsible for occupied gap. Both linemen should take a square release and get hip to hip to prevent penetration and get vertical push to create a *cavity*. The inside lineman (Rip) should always keep his eyes on his inside gap and expect a linebacker to fill it. The outside lineman (Post) should be square so to be in position to vault up to a linebacker if the defensive lineman pinches inside.

5. *Veer OT* – get vertical & go thru the inside breast of a 4 tech. Rod a 5 tech. & wash down a 4I once you block a 4I stay on him. Always make sure the HOK gets hit or chipped.

ABC Rules. How easy are the assignments? As easy as A,B,C. A simple rule: the simpler the assignments, the faster and more aggressive the line will be. The base blocking scheme as a hybrid veer scheme. It is Gap Blocking. When I was an assistant at Pace University and shadowing defensive genius, Bill Arnsparger, his rule was put defenders in gaps. So it made sense to me to put blockers in gaps as well. Here are the Veer Blocking Rules:

- The Onside Tackle has B Gap. Regardless of who is in B Gap, the OT has B Gap. If the on Guard is Covered (3 Technique) the OT doubles with the On Guard. If the On Guard is Uncovered (Zero or 1 Technique) the OT uses the Veer release previously discussed. If Defense has a 4I in B Gap, wash him down even though he is the Hand Off Key.

- The Onside Guard has A Gap. Regardless of who is in A Gap, the OG has A Gap. If the OG is Covered (3 Technique) he doubles with the OT but his eyes are on A Gap. If the OG is Uncovered (Zero Technique) he Doubles with the Center. If there is a 2I Technique or a 1 Technique, he treats it as a 0 technique. Always look to help the center
- The Center's first responsibility is a perfect snap to the QB. We use a stiff arm pendulum snap and we teach every offensive lineman to snap the ball. The Center will always have help from a Guard, so a good snap is first priority. The Center is responsible for offside A Gap. Regardless of who is there he has A Gap. If he has no one in the offside A Gap, he doubles with the Onside Guard with his eyes on Offside A Gap.
- The Offside Guard has offside B Gap. Regardless of who is in offside B Gap, he has him. If the offside B Gap is empty, the OG helps the Center with his eyes still on his B Gap.
- The Offside Tackle has offside has offside C Gap. Regardless of who is there, the OT has him. 95% of the time there will be somebody chasing the play from the backside C Gap.

The "Smoke" Call. The Smoke call is one of the most important blocking calls in the entire Triple Gun Offense. It is the call that is essential to the Cutback run by the dive back on the Gun Triple.

The Offside Tackle makes a "Smoke" call to alert the Offside Guard that is tight to the Center (to double a 1 Technique or Zero Technique) that he can't cut off the defender on him and keep him out of B Gap. The DE may have shifted from a 5 technique to a 4I. The OT and OG will execute the "Sally Technique" I learned from my year at Delaware.

The OT will rod and ride the defender toward the OG while pivoting his eyes and hips to C Gap. The OG rods the man in A gap and the EXPLODES into the man the OT is "delivering" to him almost like a trap block. This creates a great backdoor for the dive back to cut back. We use the same "Smoke" call and technique even in the pass game.

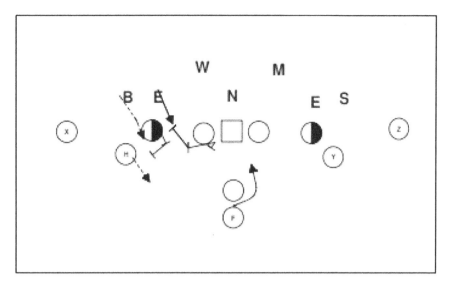

Smoke Call

Other Calls:

1. Blast Call – tells the linemen involved in double teams to stay on both double teams. Usually used for short yardage.

2. Bust Call – the On Guard telling on Tackle that he has the 3 technique alone because a Linebacker just walked up into A Gap. Or it might be an Offside guard telling the Center that he has the A Gap player alone because a Linebacker walked up into offside B Gap.

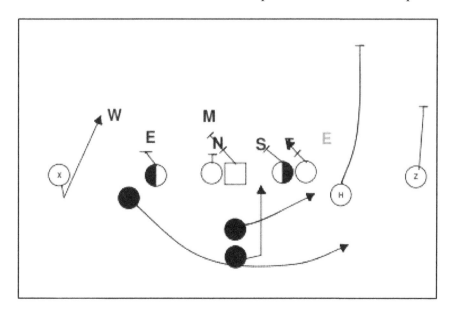

Bust Call

3. Ace Call – On Guard tells the Center that he has the Nose Alone because a 50 Linebacker walked up.LB

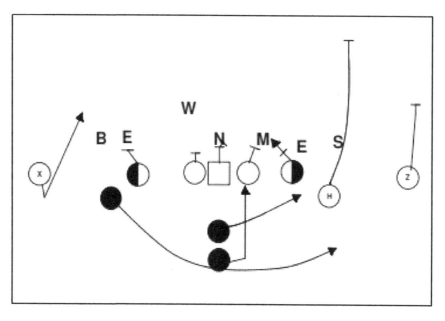

Ace Call

4. Loop Call – vs a 5 Technique – the Onside Tackle takes an outside release to block the LB. This call helps get TB in the game. The key is for OT to go through the HOK's outside breast. Rarely used.

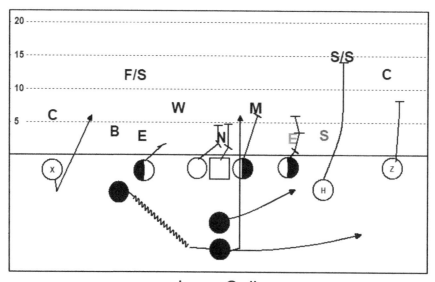

Loop Call

128

5. Down Call – The Down Call is one of the most important of these line calls. It is used if we are seeing a lot of 4I techniques or a Bears front. Defenses do this to take our Tailback out of the game on the Gun Triple.

Here's what the Down Call entails: Down Blocking: #1 Everyone cuts their splits down. So tighter splits. #2 Everyone blocks Down. #3 The Slot Seals Down & #4 the Tailback must stay frontside. There is no backside cutback on a Down" call. The Quarterback's reads are one man wider. The Pitch Key is the new Hand Off Key. The Down call turns the Gun Triple into the Wide Veer with very little new teaching.

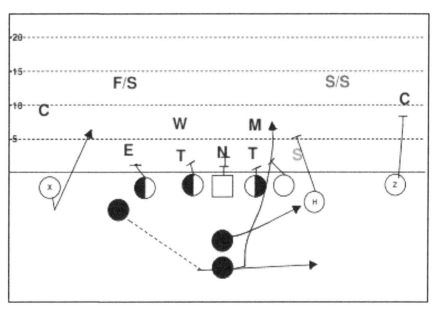

Down Call

6. Toad/Ted Call for the Tight End –"Toad" Call if the Onside Tackle is covered, the Tight End base blocks the End Man on the Line of Scrimmage. If the Tackle is Uncovered, then it's a TED call (Tight End Down) and the TE Veer releases to the first linebacker inside. Same as in the Multi-Bone).

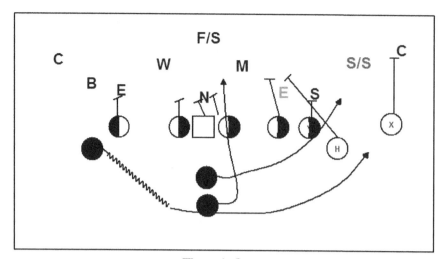

Toad Call

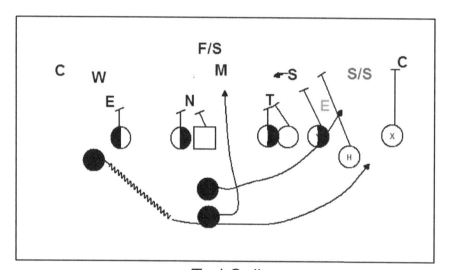

Ted Call

130

Take a look at our Veer Scheme vs the popular defenses :

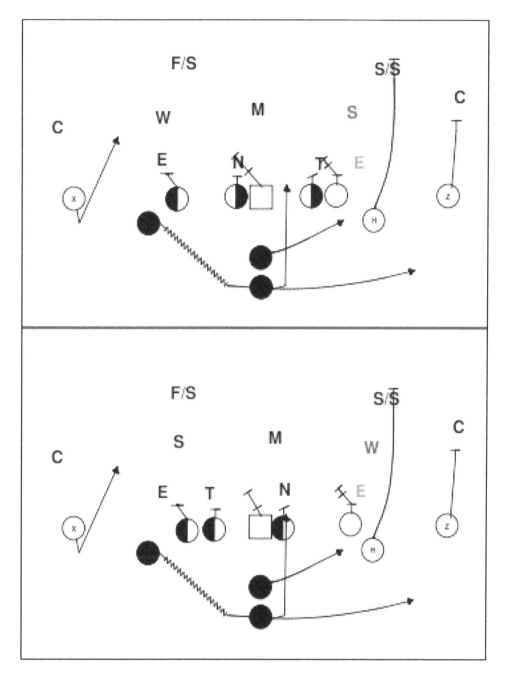

Gun Triple vs 4-3

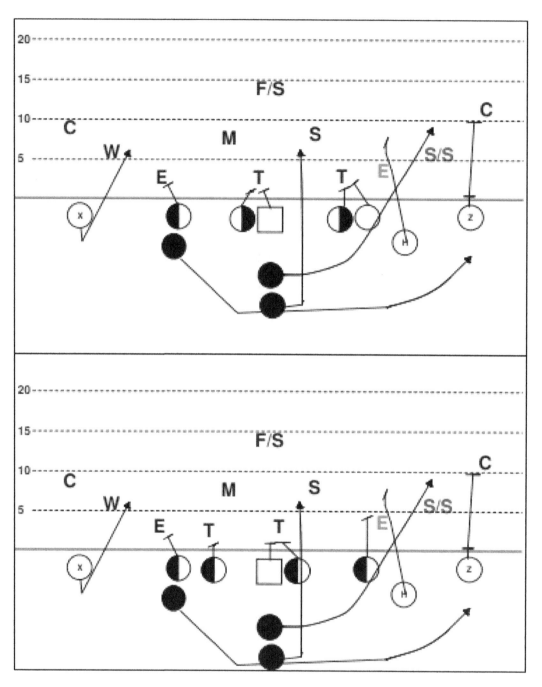

Gun Triple Seal vs 44

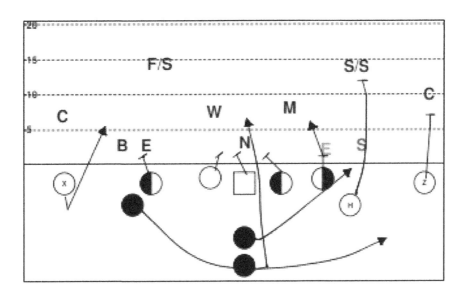

Gun Triple vs 34

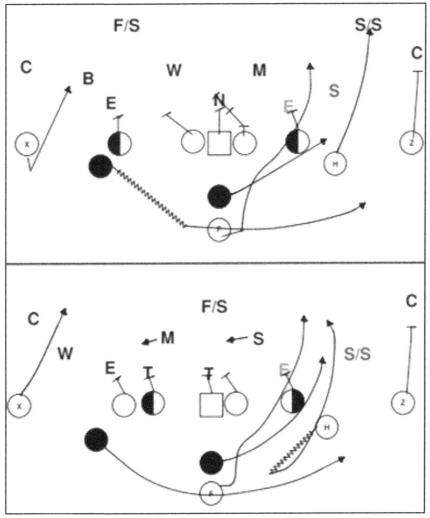

Gun Triple vs 4i

133

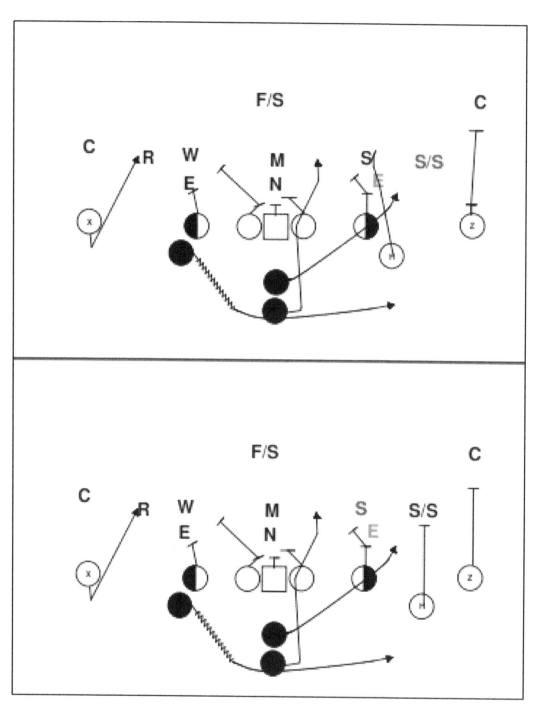

Gun Triple vs 33 Stack

134

PERIMETER PLAY FOR THE GUN TRIPLE

The easiest transition from the under center triple option to the Gun Triple was in the perimeter play. It was the same rules. The only difference was for the backside wide receiver who was a potential receiver on the Flash Screen. But for the Slots and the onside wide receiver, the rules were the same. Here's a quick review:

Objectives: Block for the pitch and put Speed in space.

Onside Slot. The Onside slot has 2 blocks, one for a 3 Shell (1 High Safety) and one for a 4 Shell (2 High Safeties)

Against a 3 Shell – The Slot seals the onside Inside Linebacker. The key is that he comes right off the tail of the Hand off Key and never let the Linebacker cross his face.

Against a 4 shell – The Slot Arc Blocks the Onside Safety. He must get width on his release and use a Stalk Block Technique. It is easier to arc from the Gun because of the Pass threat. Arc blocking is getting width & executing a stalk block. This is the rule unless a call is made, The Slot could Arc a 3 Shell Strong Safety if the QB calls Arc or if The Slot is in a Twins alignment

We could also Seal a tight 43 OLB even though it is a 4 Shell. This is a change up if the Quarterback is having difficulty with the "Stack Read"

Onside Receiver. The Onside Receiver Stalk Blocks the Defensive Back responsible for pass usually the onside CB

We use a "Crack" call against a 3 Shell which puts the Wide Receiver blocking the Outside Linebacker or the Strong Safety. Now the CB becomes the Pitch Key.

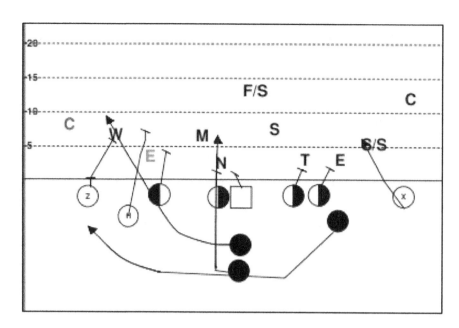

Jack Gun Triple Crack vs 44

Backside Slot. The Backside Slot is the Pitch Man. He must always expect the pitch. Catch the pitch first. Then pluck, tuck and burst. But catch the pitch first. Unless motion is called, he goes hard on the snap of the ball. His path is through the heels of the TB and then on a 5 yard highway to at least the Onside Tackle. Then mirror the QB just like he's tied to QB's hip. The Slot should look to circle the defense.

Heads up for a "Pepper Call" which the Quarterback makes if there is a level one Pitch Key that could put pressure on the QB. Pepper tells the Pitch Man he must go in motion and it tells the Onside Slot that if Whirley Motion was called it is off. Pepper tells the Onside Slot – No Motion.

Backside Wide Receiver. – The first thing the Wide Receiver does is look for Flash signal from the Quarterback. He can also signal the QB if he thinks Flash is open but it is a suggestion, the QB makes the decision. If there is no flash, the Wide Receiver must *expect* the backside cut by the dive back & block for that.

So these assignments and techniques are basically the same as the Under Center Triple Option.

The Gun Triple Mesh and QB Reads

One of the most frequently asked questions that I receive either on the clinic circuit or by phone or email is about the Quarterback/Tailback mesh in the Gun Triple. Most of the concern revolves around the quick read and the aiming point for the Tailback.

The first thing is DON'T OVERCOACH IT. Repeat; DON'T OVERCOACH IT.

When I put this offense together my number one rule was *No Turnovers*. I wanted ball security to be our number one priority. If you go back to the chapter on Meaningful Stats; the MOST Meaningful Stat is turnovers (+ 2 Turnover margin almost guarantees a win) so number one priority on the Mesh is designed for ball security and to reduce risk. The longer the ball is in the dive back's stomach, the greater the chance for a turnover. It is as simple as that. The longer the indecision by the Quarterback the greater the chance there is for a turnover. Also, the closer the handoff key is to the dive, the greater chance he has to blow up the mesh and create a turnover. Our goal is to have an efficient read not a perfect read. When you look for perfect reads, the ball stays in the mesh too long and winds up on the ground. *Better wrong than long*. A wrong read might result in a 2- or 3-yard gain but a long read might lead to a turnover.

The Quarterback's Thought Process. The Quarterback's thought process is: "I'm going to give the ball EVERY Time **UNLESS** the Hand Off Key comes down hard and flat on the TB". The definition of "Hard & Flat" is the HOK's head comes across the torso of the dive back. Only if the HOK comes down flat and hard is it a pull read. However, if the HOK is blocked it is also a PULL Read. "When in doubt - GIVE". This decision must be made on your FIRST step! "Better Wrong than Long" When in doubt – GIVE.

The Quarterback's Footwork. The QB's stance has his feet slightly tighter than shoulder width. The first and most important thing he must do is CATCH THE SNAP. Remember: Ball Security is the #1 Priority. We practice snaps EVERY DAY. After he catches the snap, the quarterback merely pivots on his playside foot and puts the ball out for the dive back to run over. His eyes go directly to the HOK and he gives the ball to the dive back UNLESS that HOK flies down on the dive back, getting his head in front of the running back. If the QB sees the HOK is on this path, he SNAPS the ball to his heart and accelerates to the pitch key. If the HOK is blocked the Quarterback aborts the mesh and turns it into a double option. If the QB sees the HOK blocked, does not even mesh with the dive back, he just SNAPS the ball to his heart and is prepared to make a quick pitch.

Coaching points:

1. By pivoting and not stepping the QB actually brings the dive back further away from the HOK. The pivot must be as quick as possible.
2. By bringing the dive back further away from the HOK – the HOK must come harder and faster to take dive. This makes the read clearer and enables the QB to make an efficient read on his first step.
3. If the HOK is blocked – there is no read – it becomes double option. But if the HOK work outside across the Tackle's block – the QB ducks inside turning it into QB ISO.
4. Ball Security is our #1 priority, and this process increases our ball security by taking the risk out of the read.

The Tailback's Aiming Point. The Tailback aim's for the front side "A" gap. His target is the playside cheek of the center. It is better for him to be too tight than to wide. He is responsible for running over the ball. His first step is a little slide step to put him in line with "A" gap. His inside arm should be up with his thumb pointing down. The pocket should be as big as possible to give the QB room to make the mesh. By pointing the thumb down the pocket opens a little wider.

If the Tailback gets the ball, he reads "A" gap. If "A" gap is open, he hits it 100 MPH. If "A" gap is closed - he runs to daylight. If it is closed from the backside, he cuts back by sliding and gliding. The slide & glide is a subtle cut made with his shoulders square to the line of scrimmage. We want him to be a north/south, downhill runner. We want him to "DRIVE FOR FIVE".

If the ball is pulled, the Tailback gets width and becomes a blocker. He blocks HOK to the onside Linebacker to the Safety. He is a runner or a blocker, never a faker.

If the Quarterback short arms the mesh because the HOK is blocked; the Tailback wraps around the Tackle's block and blocks Linebacker to Safety. He is responsible for the playside Linebacker first and then if the backer is blocked, he gets in the option alley (Hashmark, Numbers, Sideline). He doesn't have to chase because the QB will be on his hip so the defenders must come through him. Using the Tailback as a blocker is a big advantage of the "Quick Read"

Coaching Points:

1. The dive back is a RUNNER or a BLOCKER never a faker. We always want the Tailback to become an extra blocker if the ball is pulled. This is one of the main advantages of The Gun Triple over the Zone Read.

2. The Tailback (Dive back) is a "B" gap to "B" gap runner. He "slides & glides" to daylight with his shoulders square to the line of scrimmage. This is a big advantage over conventional Triple Option schemes.

3. When getting down field as a blocker; he doesn't have to chase a defender- the QB will be on his outside hip so the defender will come to him.

4. If the QB short arms him because the HOK is blocked and the HOK fights across the Tackles face – the Dive back is still looking for LB to Safety so he'll duck inside the Tackles block turning into QB ISO on the run.

The advantages of this style of this style of mesh are:

1. Better ball security. Ball security is our #1 priority because it is a Meaningful Stat – The Most Meaningful. To win games avoid turnovers.

2. Easier read for the QB, making him more effective at optioning the Pitch Key. And making him more efficient at moving the ball.

3. The Tailback/Diveback is more effective as a runner because getting the ball sooner enables him to make the back door cut or keep it playside. If you ride him into the line he cannot leave his track. He becomes a crease runner.

4. The Tailback/Dive back is more effective as a blocker. By pulling the ball sooner the TB can get width and become a blocker. This adds an extra blocker to the playside. This can be the difference between a 6 yard gain and a 60 yard gain.

5. The entire play is faster. The QB is not slowed down by staying in the mesh trying to "ride and decide". While he's riding and deciding the defense is running to the perimeter.

6. The Dive back's path constricts the defense similar to the midline option. This shortens the flank and makes the QB more effective because he becomes a North/South runner making it near impossible for the Pitch Key to use feather technique.

The most important part of the mesh phase of the Gun Triple is REPS, REPS, REPS and more REPS. Drill the QB's pivot every day, this is something that some coaches overlook.

Rhyme Time. A few helpful rhymes to help the QB read the Hand Off Key.

1. If he's in a Five – always think dive.
2. If he's in a 4 – widen your tackle some more.
3. If he's inside – no decide, go outside.

The Option Phase of the Gun Triple

The second phase of the Gun Triple or the Option Phase. The quarterback's keep or pitch decision

One of the advantages of the Gun Triple over the under center triple is the downhill path of the Quarterback after disconnecting from the dive. The angle of the Quarterback makes it very difficult for the pitch key to use a feather technique. The aiming point of the Tailback constricts the defense and this really speeds up the play and gets the ball up field much faster than under center. The Triple Gun Quarterback is heading North/South after keeping the ball. The under center QB is going East/West.

As always ball security is the number one priority. We've discussed the importance of turnovers as the most Meaningful Stat. So avoiding errant pitches is the biggest consideration in our option technique. We also want to get the ball pitched to stretch the field and get speed in space. So our approach has been to create a technique to get the ball pitched while reducing the risk.

It starts with Quarterback mechanics. As soon as the ball is pulled the Quarterback must snap the ball to his heart in a position to pitch the ball. The Quarterback should always expect the pitch key to come on him quickly. Expect a crash stunt and adjust to anything else. The QB should always check pre-snap for a tip that there will be pressure by the pitch key but regardless we want him to expect a crash stunt. If he sees a level one option key in position to crash, he calls "Pepper, Pepper, Pepper" to send the Pitch Man in motion.

The Quarterback attacks the inside shoulder of the pitch key but watches the far shoulder. He is always going to keep the ball UNLESS….the far shoulder turns toward him. If the far shoulder turns to the QB, he steps to the pitchman and pitches HEART TO HEART. If the Pitch Key gets above the Quarterback's pitch hand, he obviously must keep.

The Quarterback's thought process is: "I'm going to run for a touchdown every time UNLESS the pitch key's far shoulder turns to me, then I'm going to see the Pitch Man and pitch the ball heart to heart"

Some Coaching Points:

1. Approach a slow key fast and a fast key slow. Against a crashing pitch key just get back on your heels and make the pitch. If the pitch key backs up or feathers accelerate at him until he freezes his feet, then make the pitch. Expect a crash Pitch Key and react to a slow one. Just like a batter in baseball should expect a fastball and react to a curve ball.
2. Always SEE the pitchman. No blind pitches. Ball security is the #1 priority.
3. Always step to the pitchman but never move to the pitchman. Don't drift into the pitchman – that makes the pitch hard to handle.
4. Never pitch under stress or pitch in a mess. Ball security is the #1 priority.
5. Pitch Heart to Heart. Don't make it difficult for the pitchman to handle your pitch.

If the Quarterback is going to keep it; then he is to tuck the ball away and run for a touchdown. Once the ball is tucked away; the pitch is no longer part of the play. Ball security is the #1 priority. Once the Quarterback gets downfield he should try to get into the "Option Alley" - hash mark, numbers, sideline.

Coaching points:

1. Know the situation; down and distance is critical. Think in terms of first downs. If you are in a short yardage keep if the pitch key is in a gray area.
2. The Option Alley keeps you away from pursuit.

The Leverage Pitch. The concept of leverage pitching came about when the 43 Stack Defense came about. In the 43 Stack Defense the pitch key (the OLB) is actually inside the hand off key (the DE). Normally we "Stack Read" this defense with the thought process "I'm going to give every time **unless** one of the defenders in the stack takes dive". This read results in a lot of give reads. So we use an alternative thought process which is "I'm going to pull and pitch every time unless both defenders move outside". Then it's a give. If the Pitch Key stays inside and the DE doesn't take dive, we can turn it into a foot race between the OLB (pitch key) and our slot. We should win this race. We use the leverage pitch concept as a change up for the defense. The QB always puts the Pitch Man in motion with a "Pepper" call or call it in the huddle if he is going to Leverage Pitch.

Drills for the Option Phase

1. Pitch from a knee. Five yards apart and pitch to each other from a knee.
2. Fast Break Drill – 3 QBs, 5 yards apart – pitch to each other moving down the field. Coaching point is to step to the pitch.
3. Option Drill involves the whole backfield. Coaches play hand off key and pitch key. Run the Gun Triple but always making it a pull. Always use a shotgun snap.
4. Triple Drill – the same drill as option drill but now mix in give and pull reads.
5. Read Drill – full team drill. Work off Master Read Drill script.

Compressed Sets for the Triple Gun

I've talked for years about the use of "Smart Splits" to help the offensive line but we've also used various perimeter splits to our advantage as well. Our philosophy with perimeter splits is the same as an the old "Squeeze Box". Or as Manny Matsakis calls them "Accordion Splits. Moving your wide outs in and out like an Accordion creates a number of advantages for our perimeter attack. They include:

- Better blocking angles for the wide receivers to crack inside linebackers or strong safeties
- By bringing the Corners it's easier to circle the defense. If the receivers come in; the Corners will come in. If the Receivers widen out; the Corners will widen out.
- A great tactic is creating a new pitch key by cracking the normal pitch key. For example if you crack the strong safety in an 8 man front; the pitch key is now the corner. How much practice time do you think coaches devote to teaching their corners to be a pitch key?
- Compressed Receivers Create natural rubs in the passing game. We never teach picks because they are illegal; however, it's OK to rub against your own man to create a natural obstacle for a defender.
- By widening and tightening your wide outs splits, your opponent has one more thing to prepare for.
- Compressed sets create a different look to our basic option attack and our quick game.
- This fits with our philosophy of a "few plays run many ways". You have to execute plays, formations is just lining up.

The number of compressed sets you can use our endless. You are only limited by your imagination. However I would suggest a couple of specific reasons for getting into a particular set. What do you want from this set? Can I run the Gun Triple from it? What is my sequence of plays for this game from it? For example you may use an unbalanced compressed set and run Gun Triple, Play Action Pass and the Jet Sweep & QB ISO from it for this week. The next week you may do the same sequence from an Empty compressed set. Remember your playlist for each game must be small enough to practice daily. If you can't practice your game plan every day, you're doing too much.

Our 2X2 Compressed Package is named after playing cards. For the sake of this article we are going to stick with these basic sets. The first set is a compressed look to both sides – "Jack" – we use this to run the Gun Triple or Double Option to either side with a crack possibility. The second set is compressed to the boundary but normal splits to the field – "Queen" – we can crack to one side but still have the stalk/arc look to the field. The third set is compressed to the field and normal to the boundary – "King". We now have all our normal looks to the boundary but great crack possibilities to the field.

We add a little spice to all our sets not just compressed sets by adding the term "Wide" that tells the boundary slot to replace the Wide Receiver to that side except stay off the line of scrimmage. So for example one of my favorite set is "Wide Jack" – this compresses both wide outs but the boundary slot splits out like a flanker. This set enables us to throw the hitch to our slot (another way to get him the ball in space) and with motion bring him back into the backfield to be a pitchman.

The ability to crack on the option (double or triple) gives you some variety in the perimeter and causes the corner to play pitch. That is one more technique for the defense to learn in a week.

We use compressed sets to create easier throws for our QB. Besides creating natural rubs in the passing game; compressing the formation makes it easier to throw the corner route to the field. We also use compressed sets to create the spacing concept that has been popularized by many spread teams. The compressed sets coupled with our exotic sets gives us unique ways to run the Gun Triple without teaching any new techniques. So in conclusion adding compressed sets to your menu takes very little teaching but adds a lot to your production.

COMPRESED SETS - Jack & King

Jack

King

145

ENDS & RECEIVERS - Unbalanced

Ends

Receivers

146

FRIENDS & WIDE

Friends

Wide

147

Chapter 8
Counter Gun Triples
The Flip Triple

Anytime your offense is fast flow, like an option oriented offense, misdirection is an absolute must. Your Offense must be capable of exploiting an over-zealous defense.

Counter Options are nothing new to Triple Option teams but what is new is The Triple Gun Counter Options is that they both are Counter *Triple Options.* They are Counter Options that have a dive, keep and pitch! In addition they both require little new learning. The line blocks the same as Gun Triple. The Receivers block the same as Gun Triple and The Quarterback play is the same as Gun Triple. The only difference is in the backfield.

The Flip Triple. This Counter Option is a direct descendent of Bill Yeomen's Split Back Veer Counter Dive and Counter Dive Option. We just put it into one play and let the Quarterback read it.

This was the first Counter Triple Option we ran and it was to exploit a defense keying on motion but also defenses keying an offset Tailback.

We named it "Flip" because the motion Slot and the Tailback "Flip" assignments. In this play, the motion Slot becomes the dive back, while the Tailback becomes the pitch back.

FLIP TRIPLE

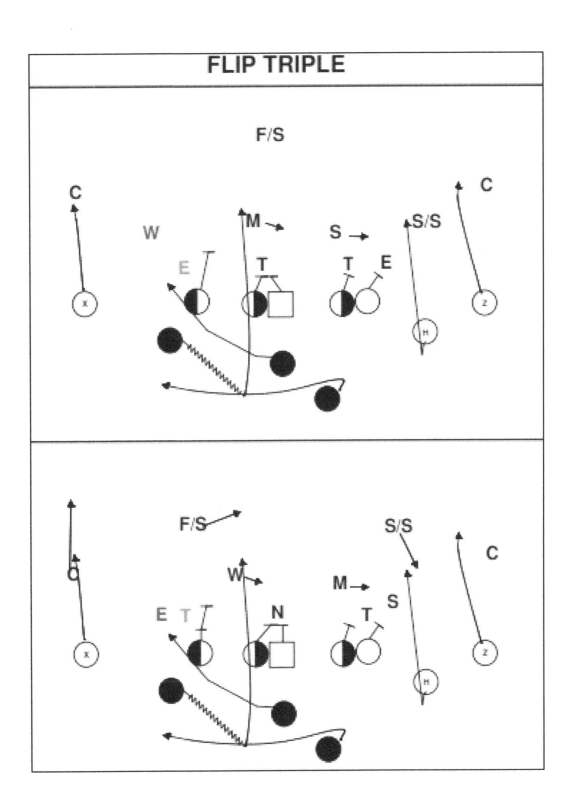

FLIP TRIPLE VS 43

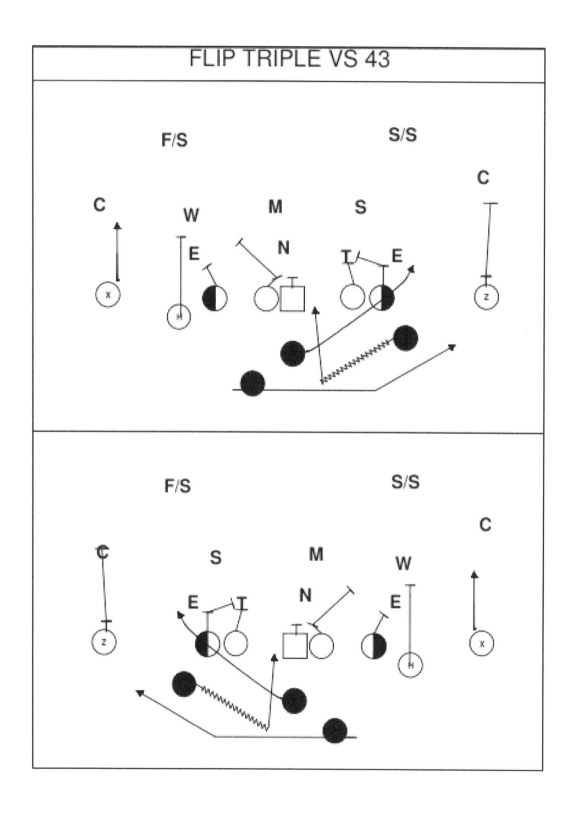

Running the Flip Triple offers numerous advantages, including the following:

- It breaks motion keys, because the play goes away from the motion.
- It breaks the perceived defensive key that the ball will always to the side of the tailback.
- It is a counter option that is read just like a triple option. As a result, the play includes a dive, a quarterback keep, and a possible pitch.
- It gives the Slot a chance to carry the ball going north and south.
- It requires only two new techniques. The offensive line, quarterback, and receiver techniques are exactly the same as the gun triple.
- Not only is it formation-friendly, it actually enhances some formations, such as Twins, Trips, Bunch, Pro, and Empty. The Flip Triple opened the door to run Gun Triple from an Empty formation.
- It counters a defense that slants its line to motion.
- It also counters a defense that rolls its secondary to motion.
- The play-action pass perfectly complements the Flip Triple.
- The Flip Triple and the Gun Triple look exactly the same at the start of the play.

Offensive Line. The offensive line blocks the Flip Triple with the exact same techniques as the Gun Triple.

The Backfield. The key to the play is for the Slot to get back to Tailback depth over the Onside Guard. He must get his shoulders square to the line of scrimmage *prior to the snap of the ball.* This is critical to the success have the play. It's better for him to be back there to early than too late. If he does get back there too early he just chops his feet until the ball is snapped.

The Tailback takes a jab step and then gets on his pitch path. This is a great way to get your Tailback the ball on the edge.

The QB follows the same rules as Gun Triple. Nothing new.

Attacking Defenses with the Flip Triple. The defense must be reacting to motion for the Flip Triple to be called. The primary key to running the Flip Triple is that it is a play that is designed to exploit defensive movement to motion. If the defense is not moving to motion, the flip option shouldn't be called. On the other hand, in that situation, a team should run the Gun Triple, and it'll have a running start, while the defense is relatively still. The Flip Triple can also be effective if the defense over play a Twins formation.

The Whirley Gun Triple

The Whirley Gun Triple gives us another Counter Gun Triple simply by using "Whirley" motion. The Whirley Gun Triple provides a lead blocker. The Whirley Slot becomes the playside lead blocker. Whirley Motion is 3 step motion executed by taking one step back, a crossover step, one more step back and then turns back to the line of scrimmage and then executes his assignment. He would Seal vs a 3 Shell and Arc vs a 4 shell.

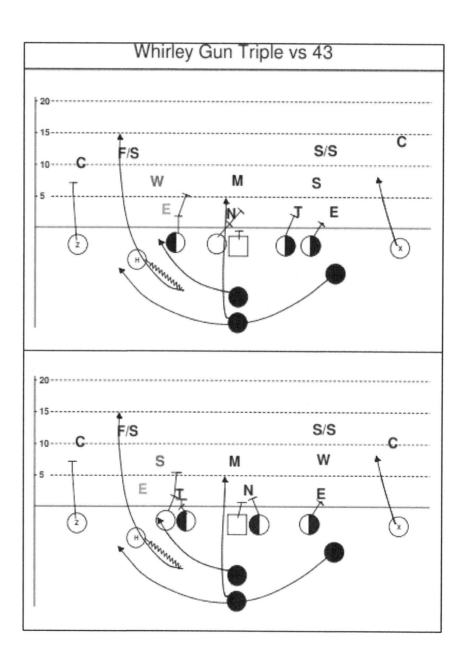

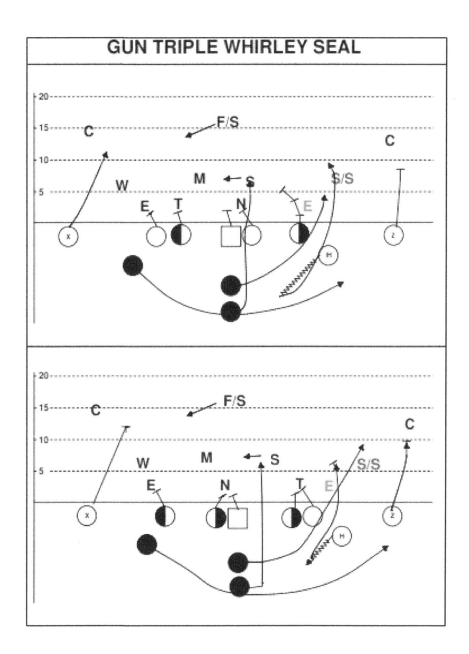

GUN TRIPLE WHIRLEY SEAL

Pepper Call. The Quarterback makes a "Pepper Call" if he sees a level one Pitch Key. This call aborts the Whirley Motion and sends the Pitch man in motion instead.

We use the Whirley Gun Triple when there are no detached Slots as in Twins or Trips. When we have detached Slots we use Flip Triple as our Counter Triple. The great aspect of these counter options is that there is so little cost involved. The line blocking and Quarterback reads are the same, the only change on the Whirley Counter Option is the Whirley Motion.

The Empty Gun Triple

The Empty Gun Triple. Running The Gun Triple from an Empty formation proved to be very productive and another nightmare for defensive coordinators. Spreading the front and removing linebackers from the front opens up running lanes for the dive back. Spreading the Defense also makes it difficult for the defense to stunt or blitz or load the box vs Gun Triple.

The unintended benefit was the Flip Motion served as a Counter Play. The other side benefit was that we could get the ball to the tailback many ways. We could hand him the ball on the Dive phase, or he could be the Pitch Man. Of course, when we talk about the Pass Game, the Tailback is in a great position to be a frequent target. Getting the Playmakers the ball is always an important part of any offense. Being able to just go to Empty Formation from our regular personnel makes it very difficult for the defense to avoid mismatches especially when we can run almost our entire offense from Empty Formation.

GUN TRIPLES FROM EMPTY

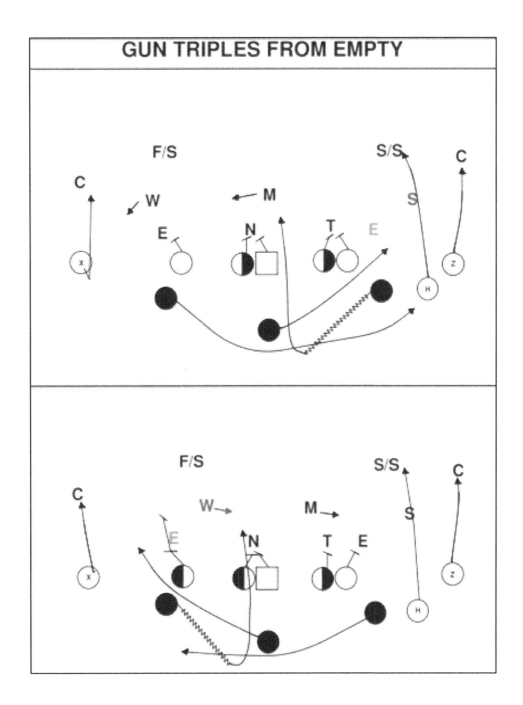

The Quarterback always has the built=in "Flash" available if the defense did not spread out with our receivers. Also, RPOs are easier to define as well.

155

EMPTY TRIPLE VS 44

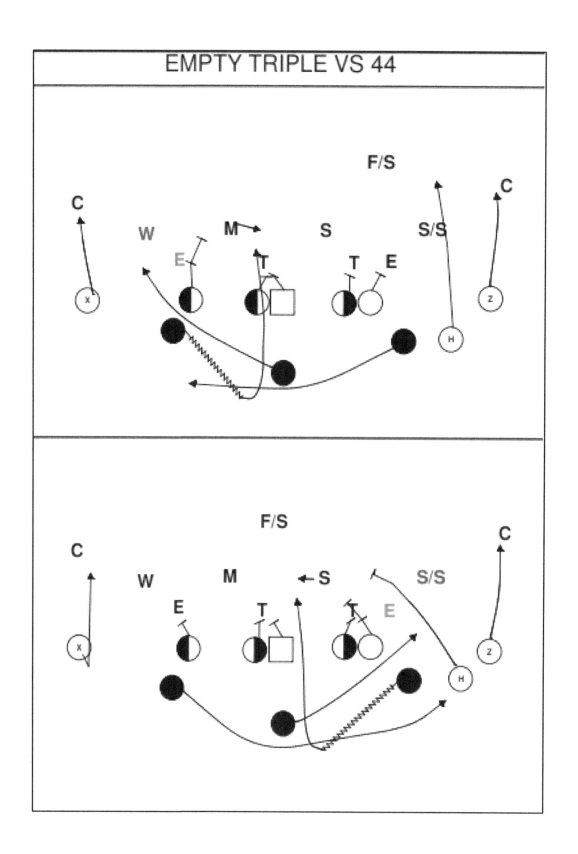

Chapter 9
Double Options
The Triple Gun Double Options

The Gun Triple is obviously the hub & core of the Triple Gun running attack. However there is a need and a place for the Double Option. Sometimes it's sometime very advantageous to use Double Options. Spreading the field and getting the ball on the perimeter is always a good thing because it stretches a defense horizontally. I always say the perimeter equals points.

Here are some reasons for investing time in Double Options:

1. Puts Speed in Space – gets the ball in your playmaker's hands.
2. Compliments Gun Triple – Flash still part of the play.
3. Doesn't allow "D" to force the ball inside. You are in charge.
4. Makes "D" defend sideline to sideline.
5. Neutralizes a great D. Line – QB off LOS – negates great 3 tech.
6. It tires a "D" out running sideline to sideline. (pursuit drill)
7. Forces LBs to play east/west & makes secondary get involved in run support. Changes up Option responsibilities.
8. Formation Friendly
9. Answer to inside blitzes.
10. Gives the Hand Off Key something else to worry about.

This fits into the Principle "Hard to block; easy to read and easy to block; hard to read" a simple and confirmed truth.

Triple Gun Double Options. The Triple Gun uses a variety of Double Options and the GREAT news is that they are *ALL* blocked with Gun Triple blocking so the offensive doesn't have anything new to learn. The only additional teaching is how we are going to handle the pitch key and hand off key. If we pitch off the hand off key we must block the pitch key. Or if we block the hand off key; the pitch key remains the same.

Triple Becomes Double One of our rules for the Quarterback in the Gun Triple is if the hand off key is blocked; it's an automatic pull. The QB doesn't even mesh with the Tailback He just short arms the dive back and attacks the pitch keys inside. shoulder. The dive back gets width and wraps around the blocked hand off key and blocks LB to Safety. So the Triple becomes a Double on the run; no audible needed. We covered this in detail in the chapter on the Gun Triple.

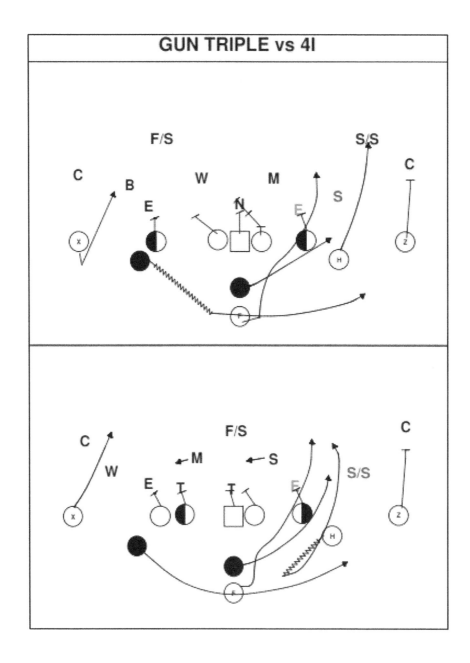

The Speed Option. The next Double Option is pitching off the hand off key (HOK). The only new teaching is now we must block the pitch key either by stalking or cracking. This is a great weapon against a soft HOK or against a defense that wants to take your slots out of the game by giving you only give reads.

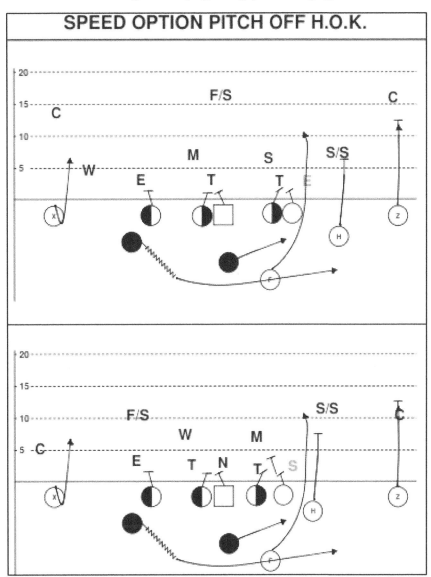

SPEED OPTION PITCH OFF H.O.K.

1. Call to take advantage of a difficult to read HOK – or an always give read.
2. O. Line blocks Gun Triple
3. Slot blocks the PK – we could use a TE
4. TB has LB to Safety
5. QB pitches off HOK. He does NOT attack the HOK, he just steps and pitches
6. Use formations to make the flank you want Nub side of unbalanced for example and we also really like running it from Empty.

NUB SPEED OPTIONS

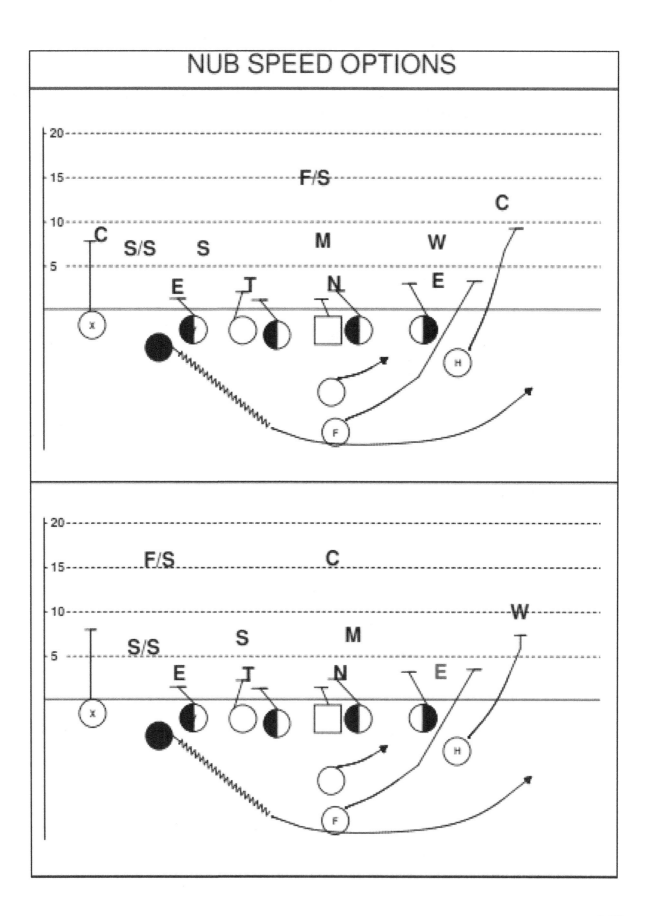

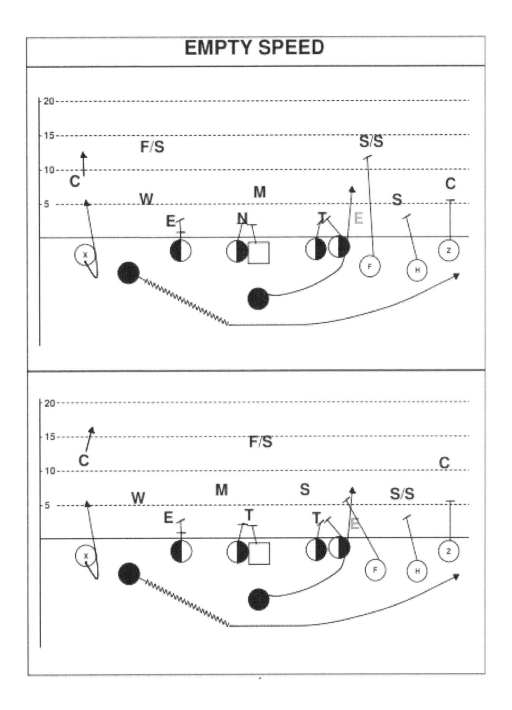

7. A "Toro" call is used vs a 43 Stack Defense. "Toro" puts the onside Slot on the playside OLB and the Tailback on the Strong Safety

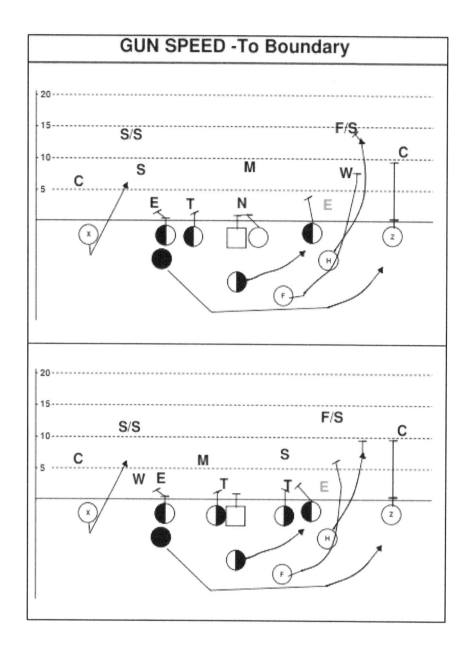

We always went into every game looking for "A pitch and a hitch" that we could always get either by motion or formation. Then we could always come back to them to get the ball on the perimeter

The Stud Option. The Stud Option blocks the Hand Off Key with the Slot and the Tackle and the Quarterback options the Pitch Key. So we use The Speed Option to Pitch off the Hand Off Key and with the Stud Option, we block The Hand Off the Key. This gives us a few ways to get to the perimeter and stretch the defense. The assignments are very simple:

- Offensive Line Blocks Gun Triple EXCEPT: On G if Covered jump reaches a 3 technique.

- The Onside Tackle - Stud Blocks with Slot (Double Team)

- The Tailback - has Onside Inside Linebacker.

- The Backside Slot is the Pitch Man.

Quarterback Reads. The Quarterback's first read is FLASH. "8 Between the Slots, throw Quicks and Hots" Next the QB checks the Inside Linebacker. if ILB turns his shoulders to the sideline and sprints, in other words his numbers disappear, the QB plants his foot in the ground and ducks up inside. With the ILB leaving so quickly there will be no defender in side. (Strategic Flexibility) If the QB sees the Linebackers numbers, he gets on the Tailback's outside hip and attacks the Pitch Key just as he would in the Gun Tripe like the Stud Option from Exotic sets like Ends and Receivers because the extra end can block the Free Safety

ENDS STUD OPTION

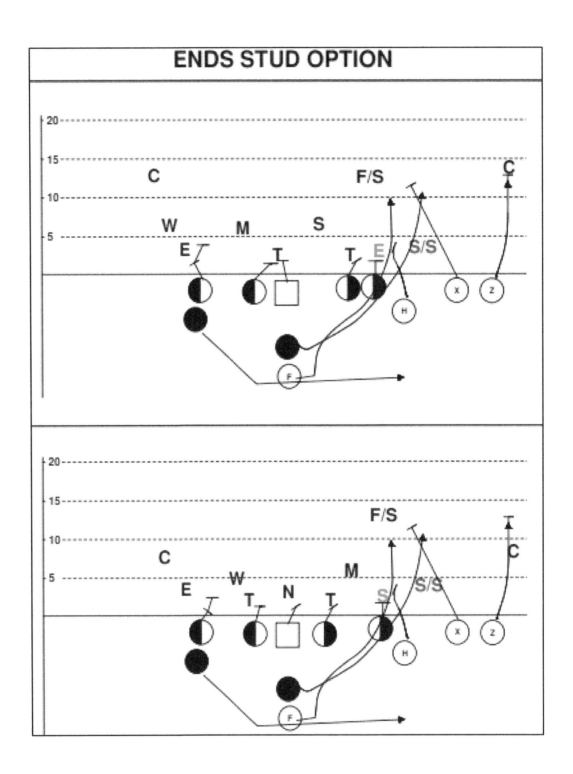

Stud RPO. The Stud Option is an easy option to run an RPO. Use an exotic formation like Receivers and read the Strong Safety if he the covers the receiver he pitches but if the SS fills, the QB throws the Dump. If the Free Safety is over the top, the QB options the SS.

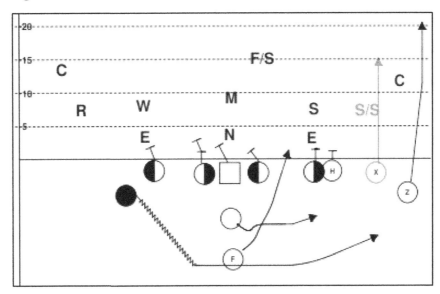

Receivers Dump RPO

Flip Speed. The Flip Speed is a Counter Speed Option. The Slot and the Tailback "Flip" assignments so the Tailback becomes the Pitch Man and the Slot becomes a lead blocker. We like this away from Twins. This is a great answer to attack the perimeter and it gets the Tailback the ball on the edge. The Quarterback and the Line just execute Speed Option.

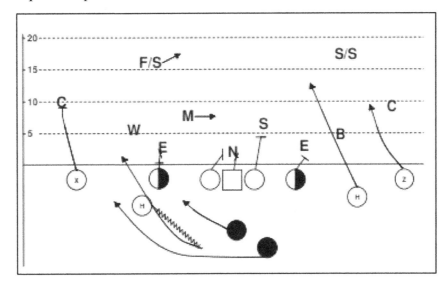

Flip Speed vs ODD

165

Whirley Speed. The Whirley Speed is a Counter Speed with a lead blocker. The onside slot executes the Whirley Motion and the onside slot and Tailback become the lead blockers for the backside slot who is the pitchman. We usually like this with a Crack block by the WR.

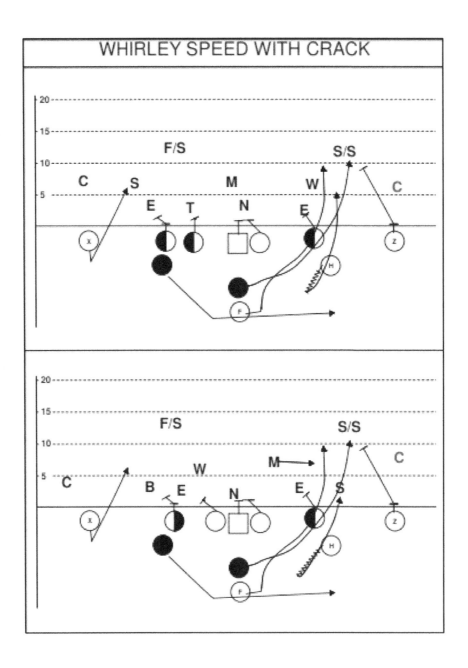

The Triple Gun Double Reads

Gun Midline and The Triple Gun Zone Read were two later additions to The Triple Gun Offense. They were used in a limited manner but proved to a nice compliment to the Gun Triple.

I was convinced to add The Gun Midline to the Triple Gun by my offensive coordinator Ralph Isernia who loved under center midline. I loved under center midline as well but did not have the same passion for it in the Gun. I was concerned about the 3 technique blowing up the mesh.

So we made some adjustments:

- The playside guard went through the *breastplate* of the handoff key.
- We used it vs 4Is so the hand off key was wider
- It was either a give or keep with no pitch involved
- We used it in 3 wide receiver sets to spread the front
- It was great in long yardage situations when the 3 technique would be rushing the passer.

Assignments:

On Tackle: Block 1st defender from 5 technique out.

On Guard: If covered – release through breastplate of 3 technique to on LB. If uncovered smoke up to On LB.

Center: If covered – base the Nose. If uncovered – block backside A gap to LB.

Off Guard: Protect B gap. If B gap is open help center eyeballing B Gap.

Off Tackle: Protect C Gap – heads up "smoke" Call

On SE: Stalk.

Off SE: Check "Flash" then cut off FS.

On Slot: If the Slot is in a Twin alignment, -he Stalks the Strong Safety. If he's a Tight Slot –he inserts for on LB.

Off Slot: Lead block inside OT's block. Motion unless in Backs Formation.

TB: Aiming point is butt of QB. Drop step & go.

QB: Open with a back step with playside foot to open up the Midline. Read 1ˢᵗ man on LOS wider than the OG, it's "give unless…" If it's a pull- tuck the ball away get North and South as soon as possible.

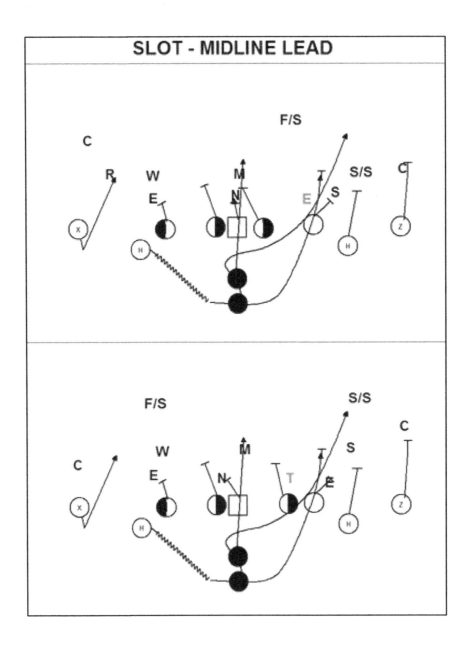

GUN MIDLINE

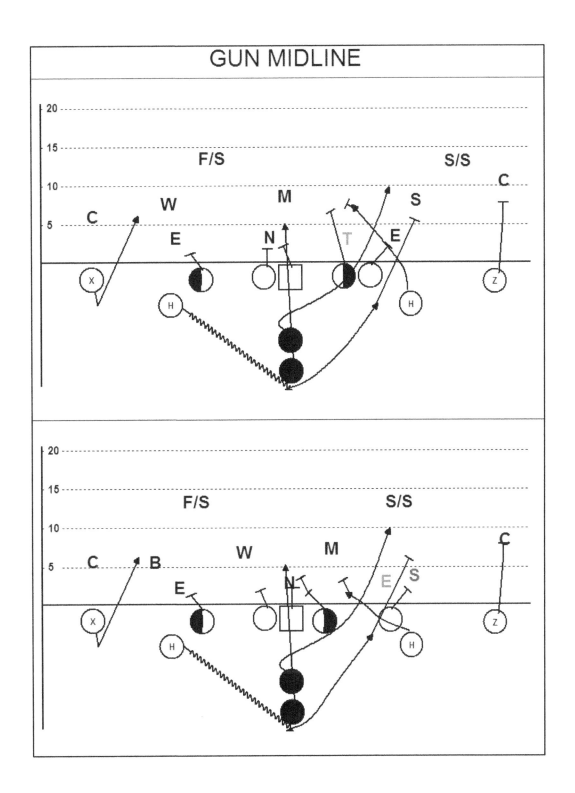

BACKS MIDLINE

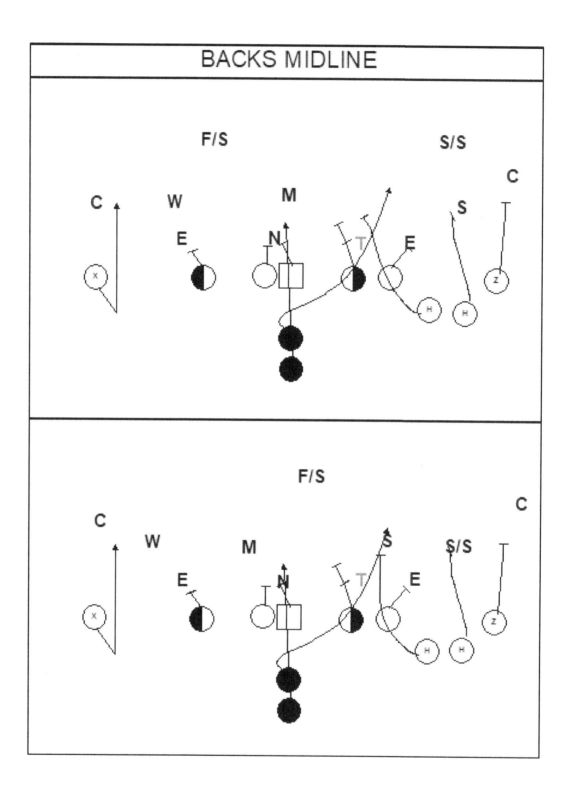

The Zone Read. The Zone read was another Double Read Play we added to The Triple Gun Menu. It was not meant to be a "Core Play" but a play to use for Play Action Passes and RPOs (Though we didn't call them that. But it was great with the Play Action Vertical Game.

When I first looked into going to the gun in the winter of 1999, I did not like the Zone Read. Though Northwestern and Tulane had done well with it, I thought it wasn't a downhill play & seemed to be stopped by simple option defensive stunts like Squeeze and Scrape.

But when Coach Isernia approached me about looking at the Zone Read at The University of Charleston, we were looking as a complimentary play to the Gun Triple *not* a core play. So we experimented with it and liked it with 3 and 4 wide receiver set.

 Here are some of the benefits of using The Zone Read as a compliment to the Gun Triple:

- Another play to hand the ball to a variety of playmakers.

- Very formation friendly.

- Very conducive for the 4 vertical Play Action Pass game.

- Simple blocking scheme which fits with "Smart Splits."

- Gives the Hand Off Key a different look.

- Very Conducive to RPOs

- The Offensive Line uses the same techniques as Veer Blocking except in the opposite direction.

- The play was enhanced by "Smart Splits"

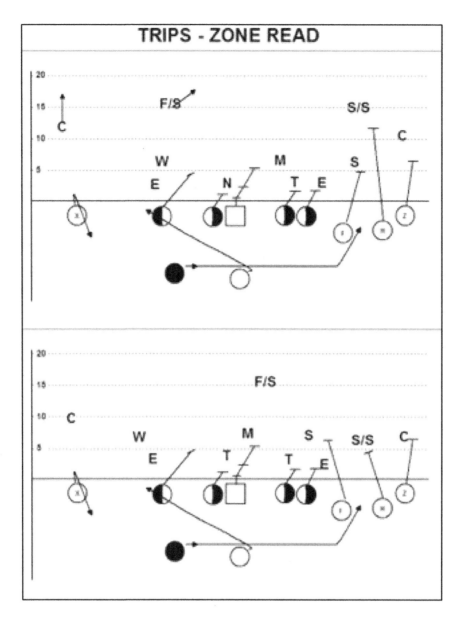

TRIPS - ZONE READ

Assignments:

On Tackle: Block man on. Target outside breastplate. (C Gap)

On Guard: Block man on. Target outside breastplate. (B Gap)

Center: Block man on to playside A Gap. Heads up for scoop call.

Off Guard: Block offside A Gap. Heads for scoop call with center.

Off Tackle: Block offside LB – leave HOK alone. Unless "On" Call. Then the Offside Tackle Blocks Man On and The QB reads the Offside Linebacker. This is the scheme for an RPO.

Off SE – Heads up "Flash" – Stalk

On SE – Stalk.

Non ball carrying backs stalk.

Tailback – If it is a "Lead" call he becomes the Lead Blocker and reads the Tackles Block.

Ball Carrier – Motion to a "T" alignment (Even with the backside OT) & come in front of the QB & chase the hip of playside tackle. Stretch the front and run to daylight.

QB: Read EMOL or the Offside LB on an "ON" call. – give unless… rule. Ride the mesh hip to hip. We want the ball handed off.

The formations are endless, but we really liked it out of Empty or some unusual set.

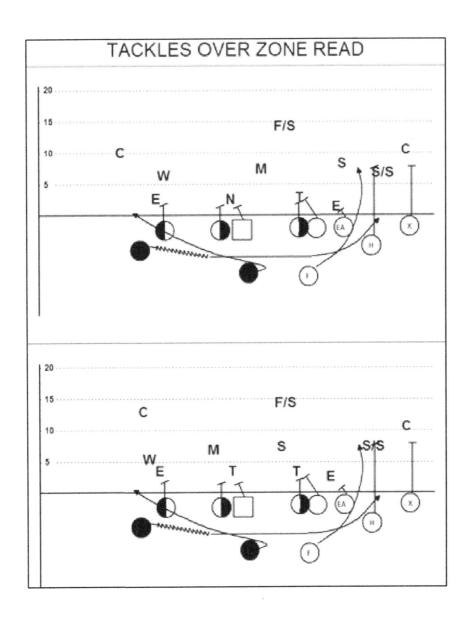

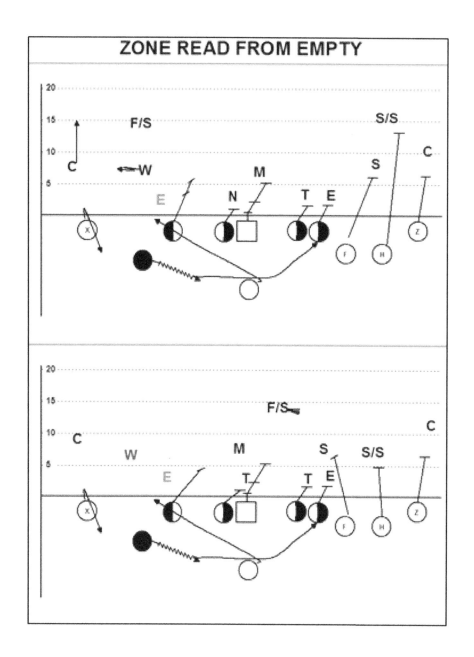

The addition of The Midline and The Zone Read were nice compliments to The Gun Triple and made our offense more diverse. The Zone Read helped open up The Vertical Play Action Pass Game which produced big plays. These plays are not core plays so should only be added *after* mastering The Gun Triple. They both had specific uses. Midline was really just used vs two 3 techniques or in a long yardage situation. The Zone Read was easier to because it was basically Veer Blocking in the opposite direction and it was installed for the Play Action Passes off it.

The Flip Zone Read. The Flip Zone Read is our Counter Zone Read. So at the start of the play, the defense doesn't know if the play is going toward the motion or away from it. Every assignment is the same except the Tailback and Slot Flip assignments. An Instant Counter with no additional teaching. There is also an RPO opportunity to the backside, especially vs a 3 Shell. This gives a simple "Read Series" to use as a change of pace.

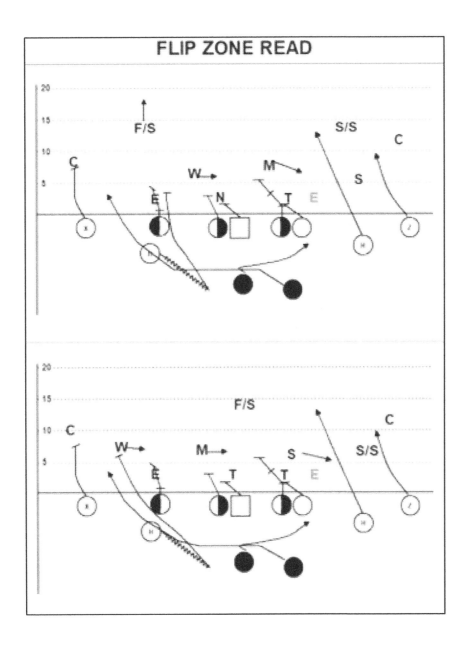

Chapter 10
Supplemental Runs
Introduction to The Triple Gun Supplemental Runs

The Triple doesn't need many supplemental runs because the Gun Triple is so good. The supplemental runs are mostly "answer plays" to exploit a defensive tactic to stop the Gun Triple. So these plays are practiced against specific defensive adjustments. So if a defense doesn't make that adjustment the play does not get used. For example if a defense is over-pursuing a reverse or counter is a good call but if a defense is not over-pursuing, a reverse probably won't work.

Some other of our supplemental plays are used to take the Quarterback out of the game to avoid extra hits and some are just a way to get the ball to a playmaker.

The supplemental runs are the following:

1. The Quarterback ISO off the Gun Triple or the Jet Sweep. This is our most frequently used supplemental run. Great is short yardage and on the Goal Line.
2. The Jet Sweep. A great way to hand a playmaker the ball and put speed in space. So effective it became a sequence.
3. The Zone Dive. This is similar to the Zone Read but the TB is either lined up behind the QB or off set behind the guard and his path is Gun Triple. It can be used off Gun Triple Action or Jet Sweep.
4. The Half Reverse is the greatest reverse I've ever run. It can be run off Gun Triple, Jet Sweep or Zone Dive action. Like the Jet Sweep, so good it became a series.

In this section we'll go into the details of these plays.

Updating the Isolation Play

The number one supplemental run in the Triple Gun Offense is The Quarterback ISO. The Isolation Play has been a staple of the I Power game for decades. John McKay's USC Trojans, Woody Hayes' Buckeyes and Bo's Michigan teams all made a living running their Tailback up the middle with a big bruising fullback leading the way.

However this was not the play of choice for the "have not" football team. To make the old Tailback ISO work, you had to be more physical than your opponent. When these power teams met equally talented teams the ISO got stuffed.

Gerry DiNardo had success with this play out of the I-Bone in conjunction with the Option. DiNardo came up with the saying *"Easy to read, hard to block. Hard to read, easy to block"* DiNardo and I have had discussions about the need for a downhill running play to complement the triple option. Coach DiNardo felt it was especially important with the Gun Triple. The combination of The Triple Option and the Tailback Isolation play was the core of the I-Bone Attack.

Many under center Triple Option teams run the QB ISO as a complement to the triple option. They refer to it as a QB Follow play, because the QB fakes to the fullback and the *follows* him through the hole. This is very effective because it doesn't LOOK like an ISO play, hence it is not defended as an ISO play. This was Georgia Tech's most frequently called short yardage play under option guru Paul Johnson.

But the QB ISO from the Triple Gun takes the ISO to a completely new level. First of all it gives us a downhill play that *looks* like the Gun Triple and secondly the QB in the Gun can read the blocking like an "I" Tailback. This adds a lot to our offense:

1. Defeats a sit and read hand off key. (Hard to read, easy to block)
2. It takes the read out of the play.
3. It takes advantage of LBs running to the perimeter.
4. It's great in short yardage.
5. We use it with both Triple Motion and Jet Motion.
6. It's a great goal line play or coming out play.
7. It's a great victory offense play.
8. The QB cutback creates a counter.

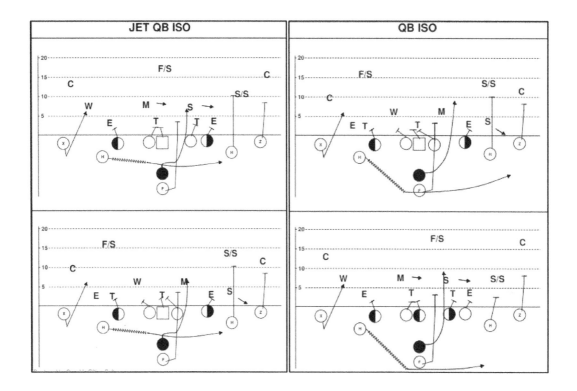

The Triple Gun QB ISO has been a great fit with the Gun Triple and the Jet Sweep. It gives us a power play and a counter play all in one. The advantage is that we don't see the hard LB fill that plagued the old I ISO teams. There are many advantages to running the QB ISO from the Gun.

1. The use of motion and the threat of Triple & Jet Sweep gets the LBs going east/west while the ball carrier is going north/south.
2. The ISO can be run to the motion or away from it. Multiple plays in one.
3. It can be run from all our formations – even Empty.
4. It can be run with all our motions or without motion.
5. We can run it to the 3 technique or the 1 technique.
6. Flash is part of the play if the "D" crowds the box.
7. It is great against a sit and read hand off key.
8. In the Gun the QB can cutback vs. overly aggressive LBs. The QB has the ability to read the blocks and make an intelligent cut. This makes it much more effective than the QB follow play
9. The QB ISO from the Triple Gun combines the qualities of the I TB ISO, The I-Bone ISO and the Flex-Bone QB follow play all in one play.

THE QB ISO ASSIGNMENTS

1. Offside Wide Receiver always checks for Flash if 8 between the slots. If not, normal triple rules (cut off)
2. Onside Wide Receiver blocks normal Triple Rules
3. Onside Slot blocks the Outside Linebacker or Strong Safety. If he's in a Twins Alignment he stalk man on. We like to use a Twins alignment to spread the front. Against a Goal line defense, he blocks man on.
4. Offside Slot either uses Jet or Triple motion. If Jet make a good fake and if triple motion keep pitch relationship in the event the ball bounces outside.
5. The Tailback has onside Linebacker.
6. Offensive Line blocks ISO RULES (which are really Veer Rules except the On Tackle blocks the Hand Off Key). Gap blocking but the Tackle blocks man on to man outside.
7. If there is a Tight End, he blocks man on, man outside.
8. The Quarterback checks Flash then fakes the play called, Triple or Jet Sweep. Then checks the blocking and runs to daylight. Against a 2 LB set he must always be aware of the cut back. Always know the front.

The QB ISO play has been a very productive play in The Triple Gun Offense. It is a low cost, low risk and very high production play. The wrinkles to it are endless and also low cost. The QB ISO is very formation friendly which allows you to dress up the pig in a lot of different ways.

Goal Line QB ISO

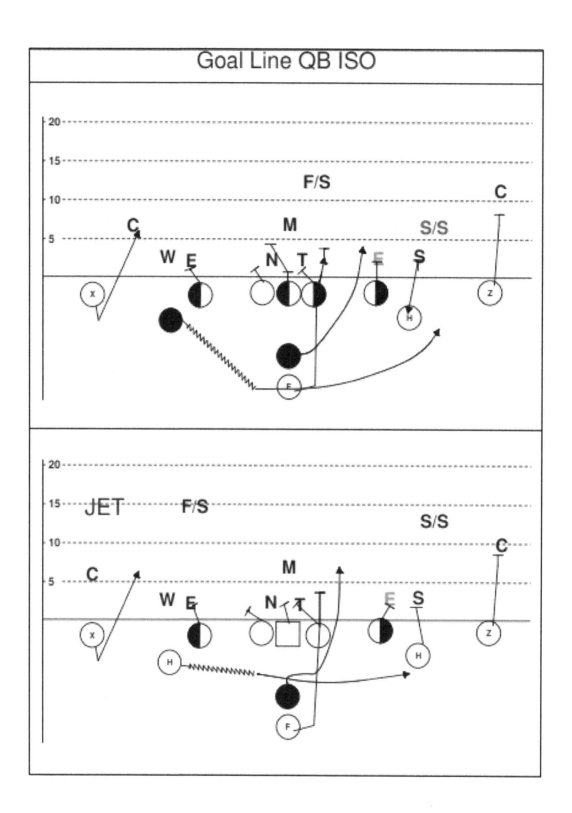

The Triple Gun Jet Sweep

The Jet Sweep was a great addition to the triple gun playbook. It has very little cost and when combined with other supplemental runs, it gives us a complete series without much new teaching.

Why the Need for The Jet Sweep.

- Power of Sequence. The Jet Sweep is easy to combine with the QB ISO, The Zone Dive, The Half Reverse, and even the Gun Triple. This gives these simple plays a new look.

- No cost. The Jet Sweep involves very little additional teaching.

- The Jet Motion can be used to disguise any play.

- Simple for the O. Line. The Blocking for the offensive line is *reach, rip and run*.

- The Sweep puts Speed in Space

- The Jet sweep compliments the Gun Triple because it defeats a hard 5 technique. If the HOK squeezes our Veer Tackle, he becomes an easy defender to reach block.

- The Jet Sweep is a great answer for defenses that try to blitz our "Smart Splits"

- The Jet Sweep is extremely Formation friendly and great with compressed sets or Empty Formation.

- The Jet Sweep attacks the perimeter without involving the Quarterback as a runner.

- The Jet Motion causes movement by the defense that can be exploited.

EMPTY JET SWEEP

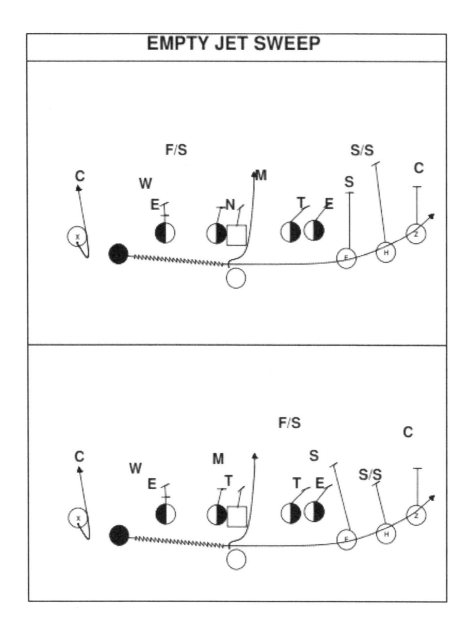

Formation Friendly. The Jet Sweep can be run just about any formation from our normal Gun Set to Empty Formation or unbalanced sets or funky sets like Empty Bunch. I like to use a compressed set so we can "Crack & Kick at the Point of Attack.

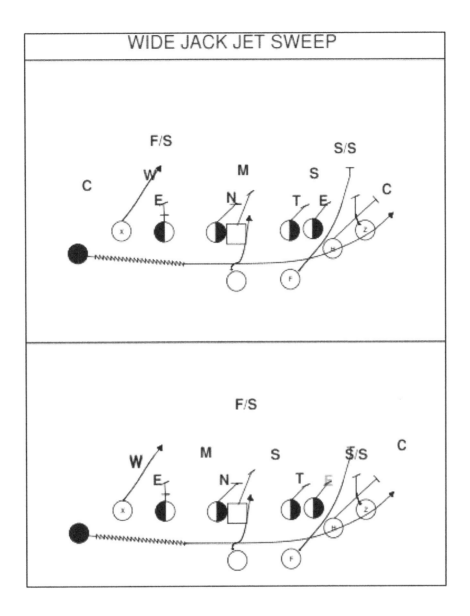

WIDE JACK JET SWEEP

Offensive Line Blocking. The line blocking for the Jet Sweep simplest line blocking ever. It's Reach, Rip & Run. The only block that must be made is the reach block on the 5 Technique. That block is made easier because our core play is the Gun Triple.

Offensive Backfield Play. There is not much teaching for the backs other than timing up the Sweeper.

The Sweeper must run full speed toward the Quarterback. The QB must have the ball snapped when the Sweeper hits the Tackle box. The Sweeper must stretch the defense and try to circle the defense. Then as the defense stretches, he can find a running lane.

The rest of the perimeter players block Gun Triple Rules.

The Tailback fakes the Zone Dive unless there is a "Lead" Call in which case he becomes a lead blocker. The Tailback can also be the Sweeper in an empty formation.

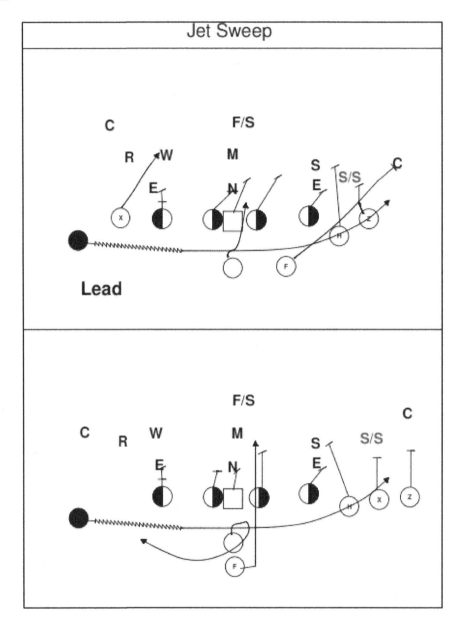

The Quarterback sends the Sweeper in Jet Motion then checks Flash. If the flash is open he can take it, if not he hands the ball to the Sweeper and fakes the Zone Dive and then a naked. We change the QB fake based on game plan.

The Dive Plays

The Veer Dive is the simplest of all the Supplemental Runs. It is the predetermined dive off of the Gun Triple. The blocking for this play is the same as for the Gun Triple, except that someone must be assigned to block the hand-off key.

Advantages of the Veer Dive Play:

- The Veer Dive is a great counter to inside LBs that try to get to the perimeter
- The play involves new techniques or schemes for the offensive line.
- The play fits in very well with the "Flash" Screen.
- The Tailback has no new reads or blocking schemes to interpret.
- The play allows the Tailback to get the ball if the defense takes him all the time on the Gun Triple.
- It can be run off Jet Sweep or Half Reverse action as well as the Gun Triple.
- Many teams are now calling this "Duo Blocking" and they block the HOK with a Tight End or H-Back.

Coaching Points:

- The quarterback looks to the Flash first. If there are "8 between the Slots, throw Quicks and Hots". If not, he gives the ball to the Tailback. A simple RPO.
- The problem with this scheme is if the Slot must block a Defensive End in a 43 Defense. This is a physical mismatch. It's OK if you use a Tight End or an H Back. The second issue is that it can't be run from a 3 Wide Receiver set like Twins or Trips. So we evolved to another Dive that better fits our personnel.

The Zone Dive. The Zone Dive has all the advantages of the Veer Dive plus many more. Here are some additional advantages.

- It is formation friendly and can be run from any formation.
- The physical mismatches now favor us..
- It Zone Blocking which tells the Line it Veer blocks TO the play not away Line protects its PLAYSIDE GAP.
- Line Blocking:

On Tackle Blocks Onside C Gap – that puts a tackle blocking a 43 DE.
On Guard Blocks Onside B Gap
Center Blocks Man on to Onside A Gap
Off Guard blocks Offside A Gap
Offside Tackle protects Offside B Gap through the man on him for the Tailback cutback

- The Zone Dive can be run off Gun Triple, Jet Sweep and The Half Reverse.

The Zone Dive is an answer play to take advantage of an overactive Linebacker. We especially like it against a 43 MLB. We can run it from Twins to reduce the front. We can also fold block the backside against a 4I.

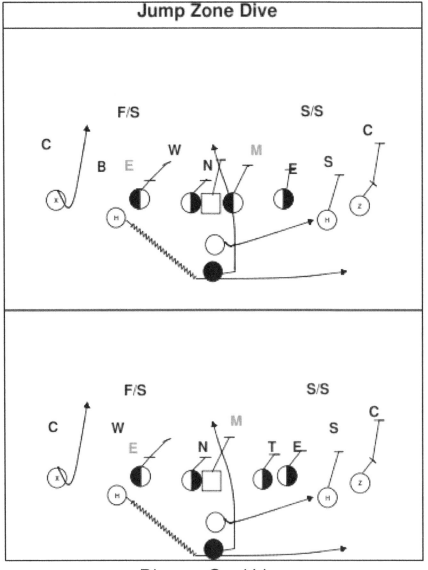

Dive on Goal Line

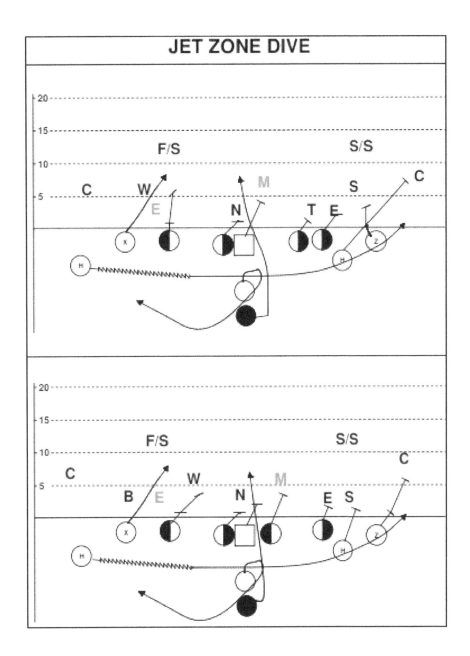

JET ZONE DIVE

Zone Dive Fake Half Reverse. The Zone Dive with the Fake Half Reverse was stolen from The Wake Forest Orbit Concept that Jim Grobe and Steed Lobotzke came up with. One way teams defend the Inside Zone or Zone Dive is to squeeze the backside defensive end to eliminate the Tailback cutback. The Half Reverse (covered next) answers that move. So by using a Fake Half Reverse, the Defense is in a conflict because they can't tell the difference.

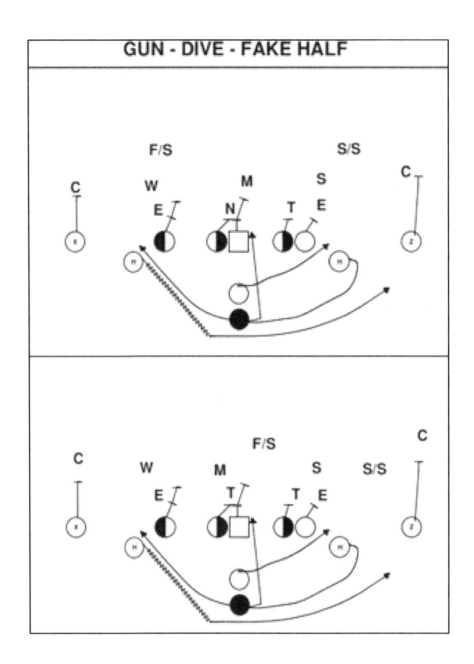

These Dives are simple answers to a defense that flies to the perimeter to stop the Gun Triple. The important part of these supplemental runs is how they form a series themselves. They can all be used in conjunction with each other to form an alternate run game without using the option.

The Half Reverse

The Triple Gun Half Reverse is the best reverse I've known because it's so efficient. It is not a feast or famine play like most reverses. It's a reverse that can be called more than once in a game. It's a reverse that is so effective that a whole series developed around it. As with the other supplemental runs, the Half Reverse fits nicely in creating a supplemental or alternative run game.

Why the Half Reverse?

- It keeps the defense from squeezing the backdoor cutback.

- It is very high production while being very low risk.

- It's part of a sequence either the Gun Triple, Zone Dive or Jet Sweep.

- It puts Speed in Space

- It makes The Triple Gun more deceptive and as Sun Tzu said "Deception is the Art of War"

Line Play. The blocking for the Half Reverse is almost the same as the Zone Dive except for the Guard to the side of the reverse. So the Half Reverse has very little additional cost.

- Tackle and Guard (opposite the Reverse) block Man on Man outside – Zone Dive Rules
- Center blocks Man on
- Guard to the Reverse Side Zone Blocks down to A Gap and helps the Center, then pulls flat down the Line of scrimmage and blocks anyone in the alley.
- Tackle blocks through man on and picks up any Linebacker.

Backfield Play

- The On Slot goes in either Option or Jet Motion full speed and makes a convincing fake.
- The Tailback fakes the Zone Dive and fills any open gap..
- The Reversing Slot reverses out then run through Tailback's heels and then catches the Quarterback's soft toss, then accelerates to the perimeter always staying wide and circling the defense.
- The Quarterback fakes Zone Dive or Jet Sweep and Zone Dive, then soft tosses the ball to the reversing Slot.

HALF REVERSE

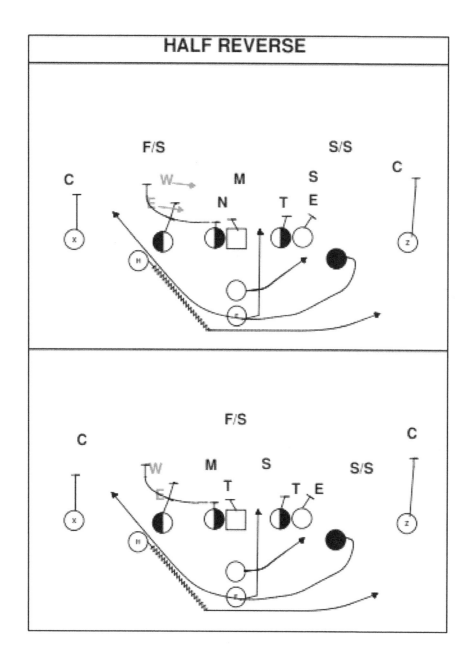

Remember the Half Reverse is still an *answer play* and is *only* effective if the defense abandons the defense of the backside of a play. If the defense is not over-pursuing it is not a good play. It is a great answer play but still an answer play.

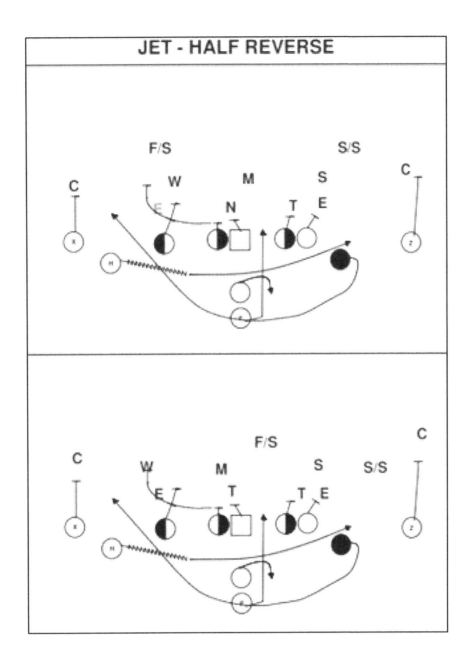

JET - HALF REVERSE

The Fake Half Reverse. When I worked for Harry Gamble at the University of Pennsylvania, he always reminded me that "They have chalk too" Meaning the defensive coaches aren't idiots. Some defensive coordinators had their offside outside linebacker key the opposite Slot for the Half Reverse. If he saw that reversing Slot come his way, he stayed home and played reverse. Pretty clever. But just when you think you have all the answers, we change the questions!

The Zone Dive Fake Half worked great. It froze the Linebackers and became a solid play. Everyone executed the Zone Dive except for the Reversing Slot. We did this off both Triple Motion and Jet Motion. Tubby Raymond would be proud.

GUN - DIVE - FAKE HALF

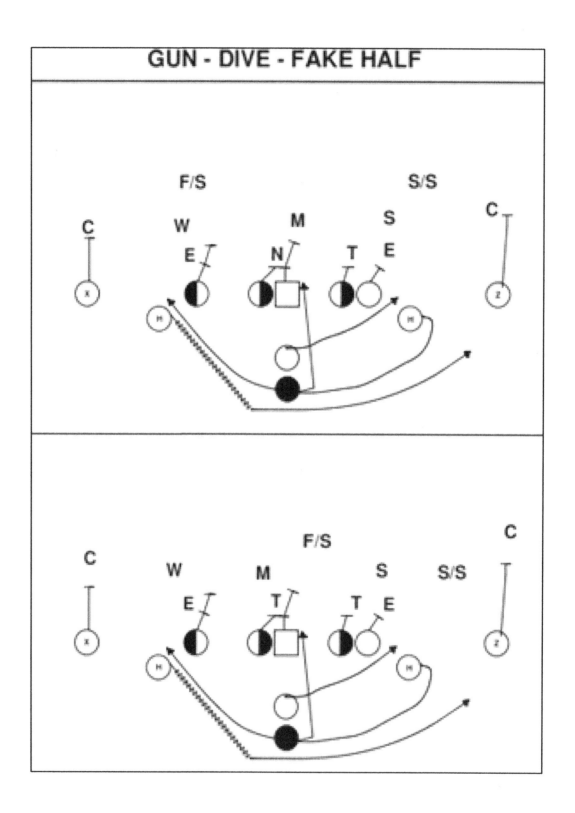

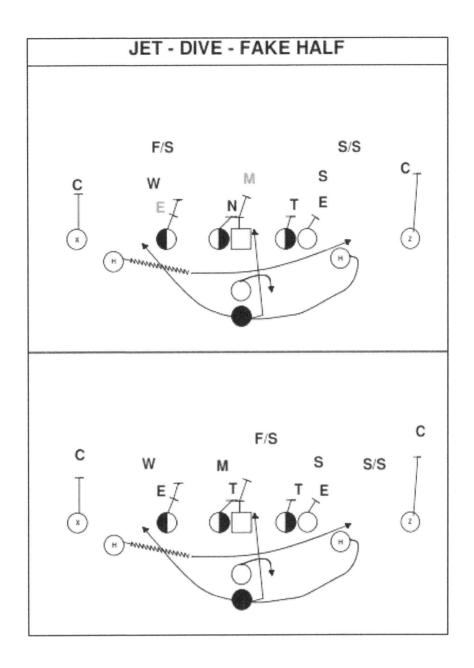

JET - DIVE - FAKE HALF

Gun Triple Fake Half Reverse. Another wrinkle was running the Gun Triple with a Fake Half Reverse. Everyone executes Gun Triple except for the Reversing Slot. The key is to do it from an Unbalanced Formation like Wingover. This was great if the Free Safety reacted to the Fake Reverse. The Half Reverse could be good to the Nub side of Unbalanced if the Defense overplays the strong side.

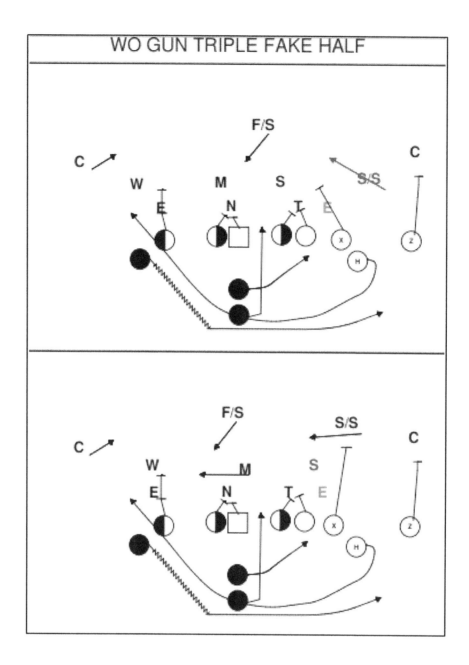

The Half Reverse has been a huge addition to the Triple Gun Package and is part of the Principle of making the defense think and not react. Football is a game of reaction and not thinking. If you think, you stink.

Hammer Time

The Triple Gun Hammer Package came about for a couple of reasons, Number One, I inherited some Tight Ends and Fullback types from my predecessor. And number two I wanted to add a simple butt kicking formation for short yardage and to finish a game. When the Tight Ends etc. graduated we moved away from this package.

The Personnel. The key to the success of this package was the personnel which consisted of the 5 O. linemen (And 6 or 7 at times) 2 Tight Ends, 2 Fullbacks or H-Backs, a Tailback and the Quarterback.

The Formations and Motions. The basic backfield lineup was the 2 H-Backs even with the QB behind the Tackles. The Tailback is lined up in his normal spot, a yard and a half behind the Quarterback). Some people call this a "Diamond" formation. We also used Hammer Strong which put the H-Backs to the same side

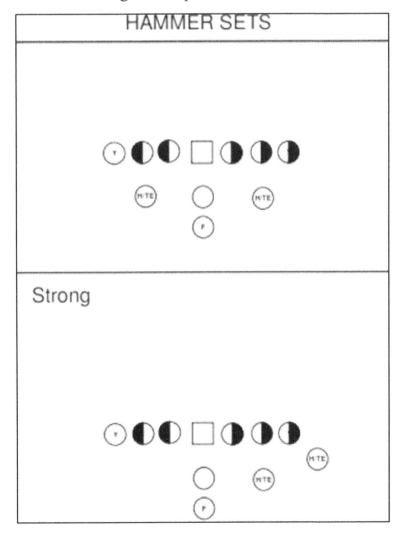

The motions are just to move to H-Back to the onside (H Right or Left) or away.

Basic Plays. We only ran a couple of plays off this and they were Tailback ISOs. The first play and the most often run was just the Double ISO. The Line blocks its ISO Blocking Rules and the Onside H-Back leads through on the Onside Linebacker. The backside Slot goes in motion and leads through any open gap. The Tailback runs to daylight. It can be run with no motion as a Single ISO as well.

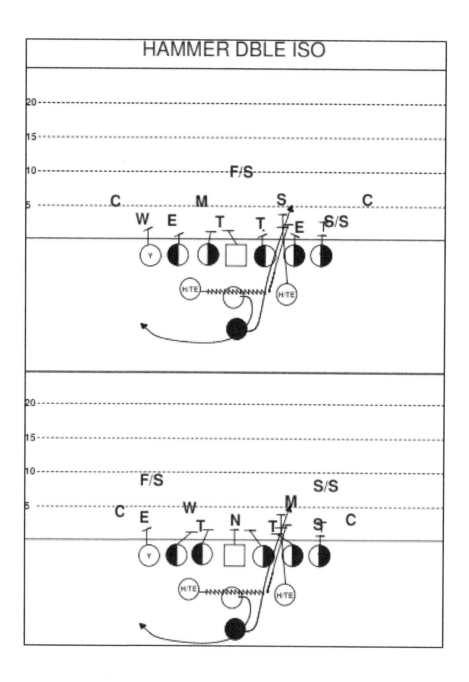

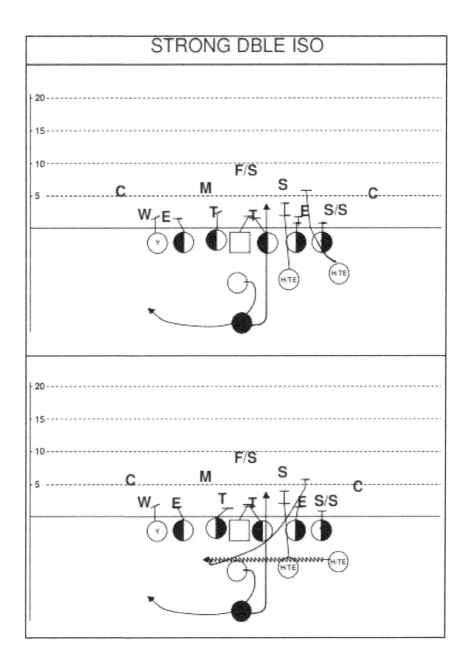

We messed around with some other plays and even some play action passes but like Tubby Raymond said "Every idea is a good idea until you practice it" The bottom line is the ISO with or without motion filled our need.

Chapter 11
Triple Gun Pass Game Overview
The Triple Gun Pass Game Principles

A big part of The Triple Gun Attack is a simple yet complete passing game. The reason we got into the Gun in the first place was to improve our pass protection so we could effectively throw the football. We have developed a handful of simple concepts that fit option quarterbacks. Each concept has a specific purpose. All our passes start with protection.

Protect first. Protection – Protection – Protection is the foundation of the Triple Gun Pass Game. Getting sacked gets us off schedule. Our base protections are 7 man protections.

- Direction is the key to protection. Our blockers must fit where the rushers are coming from.
- Our backs check release on their routes. They always block Blitz first.
- VS Heavy Blitz (8 Potential Rushers), we add to protection by a Max Call that keeps an additional receiver in to protect, all 3 backs check release.
- We throw hot only by design.

Multiple launch points. Having multiple launch points makes it more difficult to rush the Quarterback.

- *The Quick Game* has Multiple Launch points on the same play! The QB's first launch point is 5 yards behind the Center. But if the Quick Pass is covered, the Quarterback boots to the opposite perimeter.
- *The Dropback and Play Action Passes.* The Quarterback's launch point is 7 yards behind the center.
- *On perimeter passes* the Quarterback gets to a depth 7 yards behind the Tackle and then attacks the target moving downhill.

Balance high percentage throws with deep passes. In every pass, we always include a deep shot, a potential home run, that's the Quarterback's first look. (After checking for blitz) The pattern will have an intermediate route (10 to 14 yards) and a check-down route. We want to throw high percentage passes but we want the shot to hit the home run if the opportunity presents itself. If all routes are covered The QB uses his "escape rule" – run! The Quick Game escape is the Boot and the Dropback and Play Action escape is QB Draw.

Use a variety of pass actions: Quick game, Dropback game, Play Action, Boots, Perimeter Passes and Screens. Many option teams limit themselves to just Play Action and maybe a little sprint out. This limited pass attack leaves them helpless in obvious passing situations

The Flash Principle. The Flash Screen is part of every run and every pass. If the Quarterback has a pass called and he sees "8 Between the Slots, he can throw the Flash Pass and make a "Cover Guy" tackle our Wide Receiver one on one. If the CB is rolled up in a 3 Shell Defense, the Flash becomes a Fade with one on one coverage and no deep help.

Think in terms of shells and leverage rather than coverages. It's not what you know or what the Quarterback knows; it's how fast the Quarterback can process information. His reads must be simple and use unless rules. "I'm going to throw here unless…" Identify the Secondary as either a 4 Shell or a 3 Shell. Don't expect the QB to figure out if it's a loose cover 2 or a press Quarters. Instead we teach the QB to think this way "If he's deep, I'm throwing short but if he's short, I'm throwing deep"

Route Conversions are Just Common Sense. The receivers, like the Quarterback also think in terms of leverages and not coverages. The Receivers thought process is "If he's even, I'm leaving but if he's on top, I'll look to stop" To study route conversions, go to the nearest playground and watch the kids playing touch football.

Each pattern and route must be thrown with a consistent rhythm. Every route has its own rhythm and the routes must come open sequentially. Throwing the ball on time eliminates sacks. The rhythms are little different than under center and we'll cover the rhythm for each route individually later in the book.

Have a few "Cure-All" Concepts thrown many different ways. This way the Quarterbacks and receivers only have to master a few routes. Using formations, motions and different backfield actions disguise the concept but the reads and routes don't change. Nor does the protection.

Some Quarterback Tips

- Throw away from defenders not at receivers. Throw the receiver open, always make the receiver move to the ball and away from the defender covering him. Open is when the receiver is between the ball and the defender. Allow the receiver to play "The Body Game" like Charles Barkley used to rebound.
- Throw a long ball long and a short ball short.
- The quarterback run is always part of the play. When in doubt—run. Ball security is ALWAYS a must. It's always better to run for a few yards than risk a turnover. If you do run, make sure the ball is tucked away.
- Know the blitz control on every pass. The quarterback will decide how to handle blitz. Remember "Max Protection" is an option.
- Beat Man Coverage with your wide receivers and Zone coverage with your backs.

Create mismatches by motion, shifts & formations. Empty formation is a great way to isolate a Slot on a Linebacker. This is an advantage of being able to get in almost all our formations with our base personnel.

Make cover guys tackle & tackle guys cover. This is a huge pillar of the Triple Gun Offense. We try to make CBs tackle our skill guys and we always want those Linebackers covering seam routes etc. The more we put speed in space, the more points we'll score.

The Triple Gun Pass Game is a handful of concepts that are good vs any coverage. Each concept must become intuitive. The whole team must understand the concepts and how they are used. These concepts make game planning and play calling very simple.

Coverage/Leverage Characteristics

Coverage Characteristics To be an effective passing team, your team must be able to identify defensive coverages/leverages and know their weaknesses and strengths. Because in the current game many coverages morph into each other, it's important to understand leverages as well.

4-Man Shells

- *Two-deep*:
  - ✓ The strong safety backs up to the hash.

✓ The corners are flat defenders.

- *Quarters:*

  ✓ The strong safety will squat and serve a run defender. The defense may have problems in underneath coverage because only three defenders are under coverage.
  ✓ The Corners are usually off the Wide Receivers

- *Pure 4-Across Man*:
  ✓ The safeties are under 10 yards deep.
  ✓ If the safeties are split, expect a linebacker blitz.
  ✓ If the free safety cheats to one side, expect a secondary blitz. If both of the safeties are to the same side, expect a safety blitz.

3-Man Shells

- *Three Deep*:

  ✓ The strong safety is rolled up.
  ✓ The free safety is either over the ball or under the goal post. The middle of the field is closed deep.
  ✓ It should be noted that the free safety could roll weak and the strong safety could go to deep. Because this situation is still a 3-deep zone, the offense should attach away from the strong safety.

- *Man-Free:*

  ✓ The strong safety is inside the tight end, covering him man-to-man.
  ✓ The defense will rush five, unless an extra defender is in the hole (i.e., "rat" coverage).
  ✓ This coverage should be treated as a 3-man shell, regardless of whether the defense comes with a 3- or 4-man rush.

- *Press Man*:

  ✓ There is no deep secondary defender.
  ✓ A 4- or 3-man shell will be employed, depending on the number of wide receivers.

Adjust, Adapt and Advance

One of the most common questions I get on the clinic circuit is: "What do you do if you don't have a running quarterback?" Of course I would like to have a Quarterback that throws like Montana and runs like Jim Brown but somehow those guys are kind of rare. So a key ingredient to a successful offense is to adapt it to the personnel you have.

I have witnessed many coaches go to an option style attack when they have a running QB or an Air Raid or Run and Shoot Offense when they have an exceptional passer. I've also seen coaches try to install a Wing T playbook because they did not have a talented quarterback. Some of these coaches have actually had some success with this method. However, the problem is they never accumulate *"banked reps"* which is the key to building skill.

So even though adapting to your Quarterback is very important, the rest of the unit will suffer by going from a Flex-Bone Offense to an Air Raid Offense and vice-versa because all the reps your offense had at the previous offense are now thrown out of the window and you are starting at square one all over again.

OK so what is the answer? Do you keep slinging the ball around the field with a Quarterback who couldn't hit the ocean from a boat? Do you just insist on scheme over ability? How do you adapt and adjust to maximize the ability of all your players?

The way to have the ability to adapt and adjust is to have a flexible offense. This is one of the reasons I am such a big believer in The Triple Gun Offense. The Triple Gun Offense can adapt to any style of Quarterback. My first year at The University of Charleston I inherited a big, strong Quarterback that never ran the option in his life. He was a dropback passing QB. He wasn't a great runner but he was smart and tough. UC had won only a total of five games total in the previous two years. We adapted the Gun Triple emphasizing the give and the pitch and we threw the ball more frequently using our quick game almost as a run. UC went 8-3 in our first year, the biggest turnaround in conference history without an option quarterback. Our Quarterback had a great year and set several school passing records. The ability to have a comprehensive passing attack while being able to run the option from the shotgun makes it simple to adapt your style of attack regardless of your personnel.

After two years our starting QB was a 5'7'' quick running quarterback. We adapted our offense to fit his talents without changing the rest offensive unit's skill set or techniques. So everyone benefitted from *"banked reps"* and our offense continued to grow and become more productive. The 5'7" QB set the conference Pass Efficiency record twice the second time an astonishing 189. He also accounted for 89 touchdowns in his 3 years as a starting Quarterback.

My last year we had a true freshman burst on the scene and we gradually brought him along and he started the last three games of the season. In one game he came off the bench in the second quarter while we were trailing 14-0 and he led us to a 44-34 victory. In that game he became the first player in conference history to rush and throw for over 200 yards in the same game. How did he develop so fast? We did what he could do while working on the other aspects of his game. We used his strengths and compensated for his weaknesses. We stayed away from complicated audible packages and simplified his triple reads. The passing game was also trimmed to use a handful of concepts that he was comfortable with and we emphasized his escapes if he was in doubt. Ball security is always the first priority (see meaningful stats).

As you can see the exact same offense was successful with three very distinct types of quarterbacks that created three different styles of the same offense. So even though we adapted to the quarterback's abilities all the rest of the offensive unit kept using the same techniques and continued to benefit from their *"banked reps"*.

The difference between the Triple Gun and other system offenses like the pure Flex-bone or the Air Raid & Run & Shoot is it is Multi-dimensional thus it's a more flexible attack that can adapt to the personnel. If you're running The Air Raid Offense and don't have a passing QB – you better have a great punter. If you're running the Flex-bone and your QB is not a good runner, you are also in some trouble. The same is true if your QB goes down with an injury. It's easier to have a capable back-up with the Triple Gun because you can use the part of the menu best suited for that particular QB.

Another advantage of being a Multi-dimensional offense is it gives you the ability to exploit a weakness. A team may have a Cornerback playing with 2 broken legs but if you can't throw the ball, it doesn't matter. Or a team may be a terrible run defense but if you have zip for a running attack no one will ever know. A weakness is only a weakness if you can exploit it.

Our menu includes six main areas:

1. The hub of the offense is the *Gun Triple* – based on your QB's run ability you can adapt the reads (keep unless or pitch unless). This play is a complete run game in itself thus giving you more time to develop your pass game.
2. The *Quick Game* – it doesn't take Joe Montana to throw a hitch route. The Quick game is a great compliment to the Gun Triple and spreads a defense..
3. The Power Game – QB ISO and base give. (See the section on Updating the ISO
4. The *Play Action Pass Game* – another obvious compliment to the Gun Triple. This can be devastating with a talented passer but any QB can be an effective passer throwing to wide open receivers.
5. The *Counter & Jet Sweep Game* – the Jet Sweep is a great way to get outside without using your QB. The Half Reverse exploits an aggressive defense.
6. The *Dropback Game* – you need this part of the Offense even if you don't have a talented passer. Having the "QB Draw Escape" is a great weapon for a running QB.

This simple six prong attack builds flexibility in your offense while developing consistency. You get all the benefit of banked reps while having the capability to adapting the offense to the skills of your quarterback.

Chapter 12
The Triple Gun Quick Game

The Triple Gun Quick Game Pass Protection

Why the Quick Game?

- High percentage and low risk. A ball control pass. Enables a less talented team to pass against a very talented defense.

- It compliments Triple – "8 between the slots throw quicks & hots" It keeps the defense from loading the box

- The Quick Game is a great way to put "Speed in Space"

- It "makes cover guys tackle & tackle guys cover" These mismatches that favor the offense. .

- The Quick Game is not dependent on a great offensive line. It's tough to beat the O. Line in 1.6 secs.

- It's very difficult to blitz especially with the potential boot off it. There is little risk of giving up sacks.

- It's great in wet weather.

- It has multiple launch points on the same play.

- It has very simple pass protection.

- The boot part of the play is a better perimeter pass than sprint out because there is no linebacker contain.

Quick Game Pass Protection. The Quick Game Pass protection uses the same principles as Gun Triple blocking. Double team unless, never block air and always find work. The blocking scheme is a hybrid gap/slide protection that does a great job of matching blockers with the pass rushers.

Coaching Points: We always maintain are Smart Splits which helps with our double teams and the Smart Splits make it more difficult for the defense to execute line stunts. Here are key components of Quick Game blocking:

- Stay Square, don't turn your shoulders. Be able to protect your inside gap
- Stay Firm. Never get driven back into the QB's lap. It's important to stop the Defensive lineman's momentum.
- Don't move forward. Maintain the position on the Line of Scrimmage. Never lunge at a defender.
- Don't chase. You are responsible for your gap. This is not man protection.
- Don't Block Air. Same principle as the Gun Triple blocking. If no one is in your gap – Stay on the Double Team.

Assignments. The blocking assignments for the offensive line are gap oriented.

- The Onside Tackle has C Gap or the end man on the Line of Scrimmage. If possible, the Tackle should get that man's hands down.
- The Onside Guard has B Gap, if no one is there, he helps the Center.
- The Center has onside A Gap, if no one is there help the offside Guard
- The Offside Guard has offside A Gap, if no one is there help the Tackle.
- The Offside Tackle has offside B Gap, if no one is there he helps the Slot.
- It's important for the line to communicate so there is no confusion

Backfield Blocking

- The Offside Slot has the "Slam and Slide" He blocks C Gap for 2 Counts or until the Quarterback boots and then releases into the flat getting no deeper than 5 yards. As soon as he releases, he must look for the ball. His block is a hard block that's why it's called a *Slam* and Slide. When he releases off the block, he *vaults* off the block. If there is a blitz, the Slot blocks for 3 counts before vaulting off into the flat.
- The Tailback blocks away from the call, always backside. He blocks the first man outside the Slot's block. If there is no one there, he overtakes the man the Slot was blocking. It is very important that the Tailback gets in position to block as fast as he can so he is in good position to execute his assignment.

  If the Tailback is away from the call in Empty formation (Slot Empty) he is responsible for C gap but never releases. If he is aligned to the call (Backs Empty) he runs the pass route called

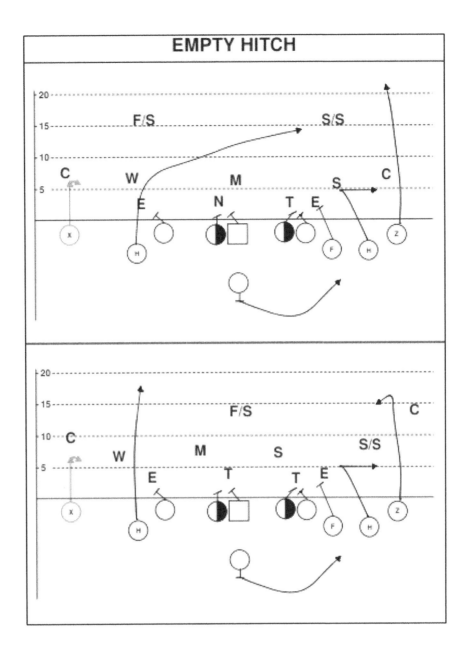

Blocking Fronts. This is the protection against the common defensive fronts. This protection is designed for The Quick Game, for it to be effective the Quarterback **must** throw the ball on time or Boot escape. The Boot escape make it very difficult for defenses to pressure the Triple Gun Quick Pass. Here is The Quick Game Protection vs common fronts.

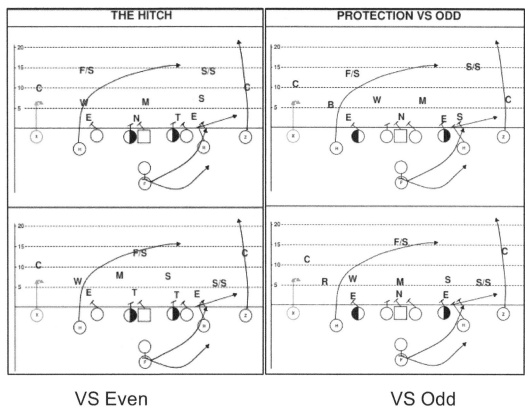

VS Even   VS Odd

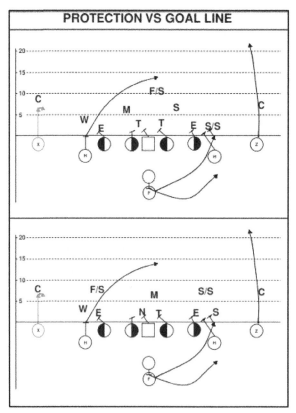

This is the pass protection for every quick pass regardless of the formation or pattern.

The Hitch Pass: The Core Pass of the Quick Game

The Hitch Pass is like a run play because it's thrown so often. It is a great compliment to the Gun Triple because if the defense crowds the box, the Wide Receiver will have one on one coverage with space to run. At the start of every game, we always looked for ways to throw the hitch and have a guaranteed 6 yards and maybe more. Any time a cover guy has to make a tackle in apace, there is a chance for a big play. The Hitch is one of many high percentage, low risk passes that allow the Triple Gun to move the chains and control the clock with the pass.

Routes. The routes are simple to run and easy to throw *but* they must become intuitive through daily quality repetitions.

The Hitch. The Onside Wide Receiver explodes downfield, forcing an outside release. He must drive downfield, with his numbers hidden (chest down, nose over toes) selling the fade. Then at 6 yards, he plants his outside foot in the ground, and gets his numbers to the Quarterback. The ball will be in the air so the wide out must snap his head around and locate the ball. Sounds simple it is, sounds easy it's not. It must be repped until it's automatic. He does not move to the QB, the ball should already be in the air. Once he makes the catch, its pluck, tuck and burst! Yards after catch are very important in the Triple Gun Offense. By doing a great job selling the fade, the receiver will gain separation and have room to run after the catch. Note: against press coverage, the Quarterback converts the hitch to a fade, always leaving himself a 4 yard lane between him and the sidelines to make the catch. If the QB boots, the wide receiver converts the Hitch to a Post.

The Onside Slot runs an "Over" route which is a crossing route. Against a 43 OLB, the Slot will run at him and then under him. This release will occupy the OLB and open up the Hitch. Then the Slot must get over the MLB or any Inside Linebacker and climb to a depth of 12 yards expecting the Quarterback to boot. If the QB boots and is forced to pull up, the Slot must gear down and stay in his vision.

The Offside Slot. Executes the "Slam and Slide" previously explained in the protection section. This is always the route for the Offside Slot regardless of the other routes.

The Offside Wide Receiver runs a "Clear" route which means we want him to occupy two defenders. Against press coverage, he forces an outside release forcing the CB to turn to the sidelines thus blinding him to the Slam and Slide route. If the CB squats, the WR will squat in the hole between the CB and Safety. Most of the time will run with the fade. If the CB is off, the Wide Receiver runs a "Skinny Post" never crossing the hash mark. So either way, the WR will take two"

Quarterback Play. The Quarterback goes through his normal pre-snap checklist first:

1. My launch point is 5 yards behind the Center.
2. My Blitz control is 7 man protection, vs 8 between the Slots call "Max" and that cause the Onside Slot to check release before running his "Over" route
3. His Read is "I'm throwing the Hitch every time unless the CB is in Press Coverage or the OLB is wide. If it's press coverage in a 3 shell secondary, the Fade might be a good shot.
4. My escape is the Boot. If the Slam and Slide is there, throw it. If not, check the "Over" Route, if it's there, throw it but when in doubt run.

The Rhythm of Throwing the Hitch. The Quarterback's timing on the Hitch Route or the Fade is "Catch, Step and Throw" The pass should be off in 1.6 seconds.

Also check out the Hitch Video.

The Hitch Away from Trips. We use the Trips formation to isolate the single receiver side Hitch. A common defensive adjustment is to play a 3 shell defense when we align in a 3 X 1 set. So the single receiver will have a 3 Deep Corner on him which makes the hitch a gift pass. The unintended consequence is the Boot off it, gives us a great Sprint Out Pass. It's a 3 level read. The #1 receiver runs the Clear Route, and the Slot runs the Slam and Slide Route. The middle receiver runs a 14 yard "Pivot Route" he goes down 14 yards and turns into the Quarterback and then slide to the sidelines.

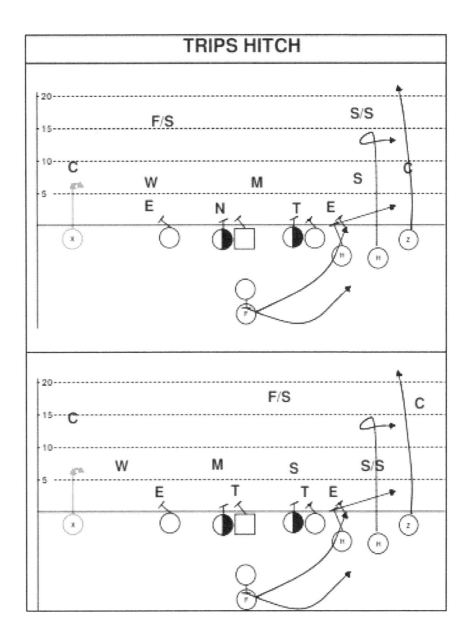

TRIPS HITCH

The Quarterback Play. The Quarterback throws the single receiver hitch unless. The only difference is that if he boots, he looks to the Slam and Slide to the Pivot Route to QB run.

The Hitch Away from Triple Motion. This another way to open up the Hitch. If the Secondary is trying to roll on our Motion, the throw to the Hitch is automatic. But if the QB has to boot he has an extra blocker leading the way. If the CB stays in a Press Position the Hitch converts to a Fade which usually results in a big play.

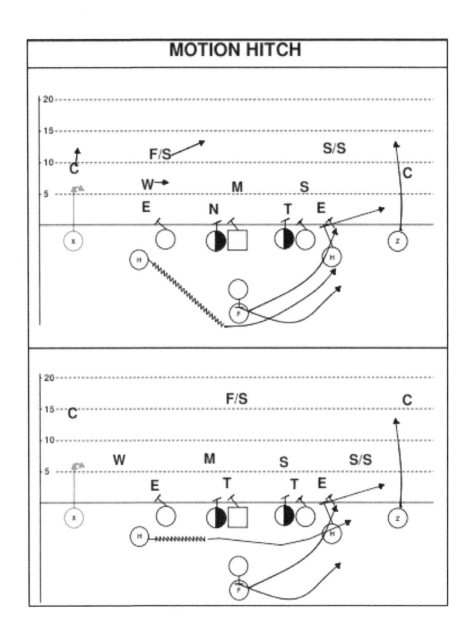

Motion Fade

Using a Wide Jack Formation. Throwing the Hitch from Wide Jack creates a scenario to throw the Hitch to a speedy Slot and causes a new look to the Boot side. The WR still wants to take 2 but in a compressed set he does it by doing a Corner Route. If the QB Boots he has a deep Corner Route with the Slam and Slide underneath. The use of formations is literally endless.

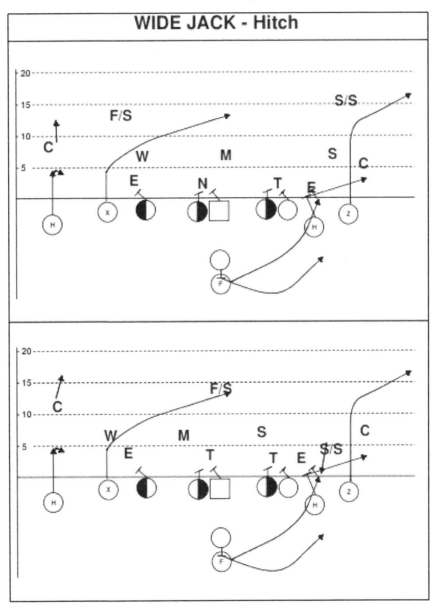

The Hitch/Seam Combo. Adding the Seam Route to the Hitch gives the play a better downfield threat and has produced many big plays. The only difference between the normal hitch and the Hitch/Seam is the Onside Slot. Everyone else just runs the hitch pass.

The Onside Slot takes an outside release and runs the Seam Route midway between the hash mark and the sideline. It's important that he looks for the ball as soon as he clears the Linebackers.

The Quarterback throws the Seam Route into a hole between the Linebacker and the Safety. This area is between 12 to 17 yards deep. The rhythm is "Catch, step and throw" Against a 3 Shell the QB reads the first LB inside the Slot this makes a "Tackle Guy" cover our Slot. Against a 4 Shell. The QB reads the CB, if the Hitch is there, throw it but if the CB is in press coverage, the hitch will convert to a fade. The QB can throw the fade because the Slot will tie up the Safety and the CB will have no help on the wide receiver. This one-on-one situation favors the Wide Receiver. If he doesn't like the looks of Fade, the QB boots.

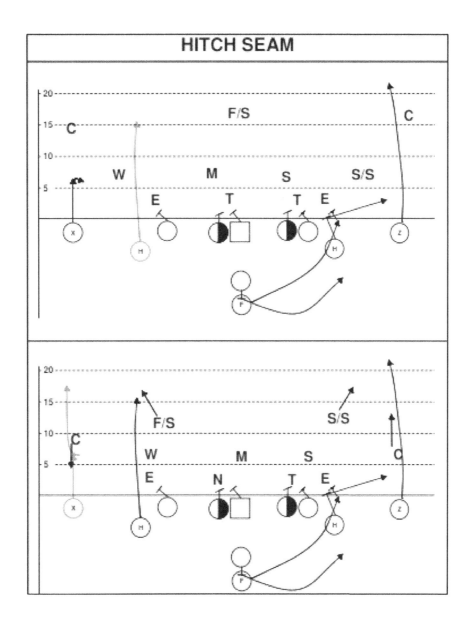

The Hitch/Seam from Empty Formation. This is exactly the same rules for everyone except the number 2 receiver to the 3 receiver side. The Tailback must stay on his block so the number 2 receiver runs a "*Snag Route*" to replace the "Slam and Slide" – The *Snag Route* is run by the receiver coming inside like a Slice Route (a 3 yard Slant) but if the QB Boots, the receiver pivots back outside into a flat route just as though it were a Slam and Slide. This is the same adjustment anytime the Quick Game is run from Empty.

EMPTY HITCH

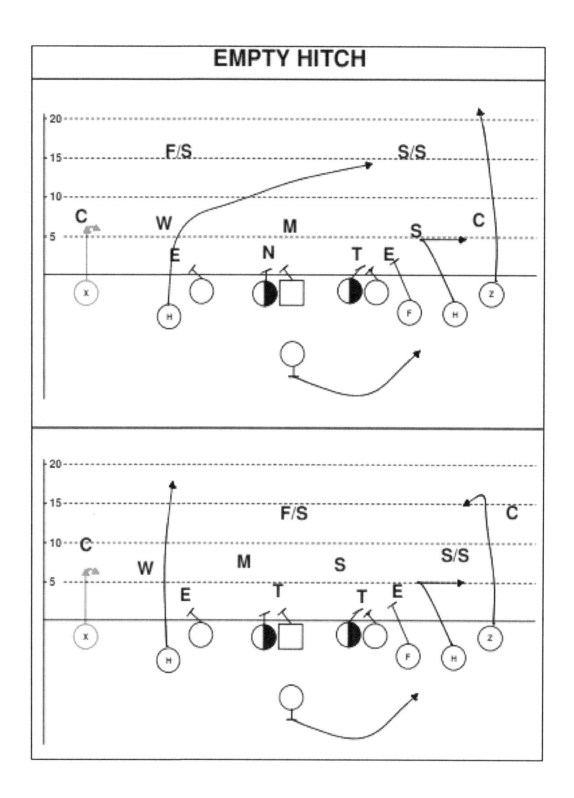

The Quick Game Fade/Stick Combo

The next Quick Game Pass is the Fade/Stick Combo. Most of the play stays the same regardless of the pattern called. The protection is exactly the same as for all the Quick Game patterns. There a couple of new routes for the Fade/Stick Combo.

Onside Wide Receiver runs the *Fade Route* which is the same fade as when the hitch converts to the fade vs press coverage except in this pattern, the Wide Receiver must take an outside release no matter what. By taking an outside release, the CB will be forced to turn away from the Stick Route and blinding him to the Slot. Against a deep CB or a 3 Shell CB, the Fade converts to a very Skinny Post.

The Onside Slot runs the *Stick Route*. On the Stick Route, the Slot explodes down field as though he was running a Seam Route, then at 5 yards, he sticks is inside foot in the ground and breaks square outside to the sideline. If there is an outside Linebacker waiting for him, the Slot pulls up and puts his numbers to the Quarterback.

This is a great short yardage route and a great stop the clock pattern.

The Offside Wide Receiver a Post/Curl route called a "Pearl Route" because the Wide Out takes an outside release then goes down 12 yards and breaks to the post for 3 steps, plants and comes back to the Quarterback looking for an open window.

Quarterback Play. The QB goes through his normal pre-snap ritual first. Then his thought process is: "I'm going to throw the Fade every time unless the CB runs with him, then I'll throw to the Stick Route. If I don't like the Stick Route, I'll Boot. If I boot. I'll throw Slam and Slide unless it's covered, then I'll throw to the Pearl Route or run. So the Quick game side is basically a 4 shell side and the Boot side is the 3 Shell side.

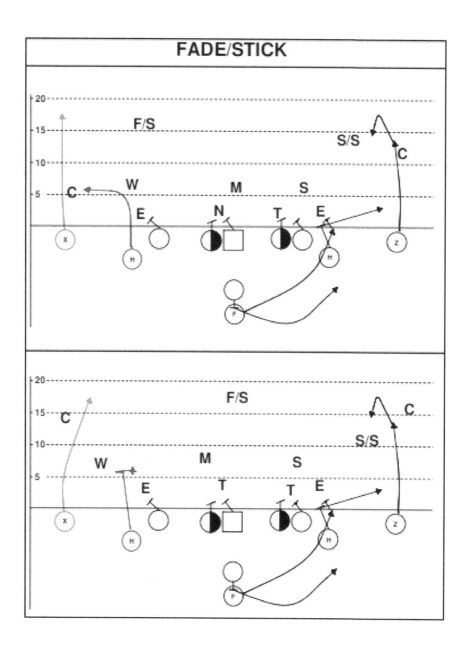

FADE/STICK

Coaching Points: If the QB is going to throw the fade, it has to be because the CB has squatted. The CB has the Safety helping over the top because Slot is running a Stick Route not a Seam. So the QB's pass must be a drill shot in the hole between the CB and Free Safety. If it is a 3 Shell with a press CB, the FS can't help so he can put some air under the fade.

Fade Stick in Short Yardage

- The rhythm for the fade is "Catch, Step, Throw" and the QB's rhythm for the Stick is "Catch, Step, Look and Throw" because the QB will *look* at the fade first.

- When the Quarterback throws the Stick, the ball should be place so it's a thumb together catch between the receiver and the sideline.
- If it's a 43 Defense with the OLB over our tackle, the Stick is a gift.

Fade/Seam Combo. Against a 4 shell secondary we might like to isolate our talented wide receiver against a press cornerback. We do this by calling Fade/Seam. The Slot running the Seam Route will tie up the Free Safety leaving the press cornerback one on one with our wide receiver.

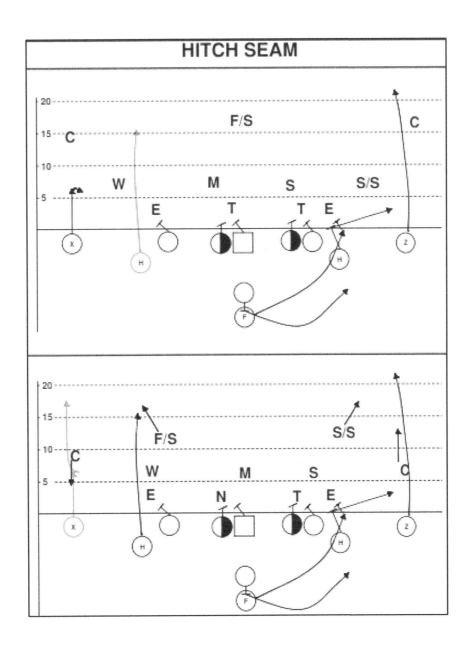

ISO Dive Stick (RPO). The Zone Read Stick RPO is another form of Option that merges the Run and Quick game on the same play. Everyone executes the Base Dive except the Onside Slot and The Onside Wide Receiver. They run the Fade/Stick Combo. The unblocked defender is the OLB.

The Offensive Line ISO Blocks leaving the Onside OLB unblocked.

The Quarterback Reads the OLB and is going to give to the TB every time unless the OLB plays run, if he freezes it's a pull. If the QB pulls he reads the Fade/Stick just like he would in the Quick Game.

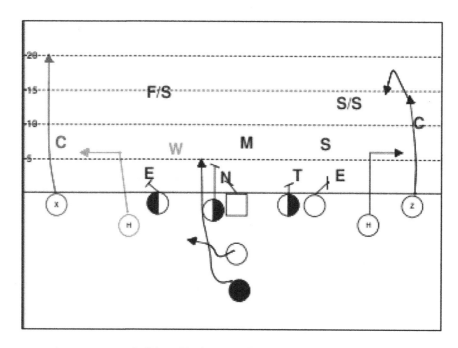

I Slot Rt Dive Stick RPO

Empty QB ISO Stick (RPO). Same concept as the ISO Dive Stick except the Defense is spread out more with the Empty set. The QB makes the same read as above but instead of handing the ball to the Tailback, he becomes the runner. I prefer giving the ball to the Tailback because I want to limit the number of carries the QB has in a game.

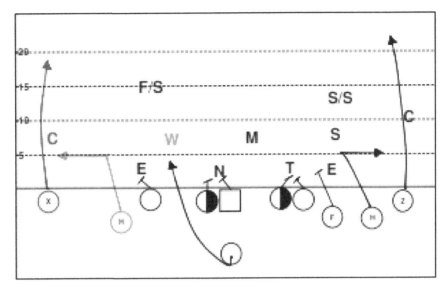

Empty QB ISO Stick RPO

The Quick Game Slice/Corner Combo

The Slice/Corner Combo is another Quick Game concept that we love in the Red Zone, in Goal line situations or as a two point play. As in all the Quick Game the Protection stays the same. The Offside Routes are still a Clear by the Wide Receiver and a Slam and Slide by the Slot. The only difference is the Onside Routes.

Onside Wide Receiver runs the *Slice Route*. On this route, the receiver steps with his outside foot like he was going to run a Fade Route. Then he plants his outside foot into the ground and rips hard back inside. Against Press Coverage, he must rip with his outside are to get inside the CB. If he takes a good first step the CB will also step outside to defend the Fade and thus opening up the inside release. After releasing inside the WR stays in the no cover zone, getting no deeper than 3 yards. If there is a Linebacker in his path (he can see the LB's eyeballs) he must pivot back toward the sidelines. If the Quarterback boots, he continues across the field on a Shallow Drag, getting no deeper than 6 yards.

221

Onside Slot runs the *Corner Route.* This route is a great Man to Man Coverage beater. Against a 4 Shell secondary, The Slot take an outside release selling the Seam Route. Then at 6 yards depth, he presses inside and gives the Safety a little "Shampoo Fake" (Head and Shoulders) the breaks to the sideline aiming for a point 15 yards on the sideline. Against a 3 Shell Secondary with no defender over him, he can convert the Corner to a Seam Route.

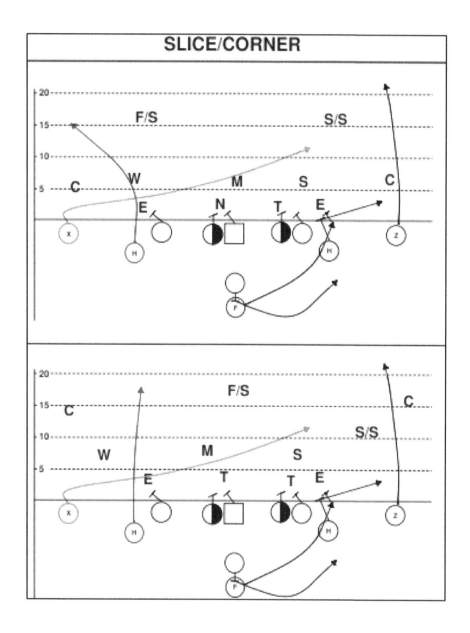

Quarterback Play. The Quarterback goes through his pre-snap checklist as he does on every Quick Game Pass.

His thought process on the Slice/Corner Combo is "I'm throwing the Slice every time *unless* the CB trails the Wide Receiver. If the CB trails the WR, the QB throws the Corner Route to the Slot.

Throwing the Corner Route. What makes the Corner route so effective against man coverage is the ball placement by the QB. Here are some coaching point:

- Throw it *after* the Slot makes his break. Every Corner Route is a little different
- Throw the ball like throwing into a kiddie Pool, nose down.
- Put the ball between the Slot and the sideline so only he can catch it.

The Quarterback Rhythms of the Throws. The QB's rhythm for the Slice Route is "Catch, Step and Throw" and for The Corner Route, his rhythm is "Catch, Step, look and Throw"

Finally, the Quarterback always has his "Boot Escape" with the Slice becoming a Drag Route giving the QB an additional Boot Target.

Chapter 13
Triple Gun Play Action Pass Game
The Triple Gun Play Action Pass Part 1

The Triple Gun Play Action Pass Game is taken to another level from any under center option systems. Every phase is simpler, more effective, and less risky. We divide the Play Action Pass Game into 2 parts. The first part is off the Gun Triple and Jet Sweep action and the second part is the play action off the Zone Read.

The Triple Gun Play Action Pass Game has many advantages, here are some of them:

- The Gun makes it more difficult to distinguish between the run and the pass.
- It creates great conflict for the Linebackers as well as the secondary.
- The 2-point stance makes it easier for the line to protect and harder for the defense to detect.
- The depth of the Quarterback in the game makes it easier to read the defense and easier to get the pass off more quickly.
- Every Pattern includes a home run shot but also a check down route which gives every pass big play potential while still being high percentage and low risk.
- There is a Quarterback run built into every pass.
- The Receiver's Route Conversions are consistent with the Principle of Strategic Flexibility.

Offensive Line Pass Protection. The line protection is the same for all of the Play Action Passes in Part 1. It is a 7-man protection scheme with the line responsible for 5 defenders and 2 backs are responsible for 2 linebackers. Assignment wise, it's the same blocking as ISO blocking.

The line still uses "Smart Splits" which makes it easier to double team and more difficult for the defensive line to twist & stunt. The Line also uses the double team unless rules. We never block air.

Offensive Line Assignments. These assignments are the same as QB ISO so the line have plenty of banked reps on these assignments.

- Onside Tackle blocks man on, man outside.

- Onside Guard blocks man on, man outside. If he has no man on him, he turns back and blocks onside A Gap.
- Center blocks man on. If there is no man on him, he blocks backside A Gap. The Center will always have help in pass protection.
- Offside Guard has man on to backside B Gap. If has no man on him, he still helps the Center before protecting B Gap. He also must be alert for a "Smoke" call by the Offside Tackle.
- Offside Tackle blocks man on to backside C Gap. If he has a man on his inside that he can't cut off, he makes a "Smoke" Call and delivers him to the Guard, then pivots to handle C gap pressure.

Backfield Protection. The Motion Slot is a check-release protection, but the Tailback is a personal protector for the Quarterback. The Onside Slot runs his route unless it's a "Max" call then he check-releases as well.

- Offside Slot runs the motion called (Triple or Jet) and then blocks anyone blitzing off the edge or outside the Onside Tackle's Block. If there is no one blitzing; he runs a Flare.
- Tailback has the first Linebacker onside. If there is no LB blitz he fits into the protection and finds work.
- Onside Slot runs the route called unless there is a "Max" call which means there is 8 defenders in the box with only 7 blockers. The Onside Slot then check releases off the Strong Safety.

MAX PROTECTION

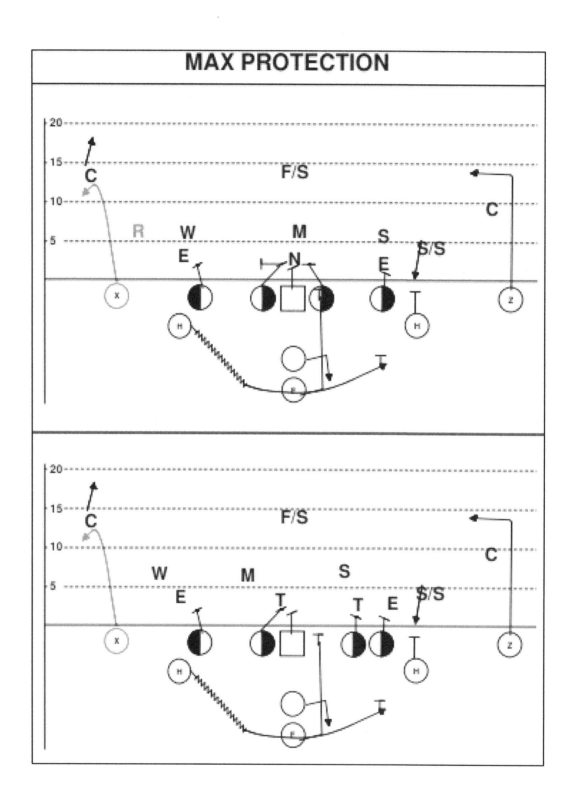

226

- *Flip Protection* is the same assignments for all except the Flip Slot and the Tailback switch assignments. So, the Tailback check-releases to a Flare and the Flip Slot fits into the protection.

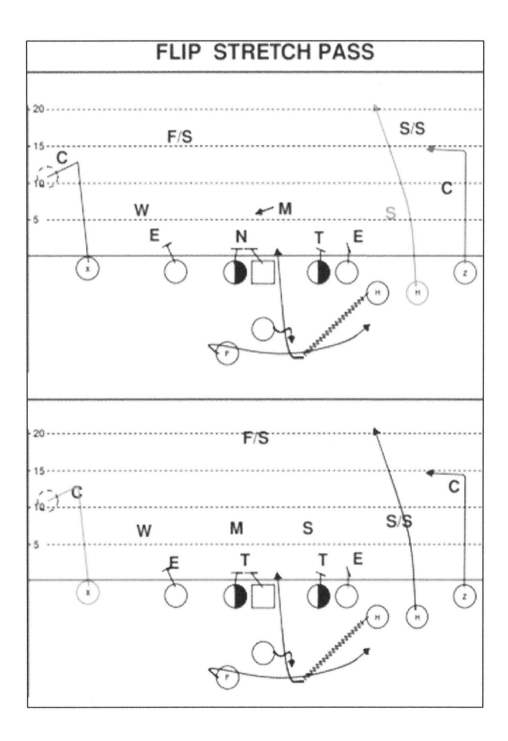

FLIP STRETCH PASS

This protection scheme is the same protection scheme for every play action pass involving Gun Triple, Jet Sweep or Flip actions.

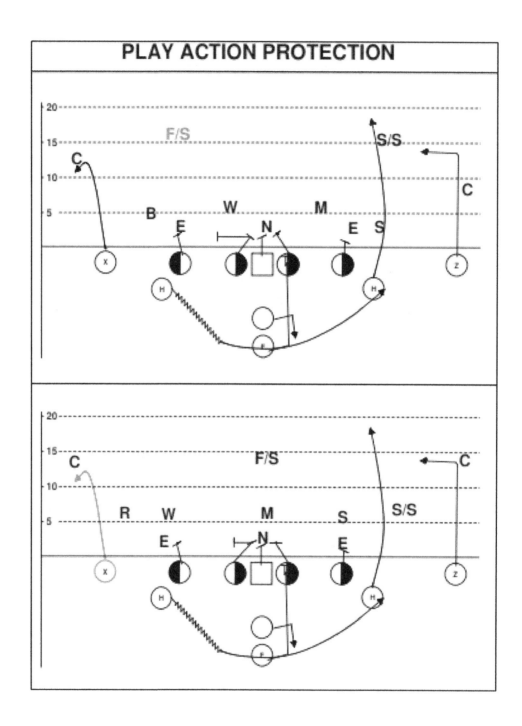

These Play Action Passes are the most frequently used passes and have been very productive and very high percentage.

The Play Action Stretch Pass

The Stretch Pattern. The Stretch Pattern is our most used pattern in the offense. We use it in both the play action and in the Dropback pass. This is our most productive pass.

The routes for the Wide Receivers are Field and Boundary Routes. So regardless of the direction of the call the Wide Receiver's routes never change. Their routes convert but never change.

Field Wide Receiver. The field Wide Receiver forces an outside release and does a Fade every time unless the CB bails or gets depth. If the CB bails, the WR breaks off the Fade at 14 yards and does an "In" Route saying parallel to the line of scrimmage looking for a window. He only moves back to the line of scrimmage after the ball is thrown to him.

Boundary Wide Receiver. The boundary wide receiver forces an outside release and runs a Fade route every time unless the CB bails and gets depth. He must remember to leave a 4-yard lane between him and the sidelines to catch the fade. If the CB bails and gets depth, the wide receiver breaks off the fade at 12 yards and comes back to 10 yards on the sideline. The WR must make the CB turn and run to get separation for the out route. He also must lean in on a CB who is running with him to "widen the field". Another coaching point is if the WR is converting to the Out Route, it is important that he snaps his head around and locate the ball because it will already be in the air on his break.

The Stretch Route. The Onside Slot is the primary receiver in the Stretch Pattern. The Stretch Pass usually run to the wide field but it's equally effective to the boundary. When the route is called to the field, the Slot takes an outside release as though he was going to Arc block the Strong Safety. His landmark is the middle of the goal post. By taking a wide release the Quarterback can lead him to his landmark and literally throw him open. If he's in a Twins alignment he doesn't need to take an outside release, but he still attacks the Strong Safety as though he was going to block him and then bend into his landmark. The ball should be caught between 15 to 18 yards.

PLAY ACTION STRETCH PASS

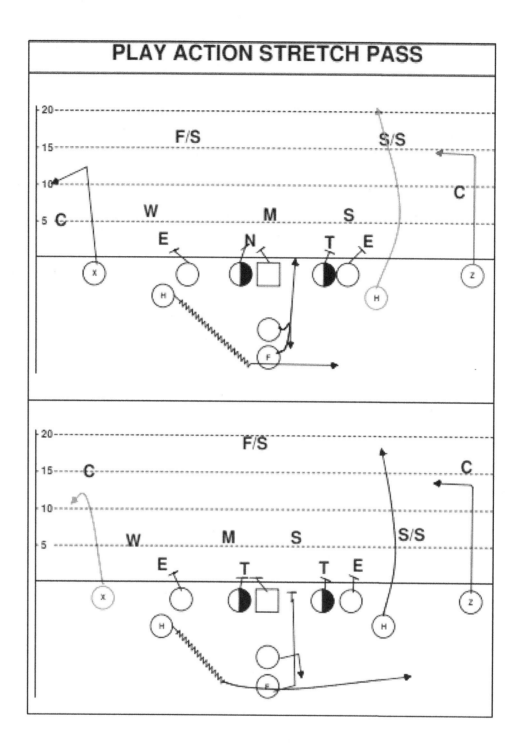

If the Stretch Pattern is called into the boundary, the Slot runs the "Seam Route" and the "hole" should be midway between the sideline and the hash at a depth between 15 to 18 yards.

STRETCH PASS TO BOUNDARY

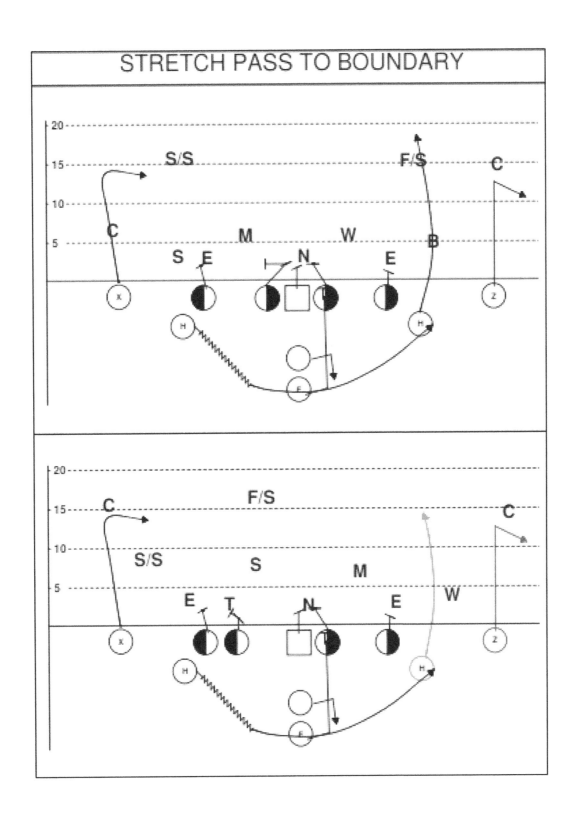

231

The On Slot must always be alert for a "Max" call by the Quarterback which means the Slot blocks the blitz by the SS or OLB to his side, If there is no immediate blitz, he runs his Stretch Route.

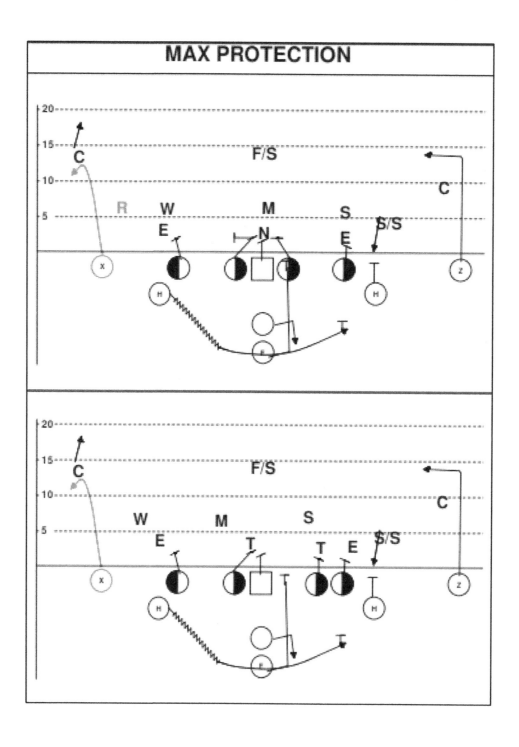

MAX PROTECTION

Quarterback Play. The Quarterback begins each pass with the same ritual. First his 4 basic questions,

- What is my launch point? – 5 to 7 yards behind the Center
- What is my Blitz Control? The protection is 7-man protection with a check release by the motion slot. If 8 between the Slots – throw Flash to the boundary Wide Receiver or make a "Max" Call and look to the Wide Receiver away from the FS.
- My keys are: is it a 4 Shell or 3 Shell? And where is the FS?
- My escape is Quarterback Draw if all are covered. Never force a pass, ball security always comes first.

Quarterback Reads

- Against a 4 Shell – "I'm going to read the Strong Safety and Throw the Stretch unless the SS covers it, if the SS covers the Stretch, I'm going to look to Z and throw either the Fade or the In Route. My check down route is the Flare. My escape is Quarterback Draw.
- Against a 3 Shell – I'm going to look for the FS. If he is over the ball, I'm going to look to the field first with the same reads as a 4 shell. But most of the time the FS is in the middle of the field, in which case the QB goes to the boundary and throws to X either on a Fade or the Out Route. If it's covered – QB Draw.

Stretch to the Boundary. On the Stretch to the boundary all the routes and reads are the same except the pass is run to the sidelines. This is very problematic for the linebackers. The Stretch to the Boundary creates one on one situations with no re-routing of receivers because of the run fake.

- Against a 4 Shell – "I'm throwing to the Slot unless the Free Safety is covering him, or the Onside Linebacker gets depth" The play action fake to the Tailback will at least freeze the LB giving the QB a shot at the Slot. But if the FS is on top of the Slot's Seam Route, the QB will go to the Wide Receiver. If the CB is pressed, the WR will be one on one with CB because the FS is on the Slot. If the CB bails and gets depth, the QB throws the Out Route to the WR.

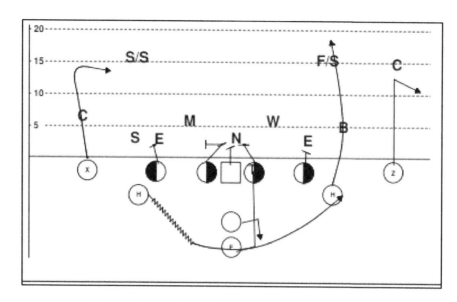

Stretch to the Boundary vs 4 Shell

- Against a 3 Shell – "I'm throwing to the Slot unless the ILB is under it (this is unlikely with the fake to the TB) then I'll throw the Fade or out to the Wide Receiver". The check down Flare is an option but if all are covered the QB Draw is the answer.

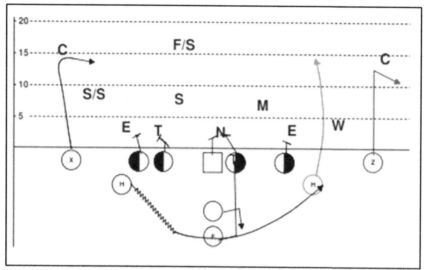

Stretch to the Boundary vs 3 Shell

Quarterback Steps and Rhythms. It's important that the Quarterback throws the ball on time because a good defense is going to recover quickly so the receiver is not going to be open long. It's also important that the ball is thrown to the proper landmark.

- The Stretch Route. The Quarterbacks steps are: Catch, Pivot, Rock Forward, Rock Back and Throw it to hole between the LBs and Safeties between 15 – 18 yards. The rock forward simulates the give to the Tailback.
- The In Route. The Quarterbacks Steps are: Catch, Pivot, Rock Forward, Rock Back, Look, Step Back gather and drill it.
- The Out Route. The Quarterback's steps are: Catch, Pivot, Rock Forward, Rock Back and Throw the Ball to a spot 10 yards on the sideline.

The Flip Stretch.   The Flip Stretch is run from a 3 X 1 set Trips or Backs. The Protection is the same and the routes and reads are the same, The only thing that's different is the Tailback and Slot "Flip" assignments. The Slot in Flip motion fakes the dive and fits into the protection. The Tailback check releases and runs a Flare. The advantage is the little misdirection can freeze the LBs. It's the same pass with a slightly different look.

FLIP STRETCH PASS

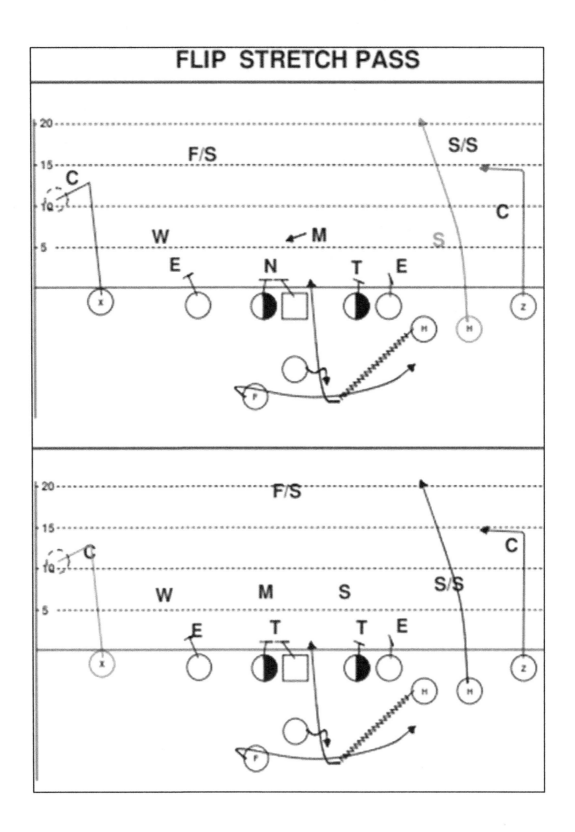

The Crossers Pattern

The Crossers Pattern. The Crossers Pattern was given to me by Larry Smith when he was the Head Coach at the University of Missouri, we were on the NCAA Rules Committee together and spent time talking ball. The Stretch Pattern was used mostly off Gun Triple and as a Dropback Pass but the Crossers is great not only with the Gun Triple but also is a great play action pass off the Jet Sweep.

Pass Protection. The pass protection is exactly the same as it is for The Stretch Pass and every play action pass unless noted.

Pass Routes. The 3 routes for The Crossers Pattern are different so this is extra teaching involved but it is well worth the investment.

- Onside Wide Receiver, The Wide receiver runs an "Over" Route across the field getting to depth of 15 yards. If he is in a compressed set (Wide Jack is a common set that we use for The Jet Sweep and the Crossers Pass) the Wide Receiver can gear down when crossing the field.
- Onside Slot. The Onside Slot does a slightly delayed Shallow Drag getting under the Linebackers at a depth no deeper than 6 yards. Against a LB Blitz, be prepared for a quick pass from the QB.
- The Backside Receiver. The Backside Receiver runs a "Deep" Route. This is a great route conversion. The Wide Receiver is going to run a Skinny Post down the hash mark. This is devastating against a 3 Shell or a $ Shell defense that rolls to a 3 Shell on motion. However, the Defense started to play inside the Wide Receiver to undercut the post. But just when you think you have the answers, we change the questions, When the Wide Receiver sees he can't get inside the CB, He pushes toward the hash and then fades back to the sidelines turning the Skinny Post to a "Go" Route.

  Another answer to this defensive ploy is to use the formation Wide Jack which switches the Slot and Wide Receiver's alignment. By doing this and running Crossers off Jet Sweep Action, the CB can't undercut the Skinny Post

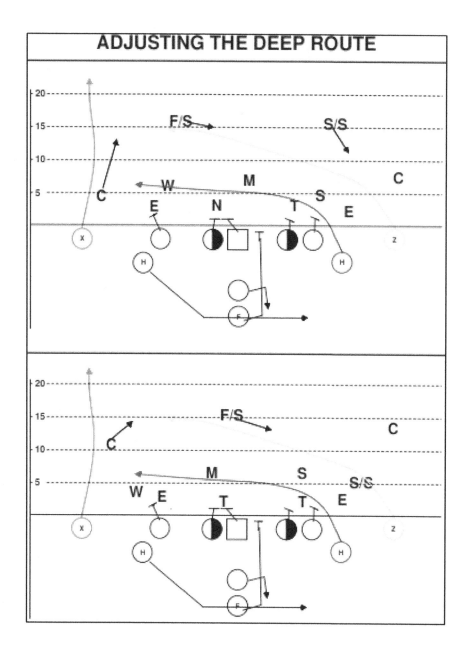

ADJUSTING THE DEEP ROUTE

Quarterback Play. The Quarterback goes through the same 4 questions he does on every pass and on the Crossers Pattern, the answers are the same except for the Quarterback's reads. On the Stretch Pattern, the Linebackers were frozen for a second creating holes in the defense. But on the Crossers Pattern it is the fast flow of the run play which moves the defense in the direction of the flow leaving them vulnerable to the receiver going in the opposite direction. The Crossers is a very deceptive pass, especially in the Gun.

The Quarterback steps are not as precise as the Stretch Pass because these are not timed routes. On the Crossers Pass, the QB fakes the run action then bounces back 2 steps and is ready to throw.

The Quarterback Reads and thought process. "I'm going to throw the Deep Shot every time unless the Free Safety is deep and, on the hash, then I'm going to throw the "Drag" unless the LBs are on it, then I'll look for the "Over" Route. Note if the CB is inside the Skinny Post, I'll throw the "Go" adjustment. The Quarterback's landmark for the Skinny Post is right down the hash mark. His Check Down Route is the Drag to the Slot but this could also be a big play.

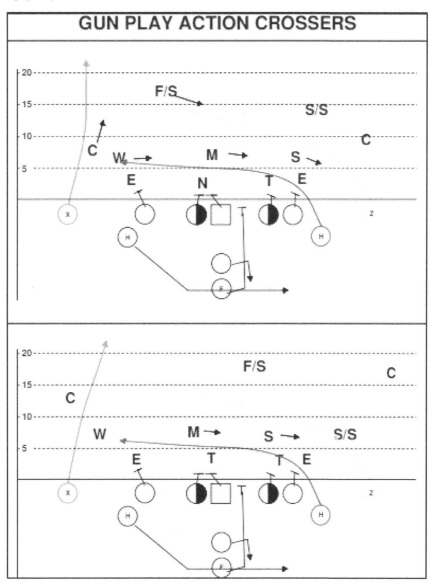

WIDE JACK JET CROSSERS

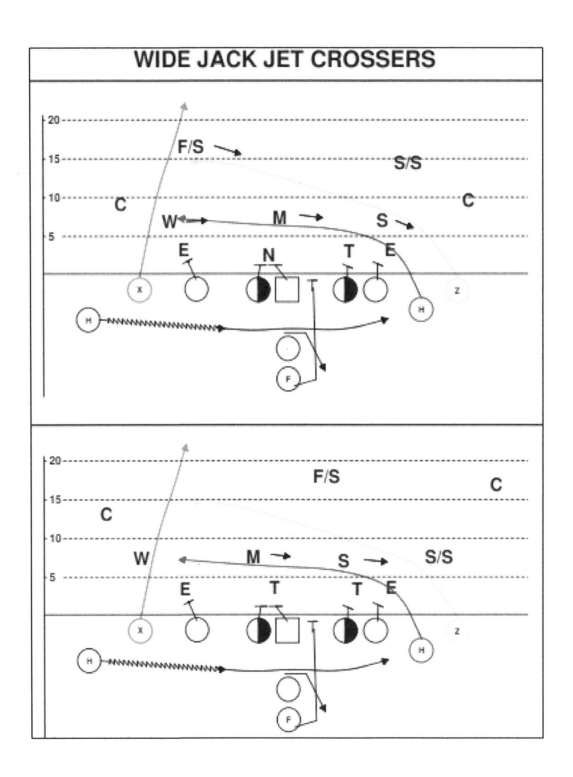

The Choice Pattern (Post/Out)

The Choice Pattern. The Choice Pattern is named because originally, we gave the Slot a "Choice" between an "Out" Route or an "In" Route. But as the offense evolved, "Choice" came to mean a 10 yard out by the Slot. The Choice Pattern is a 3 level Flood Pattern mostly to the field. This is usually off Triple Gun Action.

The Pass Protection is the same 7-man protection used in all these play action passes unless noted.

Wide Receiver Routes the Receiver Routes for the Choice Route are not Field and Boundary Routes, they are Call side and Backside Routes.

The Call side Receiver runs a Skinny Post down the hash mark unless the CB plays press. In that case the WR converts the Skinny Post to a Fade. He must force an outside release regardless of the depth of the CB.

The Backside Receiver runs a 14-yard Curl Route but is very rarely thrown to.

The Call side Slot takes an outside release just like he did on the Stretch Route. For 10 yards it should look like the Stretch Route. Then at 10 yards The Slot Sticks his foot into the ground and runs a sharp Out Route. Like a 10 yard Stick Route.

QB Reads. The Quarterback's thought process is I'm going to throw to The Wide Receiver every time unless the CB runs with on the Fade or the Safety stay deep on the Post. If the Wide Receiver is covered, I'll throw to the Slot on the Out, if he's covered, the Flare is my check down. My escape is QB Draw.

This pattern is good vs a 4 Shell and 3 Shell.

GUN PLAY ACTION POST/ OUT

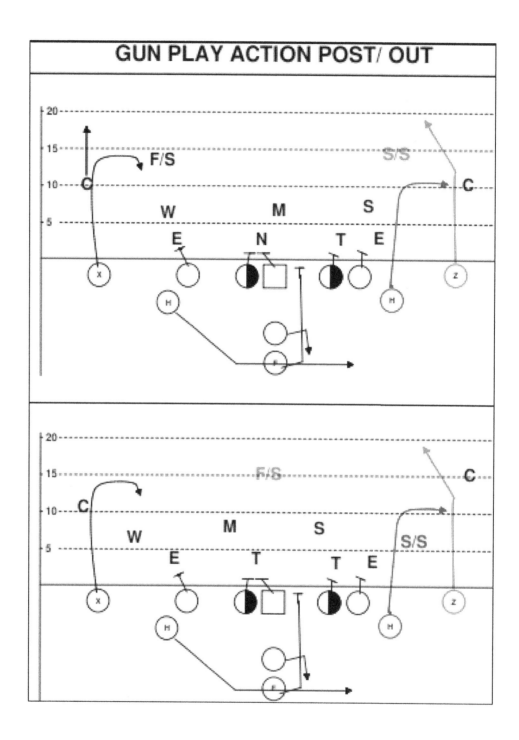

It's also best Play Action from a 6-lineman unbalanced set like Wingover.

WINGOVER POST/OUT

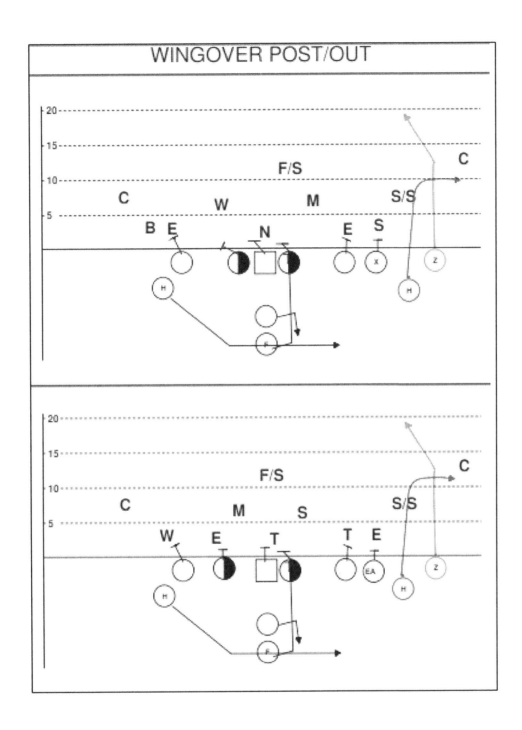

The Post/Wheel Concept

The Post/Wheel Pattern. This is primarily a boundary pattern, the only time we throw it to field is when we use an unbalanced set like Receivers. Also, we used the Post/Wheel only off the Triple Gun no other action.

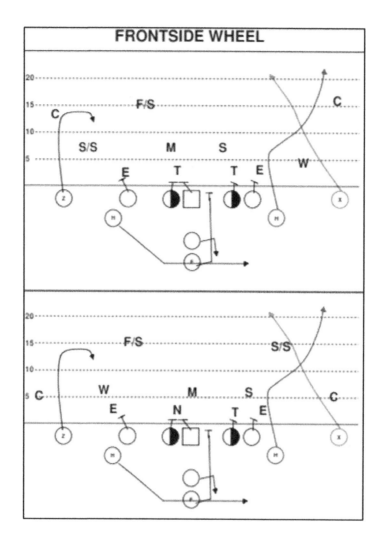

The pass protection is the same protection that is used in all our play action passes. It's 7man protection with the Offside Slot check releasing and running a Flare.

The Wide Receiver Routes are not anything new. The Offside Wide Receiver does a 14 yard "In" Route. The Onside Wide Receiver runs a Skinny Post down the hash mark unless its press coverage & then he converts to a Fade Route.

The Onside Slot. The Onside Slot runs the "Wheel Route" never getting closer than 4 yards from the sideline. The key coaching point is that the Slot releases inside as though he was going to *seal* the Inside Linebacker as he would on the Gun Triple. The he goes *behind* the Outside Linebacker so the OLB can't see him especially when the Triple Action is coming right at him. When he goes on his "Wheel" Route "if there is someone over the top, I look to stop" So if the CB is deep and has not bitten on the Wide Receiver's route, the Slot can just pull up and put his numbers to the Quarterback. This Strategic Flexibility makes this pattern a very high percentage pass.

Quarterback Reads. The Quarterback goes through his usual Play Action pre-snap checklist and the reads this pattern "Inside/Out" Post to Wheel. So, if the Post is open down the hash, the QB throws him the ball but if the Skinny Post is covered, the Quarterback finds the Slot and delivers the ball either deep or short depending on the Slot's adjustment. This is good vs both a 3 shell and 4 shell defenses but we prefer it vs a 3 Shell.

Frontside Wheel

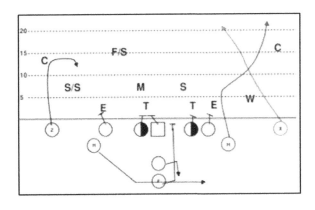   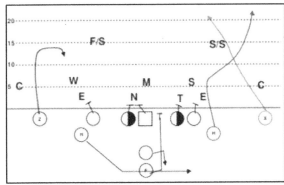

Vs 3 Shell   Vs 4 Shell

Receivers Post/Wheel. This is really the only way we will run the "Post/Wheel" Pattern to the Field. The Skinny Post stays the same, but the Wheel adjusts a little. The number 2 receiver takes an inside release like he's going to block the Free Safety but then breaks behind the Strong Safety and runs his "Wheel" down the field numbers. The Quarterback still reads "Inside/Out" Post to Wheel.

Receivers Post/Wheel

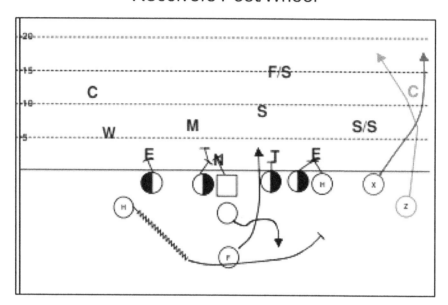

Whirley Post/Wheel. "The Whirley Post/Wheel" is a way to get a 4 shell to become a 3 shell on the Motion. If a team is rolling with motion, Whirley Motion is lethal. Nothing changes for the routes or reads except for the Whirley Motion.

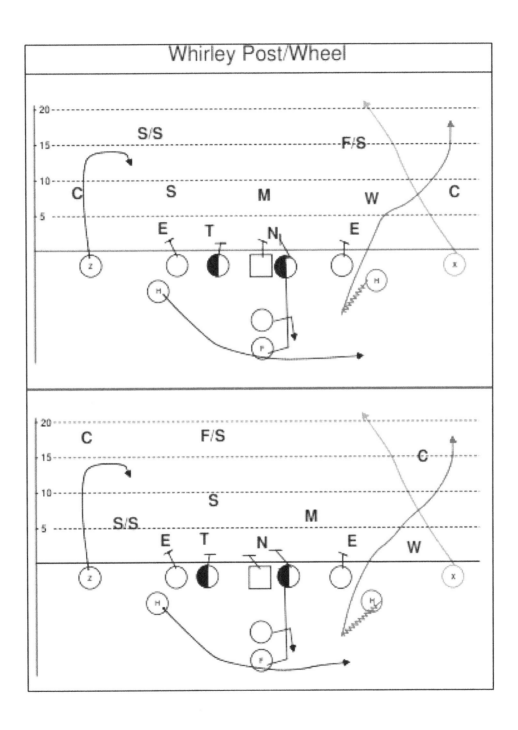

Flip Switch. The "Flip Switch" is nothing more than a throwback "Post/Wheel" Route off Flip Action The only tweak is that the Slot delays a count before releasing on his Wheel Route because there is no inside release to fake a seal block, so he just helps the tackle for a count to get out of the CB's vision

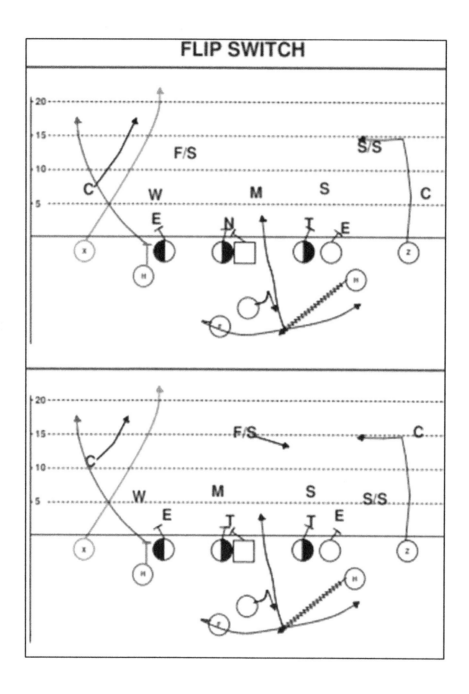

Play Action Perimeter Passes

The second part of the Triple Gun Play Action Pass Game is the perimeter play action passes. These are different because the Quarterback attacks the perimeter with a run pass option (RPO) These passes are comprised of Boots and Nakeds. I really became enamored with the perimeter play action pass in my time with Tubby Raymond and the Delaware Staff. One of the prime weapons in The Wing T arsenal was their famous Waggle Pass. But they also ran the Counter Bootleg off their Tackle Trap play that was more effective than the actual run.

We used the boot off the Quick Game from under center before I coached at Delaware but my time at Delaware really made me crave a boot off the option. Going to the Gun made that happen. But again, it had to be simple with a minimum amount of teaching.

The Triple Gun Boot from Trips (or Backs) Formation. The Trips formation was very important in keeping things simple. So was the motion. It was difficult booting into the boundary, but our "Crossers Pattern" filled that need because it gave us a misdirection pass off our base set into the boundary. So we used a 3 X 1 set with both Slots to the same side and used motion by the Widest Slot (WEB Motion) to run both the Gun Triple and the Boot off it.

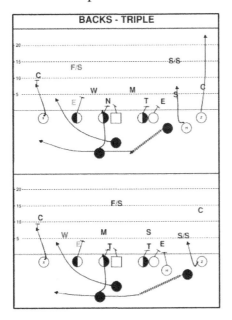
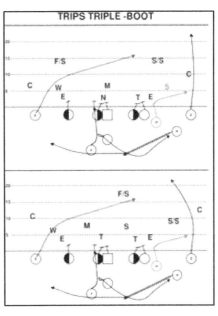

Pass Protection. The pass protection is the same as the Play Action Pass Protection used in all our Play Action Passes. The only difference is the offside Tight Slot who executes his "Slam and Slide" and releases into the flat just as he would on the Quick Game Slam and Slide. If the Slot sees someone blitzing off the edge, he blocks for 3 counts before releasing into the Flat. So, there is no new teaching. This is the reason we developed "WEB Motion" for the sake of simplicity but it added another look to the offense.

Wide Receiver's Routes. The Offside Wide Receiver runs a "Clear" Route just as he does in the Quick Game. The Onside Receiver runs an "Over" Route getting to a depth of 15 yards and staying in the Quarterback's vision.

Quarterback Play. The Quarterback Play is a little different than the other play action passes but his techniques and reads are the same as the Quick Game Boot. After he fakes the Gun Triple, he pivots out getting to a depth of 7 yards behind the Offside Tackle and then he attacks down hill with his front shoulder low and 2 hands on the ball. He holds the ball on his throwing side pec. (Same technique as the boot off the Quick Game)

- The Quarterback's launch point is the perimeter, if he's forced to pull up, he looks to the Slot then the "Over" route.
- His Blitz Protection is 7-man Protection but against a blitz the Slam and Slide Slot can pick him up for a 3 count. So, it's really 8-man protection.
- The QB is going to throw the "Slam and Slide" unless it's covered, then find the "Over" Route. We want him to take the easy throw and move the chains.
- The Quarterback's escape is QB Sweep. If the Sweep is there right away, he can take it first. We are looking for a high percentage, low risk misdirection pass.

Anytime the defense is given a conflict of assignment or is given a recognition problem, the offense gains an advantage. These high percentage plays equal first downs and clock control.

The Flip Option Boot. The Flip Boot can be run from our base Gun Formation and is another high percentage pass off a Counter Option. The protection is the same as the Gun Triple Boot as described above. The Wide Receiver routes are the same as the Gun Triple Boot and The Slot's Slam and Slide is also the same. The Quarterback's reads are the same as well. The only difference is the backfield action.

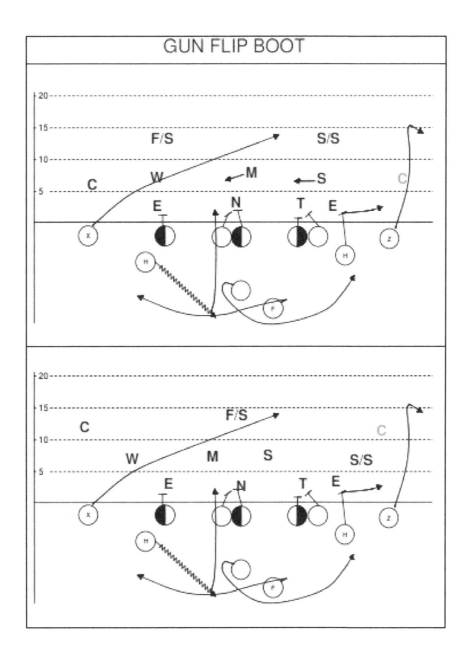

Jet Sweep Naked. This perimeter Play Action Pass is an excellent pass on the goal line or as a 2-point play. We run it from a Wide Formation which switches the Boundary Slot and Boundary Wide Receiver's alignment. This is also a frequent alignment that we use for Jet Sweep.

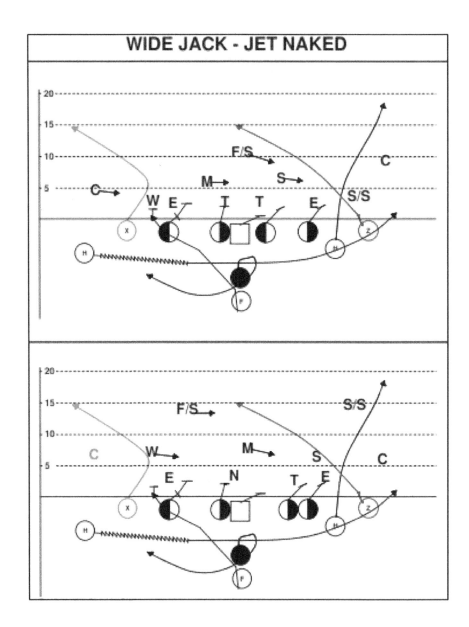

Pass Protection. The protection is just blocking the Jet Sweep. The offensive line does not pass protect; They just block The Jet Sweep. But they must sell the Sweep.

The backfield gives great fakes with the boundary Slot really selling the Sweep. The offside Slot Arc Releases as he would on The Jet Sweep and hooks up at the upright on the backline of the end zone.

Wide Receiver Routes. The field Wide Receiver runs under the field Slot and runs an over route on the back line of the end zone in case the Quarterback is in trouble. The Boundary wide Receiver runs a Corner Route to the back pylon of the corner of the End Zone. By using the "Wide" Alignment, he has leverage on the Free Safety covering him.

Quarterback Play. The QB makes good ball fakes snaps his head around and expect pressure. If the Cornerback chases the Jet Sweeper, the QB knows the Corner Route will be Wide Open. If the CB stays home, the QB will read him for the Run/Pass decision.

The Perimeter Play Action Passes create a new look for the Defense to contain and puts the Quarterback in position to use his speed to attack the flank. We're trying to get the benefit of The Wing T Waggle Pass with as little teaching as possible. These passes create additional sideline to sideline looks.

The Zone Read Play Action Passes and RPOs

The Zone Read Play Action Passes are in a separate category for a few reasons. Here's the rational for categorizing them separately:

- The main reason is that is 6-man protection not seven man protection. So there has to an answer for the seventh rusher.
- The Zone Read Passes are run from a 3 wide receiver set. Usually, Twins or Trips. We can also run them from Empty.
- The Zone Read and Zone Dive are the runs of choice for RPOs.
- The fake is designed to freeze the Linebackers but because there is no pitch dimension, the fake doesn't affect the secondary as much.
- Tailback alignment is important and can be directed by the Quarterback.

The Vertical Game. The Vertical Game was "pirated" from The Hal Mumme/Mike Leach Air Raid Offense. These guys have brilliant offensive minds and have really perfected their style of offense. There is no way practice time would allow The Triple Gun to adopt many of their concepts, but the Air Raid Vertical game seemed to fit.

- The Air Raid Vertical Attack was a relative of the Triple Gun Stretch Pass.
- The Vertical Game makes The Triple Gun more explosive.
- It destroys an 8-man front.
- It doesn't take a lot of additional teaching.
- It is simple and is formation friendly
- It can be used as a Play Action or as a Dropback Pass.

Pass Protection. The Pass protection is 6-man protection. But the assignments are still the same as the normal Triple Gun Play Action Protection. The question is "How to handle the 7th rusher?' There are 2 answers. Number one, by using 3 wide receivers, the defense will be forced to remove a linebacker from the front. I they don't there will be an uncovered receiver, or they will be in a 3 Shell Secondary. The Tailback fits into the protection after the fake just as he normally would. The second answer is Flash. It goes back to the same rule "8 between the Slots throw Quicks and Hots" So if the defense goes to a 3 shell alignment and the Outside Linebacker blitzes, the Flash to the Wide Receiver looks great.

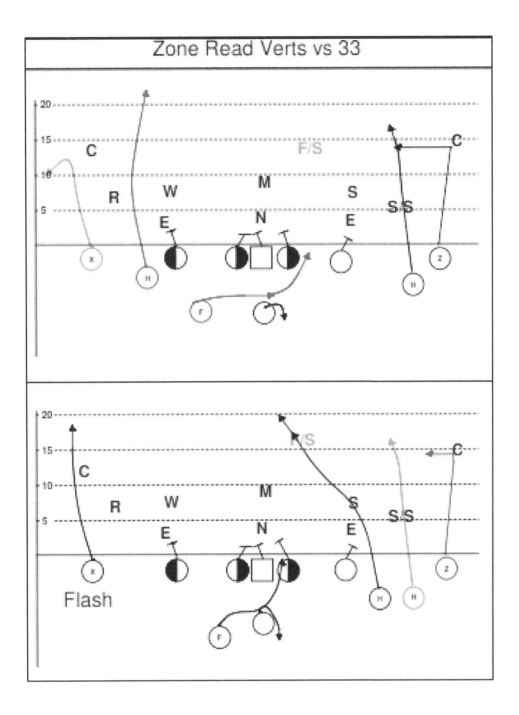

Wide Receiver Routes. Here's a big surprise and an example of simplifying the offense. Both Wide Receivers run exactly the same route as they do on the Stretch Pass and they use the same technique! The Field Receiver does a Fade/In Route and The Boundary Receiver does a Fade/Out Route. The boundary receiver is always alert for a "Flash" call

The Slots Routes. This is where some additional teaching is required. Not much but there are a couple of tweaks to make this work.

The Onside Slot. The Onside Slot or the #2 Receiver to the field runs a Vertical Route directly down the field hash mark. He must avoid any re-direct by a linebacker on him. When he clears the under coverage, he looks for the ball. (Make Tackle Guys Cover)

The Offside Slot. The Offside Slot runs a Seam Route if he is lined up into the boundary as in Twins Formation. But if he is lined up as the number 3 to the field, he bends across the field aiming for the boundary hash mark. Again, as soon as he clears the under coverage, he looks for the ball.

Quarterback Play. The QB goes through his checklist but the main thing is for him *Quarterback Play.* The QB goes through his checklist but the main thing is for him to realize that it is 6 man protection and he must be aware of blitz and of the Flash. The Quarterback reads are very simple:

- Against a 3 Shell, he reads the Free Safety. If he is over the ball he is going to look to the Slot down the Field Hash mark. But if the Free Safety is in the Middle of the field, the Quarterback is going to the boundary. He will look to the Seam unless the OLB covers him, then he'll throw the Out to the Wide Receiver. Note, if all are covered his escape is QB Draw.

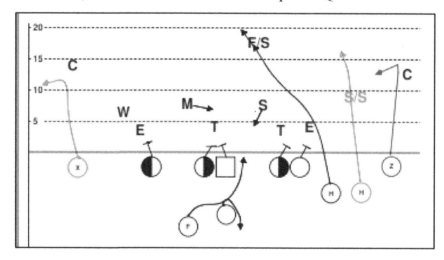

Trips Play Action 4 Verts vs 3 Shell

- Against a 4 Shell, he still reads the Free Safety. If he moves to the field, the QB will go to the boundary, and throw Seam to the Slot or to the Wide Receiver on a Fade or an Out. If the FS stays on the boundary hash the QB will go to the field and throw Slot to The Wide Receiver. Now vs a 4 Shell we like to use a Trips alignment to open up the #3 receiver and put the ILB in a bind.

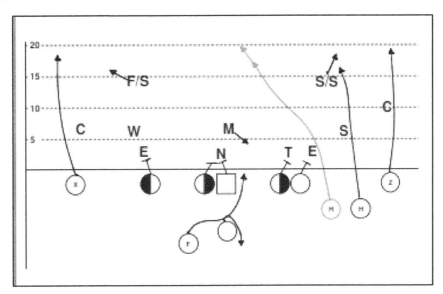

Trips Play Action 4 Verts vs 4 Shell

The Vertical Game has proven to be a big play series for the Triple Gun and with the Quarterback using QB Draw as an escape, it's very low risk.

Zone Read Switch Pass. The Zone Read Switch Pass is the Post/Wheel Combo to the boundary just as the normal Post Wheel. The Wide Receiver runs the Skinny Post (Never Crossing the Hash) and the Slot runs his Wheel Route. The Formation is Twins so there are 2 Wide Receivers to the field that both run In Routes at different depths. The Wide Receiver's In Route is at 14 yards and the Slot's route is at 10 yards. We have had the Field Slot to a Vertical but the Quarterback is looking for the Switch Route into the Boundary.

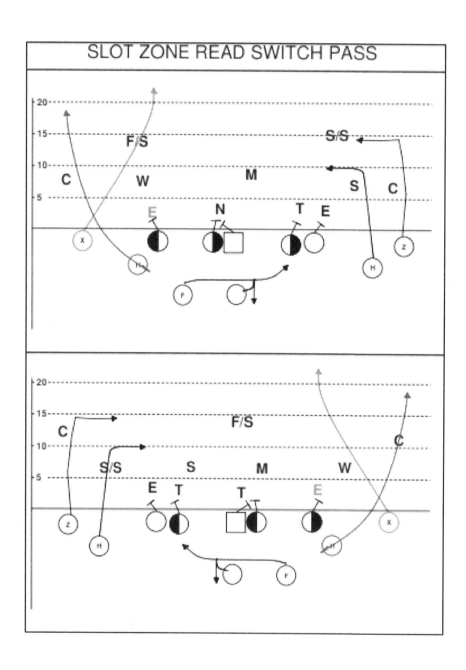

Protection. It's 6 man protection with the Tailback looking to fit into the protection and help where needed, The Boundary Slot must be aware of the Outside Linebacker Blitz and look for a Hot Pass.

Quarterback Play. The Quarterback reads the Switch like every other Post/Wheel Combo inside/out but he must recognize an OLB Blitz because Flask is not available. His Blitz Control is throwing Hot to the Wheel. We expect the CB to run with the Skinny which will leave the Wheel open early. The QB's escape is still QB Draw. Using Empty to throw the Play Action Verts Game cause additional problems for the defense

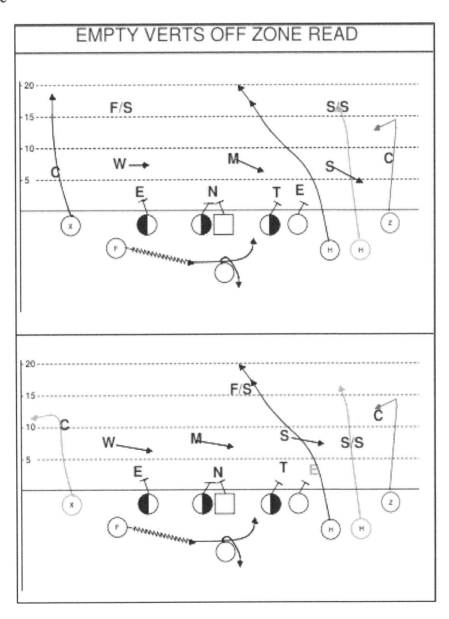

EMPTY VERTS OFF ZONE READ

Zone Read RPOs From Twins. The new buzz word that every ESPN guy uses is RPOs. A clever buzz word but the concept was really formed by The Split Back Veer Guys like Bill Yeomen who developed the "Dump Pass" which the Triple Gun also uses off the Gun Triple. But there is a simple way to incorporate the Quick Game with The Zone Read to give us additional high percentage passes to move the chains.

Pass Protection. The pass protection is our base protection with the exception that instead of the Tailback blocking the Linebacker, the QB will read the Linebacker and either give to the Tailback or throw the Quick Pass.

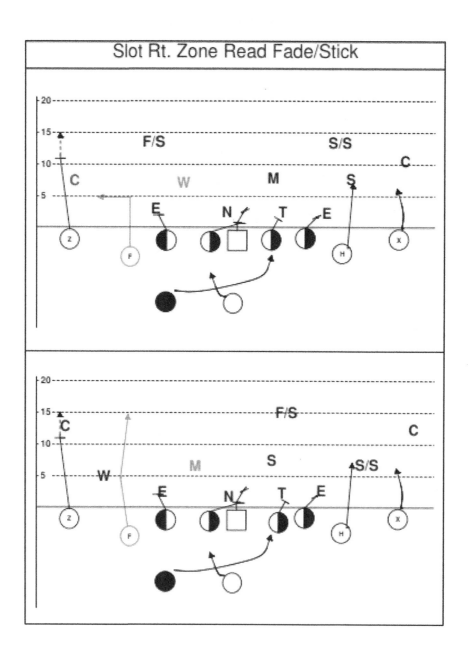

The Fade Stick Zone Read. The Boundary Receivers just run the Fade/Stick Combo. The Field Receivers run Fades (Or a tagged routes). Against a 3 Shell the Slot converts to a Seam Route. The QB alerts the Slot that it's a 3 Shell.

The Quarterback Reads. The Quarterback reads the Onside Linebacker. His read is "Give Unless…" He gives every time unless the LB stays inside, the he reads the CB just as he would on the Quick Game Fade Stick. Throw the Fade unless the CB runs and then throw the Stick; The QB's pre-snap read is if the Linebackers slide to the Twins the Fade/Stick will be the throw. If the OLB is outside the box it will probably be a give.

Against a 3 Shell, the Quarterback reads ILB and gives unless he stays, then he throws the Seam. Most likely this will be a throw.

Zone Read RPO from Trips. The Pass Pro and everything else is the same. The only difference is the Quarterback reads the onside ILB for his give throw read. The #3 route does the same route he ran with the Vertical Pass.

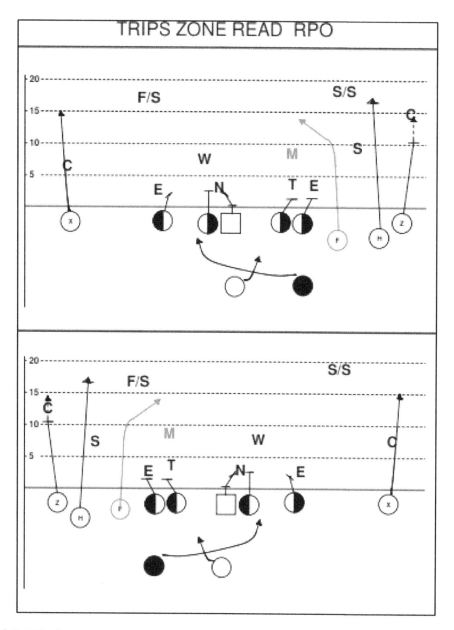

TRIPS ZONE READ RPO

Zone Read RPO from Empty. Empty formation spreads the defense and not only opens up running lanes but also passing lanes. It's also more difficult to blitz an Empty set without showing it.

Pass Protection is also the same protection we've been using from our other Zone Read RPOs. It's 6 man protection, The QB is responsible for the offside LB. The Tackle blocks the HOK and The QB reads the Linebacker.

Everyone blocks for the Zone Read Run but the Offside Receiver. The X receiver runs a Slant route by taking an outside release to give a Fade illusion. Then the Wide Receiver breaks inside on a Skinny Slant.

Quarterback Reads. The QB is going to hand the ball off every time unless the Linebacker runs with the Motion. Then the QB throws to the Slant unless the CB covers the Slant, then the QB keeps.

To the field. The RPO is effective to the field vs a 3 Shell. The number 2 receiver runs a Seam instead of a Slant. The QB reads the offside Linebacker and gives unless he runs, then the QB reads the Strong Safety for the Seam or keep.

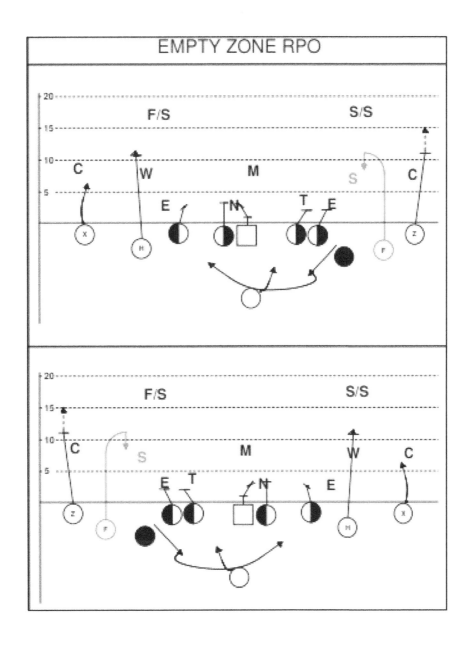

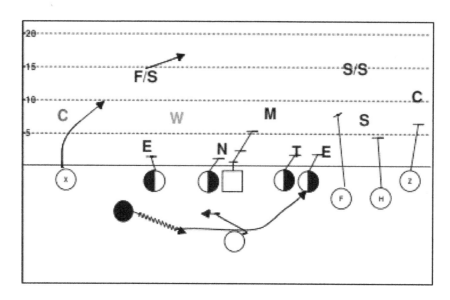

Empty Rt Zone Read Rt RPO

Jet QB ISO RPO. We run this from a "Wide" set, which switches the X receiver and the Slot to the boundary. The Slot goes in Motion and fakes the Jet Sweep. The QB Reads the Free Safety. If he moves with the Motion, the QB throws the Skinny Post to the X Receiver down the hash just as he would on the Crossers Pattern. Of course if the Free Safety doesn't move he runs QB ISO.

The RPO game is limitless. The Triple Gun has a built in pass (Flash) on every play. We'll get into more RPOs when we get into our "Dragon Package"

Wide Jack Jet QB ISO RPO

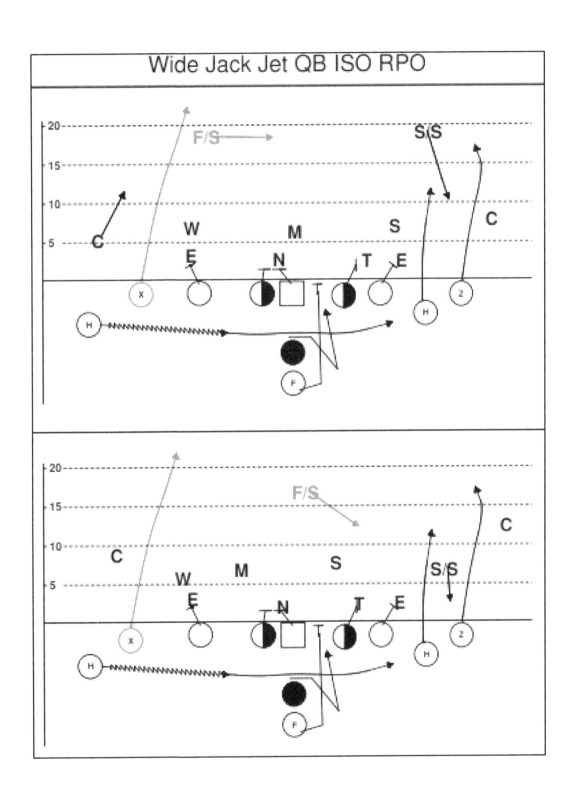

Chapter 14
The Triple Gun Dropback Pass Game

The Triple Gun Dropback pass is not a frequently used part of the offense but a very important part of the offense. It is important because it bails the offense out of tough situations. The Dropback pass uses as many crossover skills as possible. And is kept as simple as possible so it doesn't take up a lot of practice time.

Why The Dropback Pass? Many option coaches question me about the necessity of a dropback pass game. But one of the advantages of the Gun Triple being so good is that there isn't a need for many other run plays and that gives us more time to work on the pass game. The key is to keep it simple and use "Strategic Flexibility". Homer Rice combined The Split Back Veer and the Dropback Pass in the 60s so it was going to be easier to combine them in the Gun. Here are some reasons for the Dropback Pass as part of The Triple Gun Offense.

- It is the answer in long yardage and 2-minute situations.
- It is our "Come from behind" weapon.
- It stretches the field both horizontally and vertically.
- It uses the same routes that we use for Play Action Passes.
- It's the same reads and throws for the Quarterback.
- It puts Speed in Space
- It makes "Cover Guys Tackle" and "Tackle Guys Cover"
- We detach Slots to use the same personnel for the Dropback pass
- We Combine the Dropback Pass and The Quick Game to give us a great built in blitz answer.

Dropback Pass Protection. It all starts with protection. The most important parts of The Triple gun Passing Game are Ball Security and Pass protection. Our Dropback Pass protection has many similarities to our Play Action Protection but it needs a special period daily to make it dependable. The base scheme is 7-man protection but 6-man protection is also used with blitz answers.

Dropback Pass Pro Basics.

- Maintain Smart Splits and Double Team when possible.
- Direction is the key to protection, directing the protection to where the rushers are coming from.
- Big on Big is the base protection. The Offensive Line has the 4 down linemen and the Middle Linebacker. The backs check release off their Outside Linebackers.
- Vary between 7- and 6-man protection. 6-man protection uses the Quick Game as its Blitz answer.
- Add to the protection by calling "Max" against 8-man pressure.
- Free Release the Tailback by calling "Hot" – if his Linebacker comes, the Tailback is the hot receiver.

7 Man Dropback Pass Pro against Basic Fronts. These are the way the 7-man Dropback Protection looks against the most common defensive looks. Again, the threat of the Option keeps defenses from getting into exotic pass rush fronts.

- The 43 Defense. This is simple, the Call side Guard and Tackle have man on man outside. Against a DE and DT Twist, they exchange their men. The Offside Tackle has man on. The Center and the Offside Guard have the Nose and the MLB. If the MLB drops, double the Nose. The Tailback Number 3 to the field) has check release Flare on the OLB to his side. The Offside Slot (Number 2 to the boundary) has a check release Stop Route.

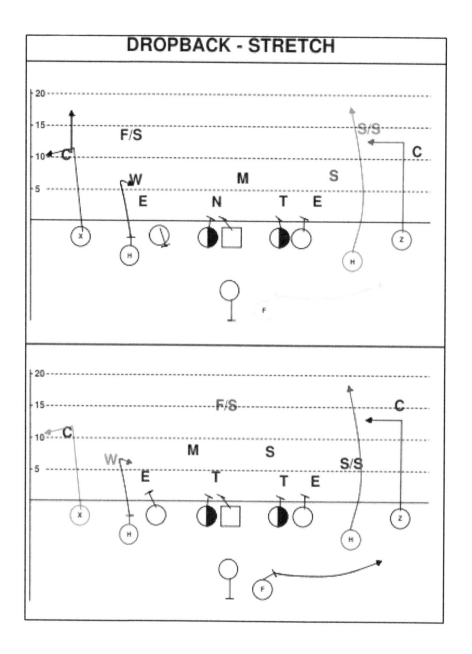

- The 44 Defense. This is exactly the same as the protection of the 43 defenses. The only difference is if the Strong Safety creeps into the Box. The Quarterback can call "Max" if the formation is basic Gun. The Onside Slot then Check releases on the Strong Safety. If he comes, he blocks him and if he doesn't, he runs his route.

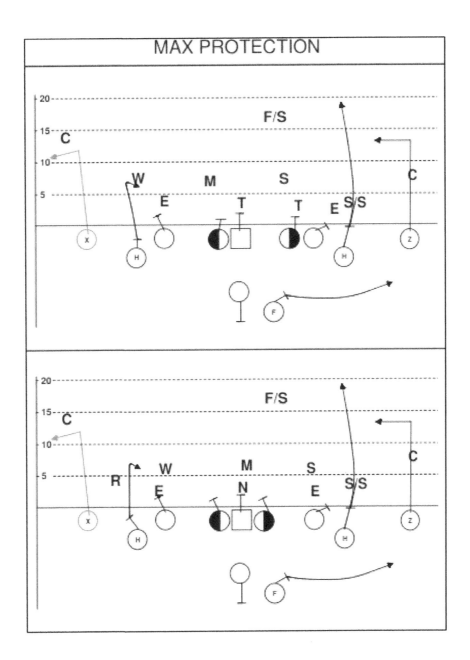

MAX PROTECTION

- If the formation is a Slot set, the Quarterback can't call "Max" but the Free Safety must get out on the Slot giving up the element of surprise. The Quarterback can "Slide" the Protection to the Right (Ricky) and the Offside OLB is now the Hot read. We only have 7 to block a possible 8 rushers but we block the most likely rushers.

269

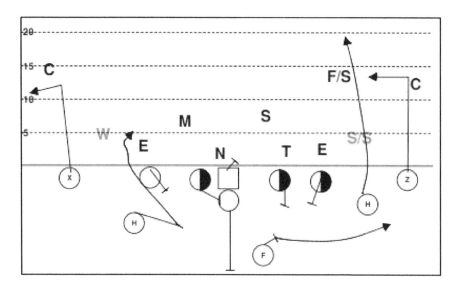

Dropback Stretch vs 44 SS Blitz

- The 34 Defense. Using a detached Slot makes this protection a lot easier. But if we were in a Gun Set with no detached Slot, we would block "Solid" The Line would block Man on and the Backs would Check Release on the OLBs. The Guards have the ILBs over them. If they Blitz they block them, but if they don't, they help the Center on the Nose. The Smart Splits makes that an easy block.

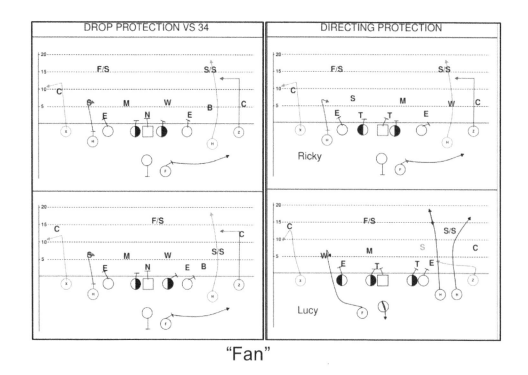

"Fan"

With a detached Slot, it is much easier to read the defense. If it's a 4 Shell, there is no need for a call. It's our base protection. The On tackle has Man On. The On Guard has no man on, so he doubles the Nose to the Off ILB with the Center. The Off Tackle has Man On but if the Tackle sees the OLB on the line of scrimmage, it's a "Smoke" Call. The Backs Check release on the LBs to their side.

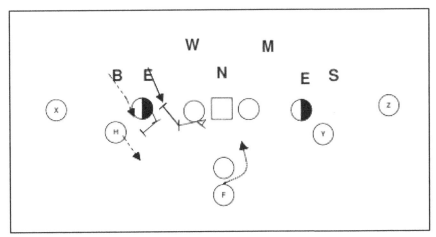

Smoke Call

If the Defense is in a 3 Shell then we have to make a call to "Fan" the Protection. "Rat" to the right and "Lat" to the left. In this example, the call is "Rat". The Right Tackle fans to the end man on the Line of Scrimmage. The Right Guard Fans to the first man outside him which is the DT. The Center and Left Guard combo on the Nose and the off ILB. The Left Tackle has the man on. The Tailback check releases on the ILB. The Slot check releases on the OLB.

Using these calls against a 34 Defense takes the guesswork out of which of the 4 linebackers are blitzing and gets as many backs as possible into the pattern.

- The 33 Defense. The 33 Defense has gained popularity in the past few years because it has so many blitz possibilities. But there is an old adage: Attack simplicity with complexity and complexity with simplicity. Detaching a Slot helps to simplify the protection. It's very similar to blocking a 34. The On Tackle blocks Man on. The On Guard combo with the Center to block the Nose and the MLB. The Off Guard helps the Center but is responsible for the OLB. The Guard must also be alert for a "Smoke" call. The off Tackle has

271

Man On. The Tailback check releases on the OLB to his side and the Slot check release on the OLB to his side.

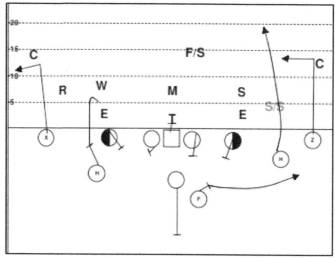

Dropback Protection vs a 33 Defense"

- The Bears Defense. The Bear's Defense is very weak against the option so we don't see it too often. It is also weak against the Quick Game which is also one of our staples. But if you run into it make a "Bears" call. This tells the Guards and Center to "Wad Up" and they have the 3 defenders lined up on them. The Tackles have the 2 Outside Rushers and the TB and Slot have the Linebacker to their side.

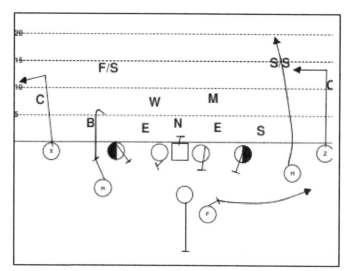

Dropback Protection vs Bears

This is the 7 Man Dropback protection against the common defenses which depends on the check releases by the backs.

6 Man Dropback Protection. This protection is a great way to free release another receiver into the pattern. If there is a 7th rusher, the Quarterback must handle it. One way we do this is by having the backside of the Pattern to be a Quick Pattern. So the Quarterback has a Dropback Pattern to the Call-side and a Quick Pattern to the "Hot" side. So, either by a "Hot" Receiver or a Quick Pattern, the blitz will be handled. Remember anytime the defense removes the 7th rusher from the front, there isn't a need for any "Hot" but the QB can throw to the Quick side because he likes the matchup.

- Against a 43 Defense. If the Defense removes the OLB to cover up the #2 to the field, it's normal protection. But if they keep 7 in the box and roll up to a 3 Shell, then adjustments must be made. The Hot Linebacker is the backside OLB. If the OLB comes there is really no one on the Slot. We can run Hitch/Seam backside or Slice/Seam or Fade/Stick.

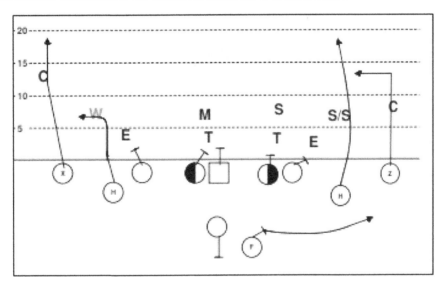

Slot 60 Stretch Stick

273

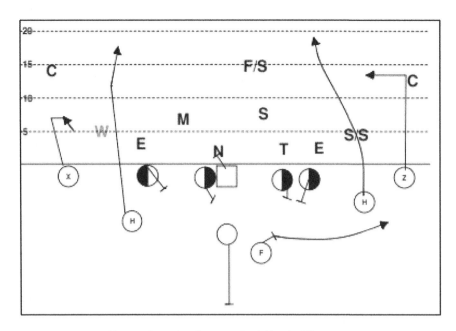

Dropback Stretch Hitch/Seam

- Against a 44 Defense. We couldn't block an 8 man rush with 6 man protection but somebody would be wide open for a TD. Not likely for a defense to gamble like that. So basically it would be the same answer as a 43 Defense with 7 in the box. The Hot Read would be boundary OLB. If he blitzed the Quarterback would throw to the Slot or give a Flash signal. Note if the FS was into the Boundary, the Strong Safety would have to cover the field Slot.

- Against a 34 Defense. The detached Slot helps identify the coverage and blitz possibilities. Against a 4 shell defense, the field OLB is probably removed from the front giving us 6 to block 6 and no need for a Hot throw. . But the danger is the Strong Safety rolling up just before the snap and the OLB blitzing. This is a standard Zone Blitz that everyone runs. The question is can the Free Safety get to the #2 receiver and still disguise the blitz? The call the Quarterback makes is a "Ricky" call which slides the protection to the field and puts the Tailback on the outside rusher. That means the backside OLB is the "Hot" read. The Guard Center Guard have the 2 ILBs and the Nose. And the Tackles have the DEs. If we were going in the other direction the call would be "Lucy". If a team was a heavy Zone Blitz team and we wanted to challenge the Free Safety, we could check to 7 man protection.

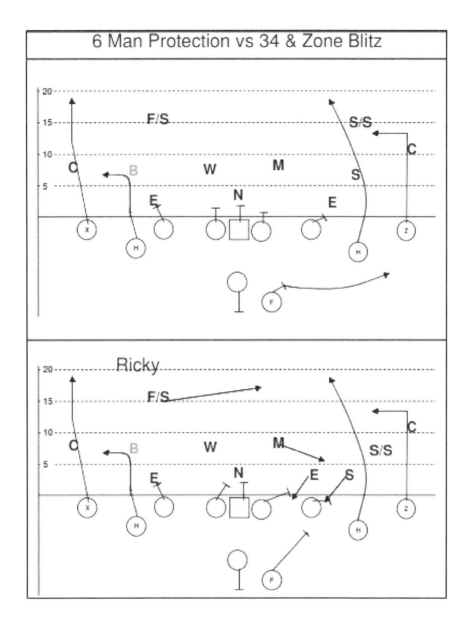

6 Man Protection vs 34 & Zone Blitz

- Against a 33 defense. Blocking the 33 with 6-man protection is the same as 7 man except we are turning the offside OLB loose and making him the "Hot" read. The Tailback dual reads the stacked OLB and the Strong Safety. Again, we can't block 8 or 7 with 6-man protection so using a detached slot simplifies it. With the Strong Safety showing Blitz, sliding the Protection that way (Ricky/Lucy) puts the Tailback on the Strong Safety and the backside OLB is "Hot."

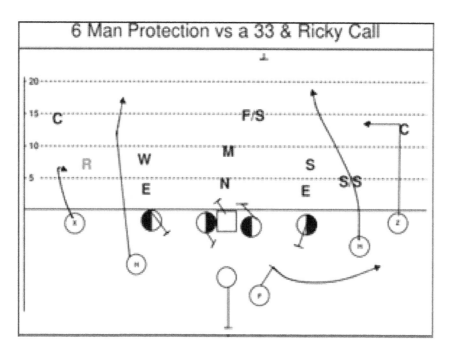

6 Man Protection vs a 33 & Ricky Call

Obviously the biggest thing in a dropback game is protection. Everything else is pretty simple and works great in those 7 on 7 leagues but blocking the pass rush is a whole other story. So if you want a dropback pass game in your offense, you must commit time every day to pass protection and blitz pickup.

The Stretch Pattern and Variations

The Stretch Pattern is a "cure-all" pattern, meaning that it's good regardless of the coverage. It is the core pass of the Play Action Game. It's so effective as a Play Action Pass, it's easy to see why it's also the core pass of the Dropback Game. The Stretch pattern is thrown with both 7 Man and 6 Man Protection. It's also thrown from multiple formations. We covered the protections, now we'll work on the routes and reads. The Receivers are numbered as Boundary and Field Receivers so it's easier to flip the protection without changing the routes. So the widest receiver to the field is #1 (usually a Wide Receiver) the #2 receiver is usually a Slot and the #3 receiver is usually a Running Back. The widest Receiver to the Boundary is #1 and the second widest is #2.

Stretch Pattern with 7 Man Protection. The stretch pattern with 7-man protection is the most frequently used Dropback Pass. The great thing is the routes are the same as the Play Action Stretch. This is an example of crossover skills.

- Wide Receiver Routes. The field Wide Receiver runs a Fade unless the Corner bails, then the Wide Out breaks the Fade off at 14 yards and does an "In" Route. The boundary Wide Receiver runs a Fade unless the CB gets deep, then the WR breaks off the Fade at 12 yards on an "Out route and works to the sideline at 10 yards.
- The Slot's Route (#2 to the field). The Slot runs the "Stretch" route getting to the middle of the goal posts. This is the same as the Play Action but in the Dropback pass, it's usually from a Twin alignment.
- The Tailback (The Field RB) (#3 to the field) check releases on the Linebacker in the protection. If no blitz, he runs a Flare. Coaching Point: he must always be alert for the calls that change the protection.
- The Slot (Boundary RB) (# 2 to the boundary) Check releases on the boundary OLB. If he comes, the RB blocks him but if he drops the RB runs a 5 yard "Stop" Route.

So except for the RB patterns, the routes are exactly the same as the Play Action Stretch Pattern. We use the Number 2 to the Boundary and number 3 to the field because it might be a Trips set where the Slot and Tailback switch spots.

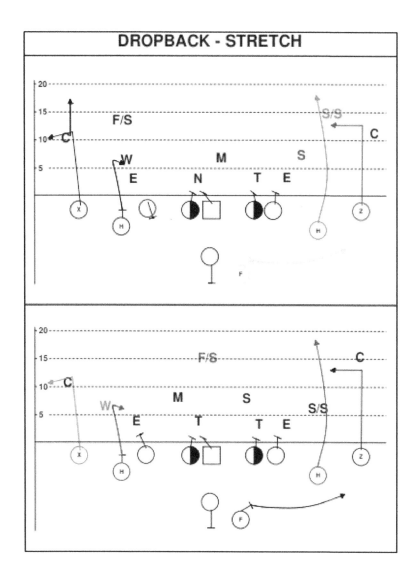

DROPBACK - STRETCH

Quarterback Play. As in the entire offense, the Quarterback is the trigger.

1. The Dropback Check list for The Stretch Pattern with 7 Man Protection.
   1. Launch Point – 7 yards behind the Center.
   2. Blitz Control – We can block 7, if there is 8 in the box, think flash or direct the protection toward the Free Safety "Ricky Call".
   3. QB Reads against a 4 Shell throw the Stretch to the field unless the Strong Safety jumps it. Then look to the WR on either the Fade or In Route. If that doesn't look good think Flare. When reading the OLB, "if his shoulders are square throw the flare" If his Shoulders are Square that means he has got into position to defend the "In" Route.

Stretch vs 3 Shell

> Against a 3 Shell. The QB looks to the boundary and throws the Fade unless the WR breaks it off. Then read the OLB. Throw the "Out" unless the OLB is under it, then throw the Stop Route.
>
> 4. My Escape is Quarterback Draw. Remember Ball security is our #1 Priority.

Other Formations. The same play with some "Smoke and Mirrors" can look like a whole new play without any new teaching. Detaching a Slot from the formation makes sense because it's easier to identify the coverage. So, Slot is our basic Dropback set. Trips formation can give a counter look by using "Flip" Motion. No new teaching, except the Tailback must learn the Stop Route.

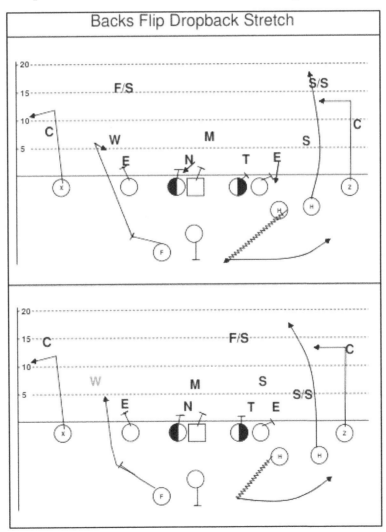

Whirley Motion is also used from Slot formation to give the illusion of the start of Gun Triple.

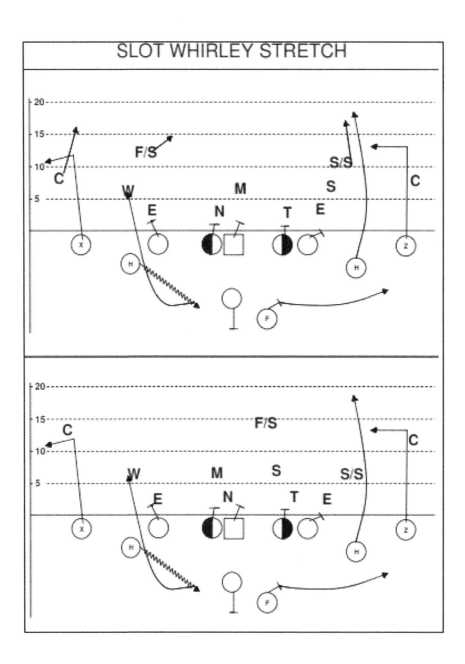

280

We can also use Empty to further spread the defense and use motion to confuse the defense.

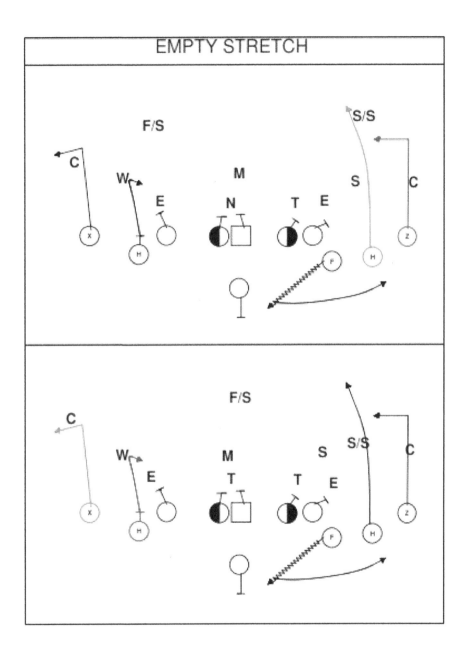

EMPTY STRETCH

The Stretch Pattern with 6 Man Protection. To free release a running back we must use 6-man protection, so the Quarterback is responsible for the 7th rusher. This is great against a defense that reduces their front against a 3 wide receiver looks. It's also a must to throw the Vertical Game.

- The Vertical Pattern is the main reason for 6-man protection. The routes are the same as the Play Action Vertical Pass off the Zone Read except the Tailback check releases and does a Flare.

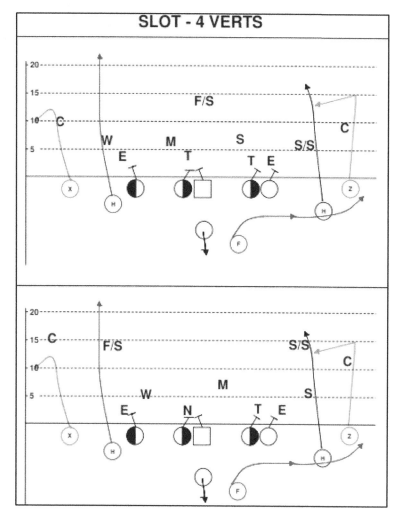

- If there is no blitz, no problem but if a 7th rusher is creeping into the box, the Quarterback calls "Ricky" which kicks the protection to the rush and makes the backside OLB Hot, Now he can throw either Flash or Hot to the Slot. If we are in a "Wide" set the Slot is doing the Flash and the Wide Receiver is doing the Vertical.

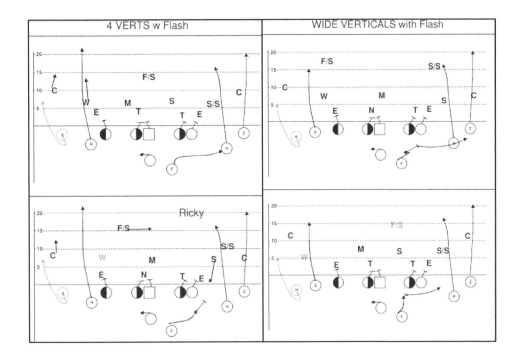

Combining The Quick Game and The Dropback Pass. This little wrinkle gave us many more opportunities to use the Dropback game because it provided a high percentage pass pattern into the boundary. And the great part is it didn't cost anything to do. The Quarterback and receivers already knew the quick game routes and reads and the protection was still 6 man protection. So, to the field side was the Stretch Pattern and to the boundary side was one of three quick game patterns as a Blitz answer or a throw the Quarterback favored. The 3 combinations were:

- The Stretch with the Hitch/Seam. This is great against a 3 Shell Secondary, but also effective against a 4 shell. The QB's hot read is the boundary OLB. Note: against a 4 Shell the defense would have to add a 7th rusher to the box.

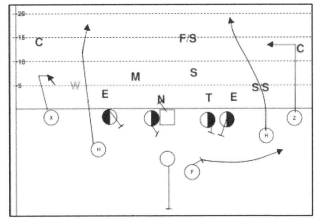

Dropback Stretch Hitch/Seam

283

- The Stretch with the Fade/Stick. Great vs a 4Shell or a 3 Shell. QB keys the OLB for the Hot read but a high percentage throw anytime the Slot can out-leverage the LB.

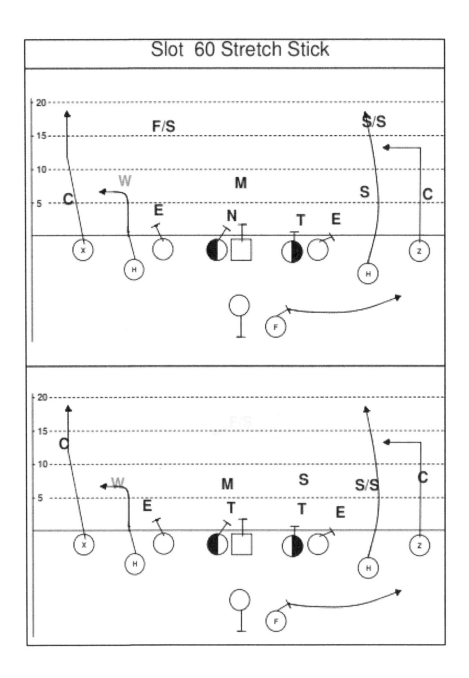

- The Stretch with the Slice/Corner. An excellent pattern vs the Blitz regardless of the secondary shell. The Slot adjusts his route from a Corner to a Seam vs a 3 Shell. The Slice is always a high percentage pass and the Stretch is still a possibility

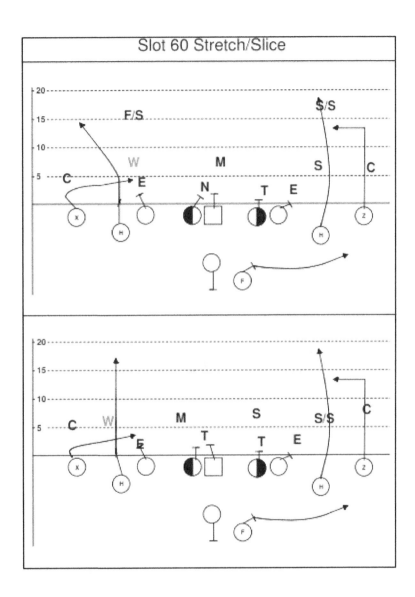

Slot 60 Stretch/Slice

Combining the Quick Game and Dropback Pass with the Houston Pass. The Houston Pass is one of 2 passes in the Texas Package. We named it Texas because the passes are run from either a Trips or an Empty formation. The Houston is basically Stretch for all the receivers except the Number One and Number Two receivers to the field. They execute The Slice/Corner Pattern.

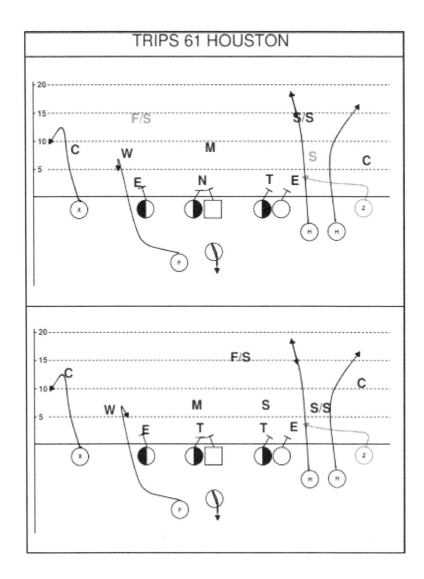

- Against a 4 Shell, the Quarterback reads the Free Safety on his first step and goes to the side away from the FS. Pre-snap the Quarterback checks if there are any blitz possibilities to the field. The OLB to the field would be the 7th rusher. The answer is a quick throw to the Stretch or the Slice Route coming from the wide side. If no Blitz, the QB reads Stretch to Slice off his third step If he doesn't like it – then QB Draw. If the Free Safety leaves the hash and moves to pick up the Stretch, the QB throws the Out Route to the Stop Route reading the OLB.

- Against a 3 Shell, the Quarterback checks any Blitz possibilities to the field. Now the Number Two Receiver's route becomes a Seam down the hash. So if the Strong Safety runs with him the Slice is wide open. If the SS doesn't run with the Seam in cover #2 – it could be a TD. The QB throws the Seam on his first step unless the SS runs with the Seam. If there is no Blitz, the Quarterback takes his 3 step drop and reads the OLB to the Boundary and throw the Out unless the OLB runs under it, then he throws the Stop route.

- Coaching Point: Against Press Coverage, the Out Route Converts to a Fade.

The Houston Pass can also be run from Empty with no changes.

The Stretch Pass is my favorite pattern because the reads are so simple and adjust against any defense.

The Choice Pattern and Its Variations

The Choice Pattern is so named because the Number 2 receiver to the field has a *Choice* of running a 10 yard Out route if he lines up tight or a 10 yard In route if he lines up wide. The Routes for this pattern are the same as for The Play Action version. However most of the time we throw the play action pass, the number 2 receiver is tight and most of the time we throw the Dropback version, he lines up wide. Here are the routes.

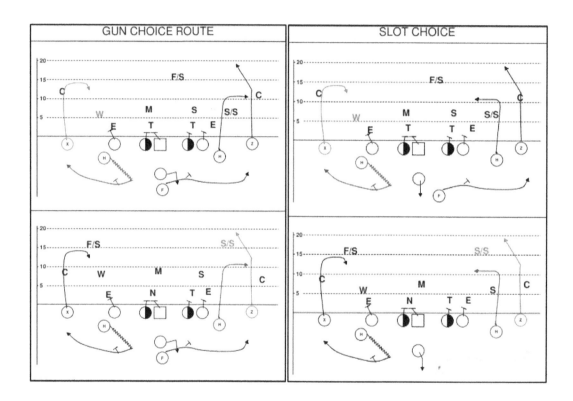

- The Number 1 receiver to the field runs a Post unless it's press coverage then he converts to a Fade.
- The Number 1 Receiver to the Boundary does a Fade unless the Corner is deep, then he converts to a 12 yard Curl.
- The Number 3 to the field runs a Check-release Flare as does
- Number 2 to the Boundary.

The Choice Pattern with 7 Man protection. The protection is 7-man protection if there is an 8th rusher, the Quarterback must direct the protection to the 8th rusher and throw flash away. The. Choice Pattern is a 3 Level Read to the Field and a Curl/Flat combo to the Boundary.

Quarterback Play. The QB's launch point and Blitz control are the same as with all Dropback Passes with 7 man protection. The reads are a little different.

- Against a 4 Shell Secondary, the Quarterback is going to throw to Number 1 to the field deep on either the Fade or the Post *unless* the Strong Safety is deep. If the SS stays deep, the QB is going to read the OLB and throw to Number 2 on the In route or if the OLB's shoulders are square, he throws the flare. If the MLB gets out in the perimeter – QB Draw.
- Against a 3 Shell Secondary, the QB finds the Free Safety, if he stays over the ball, the QB can still go to the field but if he is under the goal posts (Most Likely) the QB will throw the Curl to Number 1 unless the OLB is under it, then he drops it off to the Flare. If he doesn't like either – QB Draw. Coaching point if Number One to the boundary has press coverage with no Free Safety help, the Quarterback can take shot at the Fade

Adding The Quick Game to the Choice Pattern with 6 Man Protection. The advantage to having a Quick Game side is that it's not only a great Blitz answer but it provides with a high percentage throw against soft coverage. We only use 1 Quick Game Combos with the Choice Concept and really my favorite is the Slice/Corner. The QB is responsible for the 7th rusher, so he directs the protection to the 7th rusher and to the Free Safety.

- The Slice/Corner Combo. This works great with the Choice Concept because if there is no blitz, the Slice actually replaces the MLB. If the MLB is getting into the perimeter, there is no one to cover the Slice. It's getting a 4th receiver to the field. Against a 3 Shell it puts the ILB in a no-win conflict; get depth on the Seam and the Slice is open, stay low and the Seam is open.
- The Hitch/ Seam and Fade/Stick can be added but are not really needed.

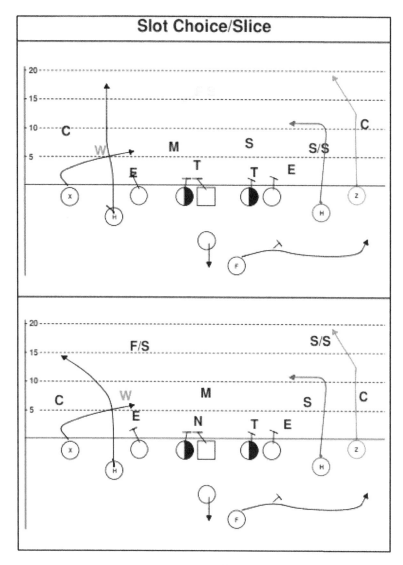

Slot Choice/Slice

The Dallas Concept from a Trips Formation. Dallas and Houston are the 2 Texas concepts we use in Trips to get a more receivers in the pattern. Houston is a variation of the Stretch Pattern and Dallas is a variation of the Choice Pattern. The Number 1 and Number 2 receivers to the boundary execute the same routes as the Choice Pattern. The Number One Route to the Field runs a Fade unless the CB is deep, then he converts to a 14 yard In route. If he sees Blitz, he can convert to a Slant. The Number 2 receiver to the Field runs a Slice Route. The Number 3 receiver to the Field runs the Stretch Route.

- Against a 4 Shell the Quarterback checks for Blitz from a 7th rusher which will be OLB to the field and the Slice is his blitz route. If no Blitz, he looks at the ILB and throws Stretch to Slice. He throws to the Stretch unless the ILB covers it the dump it to the Slice. If nothing looks good – QB Draw.

- Against a 3 Shell. Check for a 7th rusher and the answer is the same as the same as a 4 Shell. If no Blitz, he has the Curl/Flare read to the Boundary. Throw the Curl unless a LB is under it, then throw the Flare. He also has the Slice coming into the boundary late. If all covered – QB Draw. Note: anytime the Boundary Receiver faces press coverage, he runs a Fade.

The Dallas Concept is a good wrinkle for the Choice Pattern because it provides the Offense with Quick Game to the field.

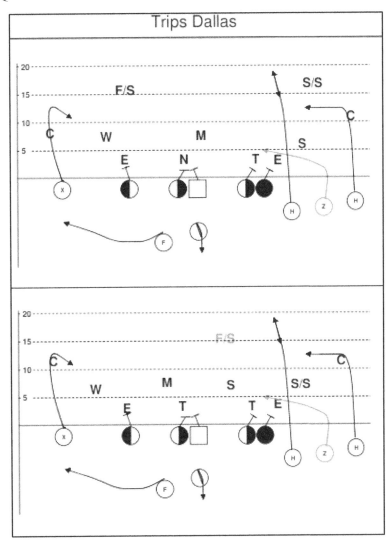

The Triple Gun Dropback game has been invaluable in long yardage and come from behind situations. It's simple and efficient as long as you can protect it and always remember Quarterback Draw is part of the play, there's no reason to force a throw.

Chapter 15
The Triple Gun Screens and Draws
The Screen Game Overview

The Triple Gun Screen is a very important part of the Triple Gun Offense. It helps The Triple Gun control the clock through the air as well as on the ground. The Triple Gun Screen game is another group of high percentage passes that are chain-movers and clock-controllers. Let's look at some the benefits of The Screen Package.

- It's not dependent on a dominant offensive line and neutralizes a good defensive line.
- It puts speed in space and makes the big guys chase. Making the defensive line chase takes away their legs. It's like doing pursuit drill all game for the defense.
- It helps to control the pass rush and defensive blitzes. By discouraging all out blitzes, there is less pressure on the Quarterback in long yardage situations. This also helps pass protection.
- The Dropback Game and the Play Action pass threaten the defense vertically while the screen game threatens the defense horizontally. It's hard to defend both at the same time.
- It keeps the defense from loading the box. "8 Between the Slots throw Quicks and Hots" So both our run game and pass attack benefit.
- Screen are chain-movers and clock-controllers.
- The Screen Pass is high percentage and very low risk.
- Screens are great "Sling Shots" against teams with superior talent.
- Screens make "Cover Guys Tackle"
- Paired with Runs, Screens become Great RPOs.

Types of Screens. The Triple Gun employs 2 types of screens. The conventional type of screens with linemen leading the ball carrier downfield, but even those screens have multiple screen possibilities in each one. For example The Triple Screen is 3 screens in one play!

The second type of Screen is really part of a run play. These are RPOs before someone clever started calling them RPOs. So we attach a pass to every to every run to keep the defense from loading the box. We'll start with these types of screens. We started this concept in 1999 when we installed The Triple Gun.

The Flash. The Flash Screen is technically not a screen because it does not have a "Screen of Blockers" in front of the receivers but it is more of an RPO behind the line of scrimmage with everyone except the Wide Receiver running the called play.

The Wide Receiver running the Flash takes 2 quick steps forward and then moves back behind the line of scrimmage with his numbers to the Quarterback. Once he receives the ball, he goes one on one with the Cornerback and makes a "Cover Guy" make a tackle. If the Cornerback is playing press, the Flash converts to a fade. If the Quarterback doesn't throw the Flash, the Wide Receiver gets downfield as a blocker. It's as simple as that. There is no audible involved, Flash is just built into the play.

The Flash is always available on any run or pass. It was originally used to keep a 44 OLB from stopping the Gun Triple Tailback cutback. But it evolved and was useful against any defense. Here are some of the reasons for throwing the Flash.

- "8 between the Slots throw quicks and hots" if the 44 Defense OLB creeps into the front, Flash is the answer. If the CB plays press coverage with no Free Safety help, it's a good time to take a deep shot with the fade.
- If the Defense bounces LBs to motion (either Jet or Option motion) the Flash will create another one on one situation.
- If it's a 4 Shell Secondary and the roll to a 3 Shell on motion, Flash is an answer.
- If the Cornerback is playing deep off the ball, the QB can look to the Wide Receiver and take the easy pass. This can be done anytime.
- If it's a pass play and the defense has too many in the box (7 men in the box with 6 man protection) Flash is an answer.
- Flash always creates a situation in which a "Cover Guy" must make a tackle.
- And it's also part of The Dragon Package.

We never called this an RPO but it certainly was a Run/Pass Option. Take a look at the 2 Gun Triple Flash videos.

The Bubble. The Bubble Screen we used to pair up with Draw Plays and The Zone Read. It was used for a similar reason as the Flash, if the defense loaded the box against the Draw, the Quarterback had the Bubble Screen as an answer. The difference is that the receivers involved in the Bubble phase always ran the Bubble while the rest of the offense ran the Draw. (Tailback or QB Draw). There is no audible involved, the Bubble is just part of the play.

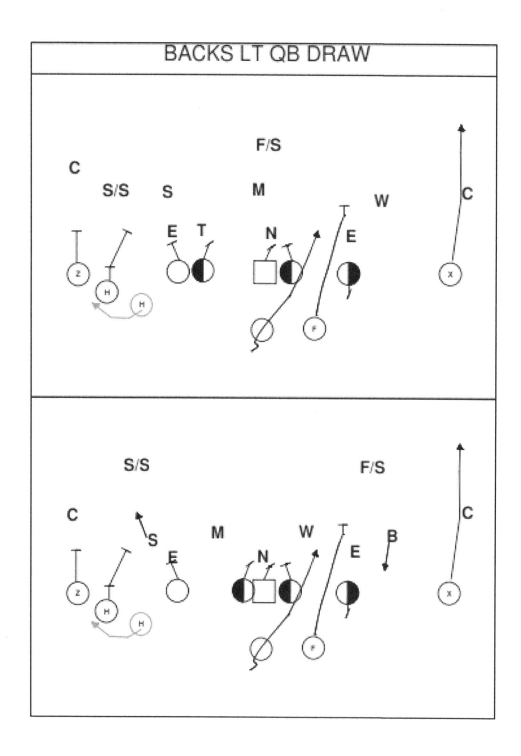

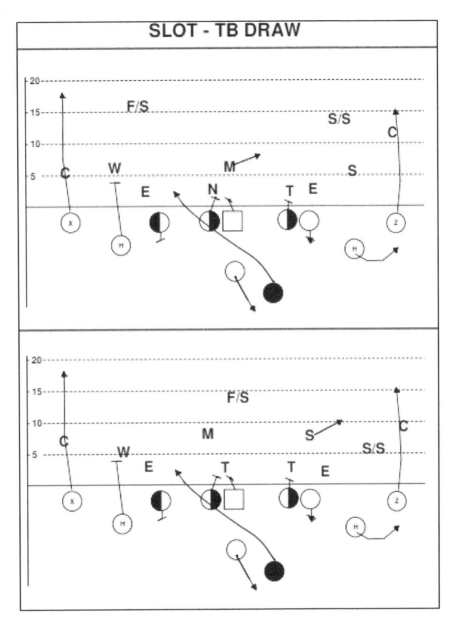

The Bubble Receiver is the Receiver closest to the Quarterback and his steps are: Step back with his outside foot, crossover with his other to get depth and the look for the ball. If he gets the pass, he stretches the defense to the perimeter. The blockers block as they would on an option play.

Note: some teams have the Bubble Receiver back up like it was Flash, I've never done it but I have seen it work.

The Bubble is a high percentage pass but not a big part of The Triple Gun Offense because we don't run that many Draws in a game but it does give The Quarterback a way out of a bad call. The Bubble is also part of The Dragon Package.

The Uncovered Pass. A third of these hybrid RPOs is the "Uncovered Pass" Simply put if the Quarterback sees an inside Slot Receiver uncovered, he signals him and then just catches the snap and throws him the ball. This doesn't happen often but when it does, a big play is possible. Any time there is "Speed in Space" it could be a big play.

These are 3 very high percentage; low risk plays that help a Quarterback control the clock with the pass. These are plays that also break down a defense's morale. These are plays that all make the defense chase.

The Triple Screen

The Triple Screen is the single best screen in football because it is 3 screens wrapped up in one play. It's the Triple Option of screens. Here's why it is an essential weapon of The Triple Gun Offense.

Why The Triple Screen? Here are some of the benefits of The Triple Screen:

- It complies with the Strategic Flexibility Principle because it changes after the snap.
- It looks like the Dropback Pass at the start of the play so defenders get depth not width.
- It puts "Speed in Space" and makes defensive linemen chase the ball and that wears them down.
- It gets the Tailback the ball. One year our Tailback caught 51 balls.
- It is formation friendly so it's easy to disguise the play.
- It complements the Dropback Pass because it attacks the defense horizontally, while the Dropback pass attacks vertically.
- It's high percentage, high production, and low risk.
- It helps pass protection because it neutralizes the defensive line.
- It gets the playmakers the ball.

Blocking The Triple Screen. The blocking for the Triple Screen is simple but must be practiced to maximize the effectiveness of the play.

- The On Tackle shows pass, then releases *flat* down the line of scrimmage and blocks the first defender he comes to.
- The On Guard blocks the protection for 2 counts and the releases to block the MLB

- The Center blocks the protection for 2 counts and the releases opposite the On Guard and blocks the MLB. If the MLB drops to the On Guard's side the Center finds work downfield.
- The Offside Guard blocks the protection for 2 counts and then releases to block the offside OLB.
- The Offside Tackle sets, butts and cuts the End Man on the Line of Scrimmage.
- The Number One Receiver to the call blocks the same rules as Gun Triple.
- The Number 2 Receiver to the field Seals the first man inside of him. He releases down field to give the illusion of the Dropback pass but keeps his eyes on his target and when he settles, he blocks him.

The Receiver Play in The Triple Screen. The receivers' first responsibility is to catch the ball. There is no play if there is no catch. The second responsibility is to get up field and gain yards after tucking the ball away.

- The Number 3 Receiver to the field (usually the Tailback) runs a Flare route and immediately looks for the ball. The route must be parallel to the line of scrimmage with no bellying back. Once he receives the pass, he must pick up the Tackle's block.
- The Number 1 Receiver to the boundary takes 3 quick steps up field, then comes back behind the line of scrimmage and toward the center and looks for the ball on the tunnel or jailbreak screen. Once he receives the ball, he must get north and south and get yards.
- The Number 2 Receiver to the boundary does Whirley Motion and eyeballs the Cornerback. If the Cornerback follows Wide Receiver, the Slot makes a "Ball" call. He's being the Quarterback's eyes. After making the "Ball" call, he runs his Flare Route to the boundary.

Quarterback Play in The Triple Screen. Like with the Gun Triple and most of this offense, the QB is the trigger of the play. Once he receives the snap, he starts his 3 step drop but is prepared to throw the ball on his first step.

- The Quarterbacks first read is the onside End Man on the Line. His thought process is "I'm going to the Flare every time unless the End Man covers him. If he is going to throw the Flare, he delivers it as soon as EMOL comes to him. He is going to have a high release and put the ball shoulder high to the Receiver's up field shoulder.

- If the End Man (EMOL) covers the Flare, the Quarterback continues to drop back while flipping his hips parallel to the line of scrimmage. He find the offside Wide Receiver on the Middle Screen and delivers the ball with a high release face high. He throws this middle screen unless he hears the backside Slot make a "Ball" call.
- If the Quarterback hears a "Ball" call he flips his hips to the target and throws the Flare to the backside Slot.
- If the Quarterback doesn't like any options he throw the ball at the feet of the middle screen receiver. This is his escape on the triple Screen.

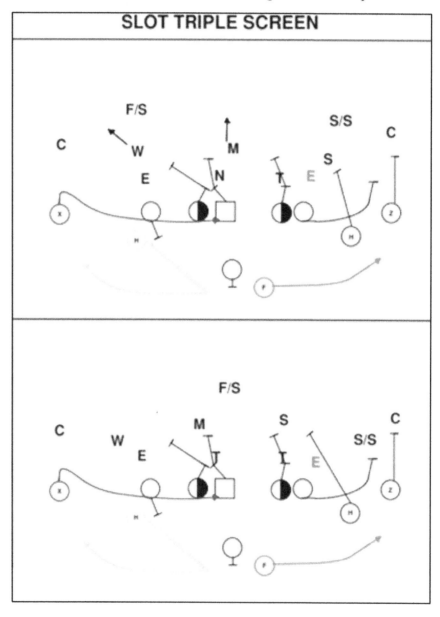

SLOT TRIPLE SCREEN

The Triple Screen against Common Defenses. The Triple Screen is good against any defense and is a great weapon vs the Blitz.

- The Triple Screen against a 43 Defense. Against a 4 Sell Defense, the Twin Slot can block the OLB or he can release downfield for the Strong Safety if the OLB is too close to the Line of Scrimmage. The On Tackle will block the OLB or the SS based on the Slot's block. We have used a TE instead of a Slot and run this from a Pro formation.

- The Triple Screen against a 44 Defense. Nothing really changes vs a 44 Defense except from a Slot Formation, a "Loop" Call by the Slot. The Slot blocks the Strong Safety and the On Tackle "Loops" for the On ILB.)

- Against a 34 Defense, the blocking stays the same unless they get in a Cover 3 Look with the Strong Safety rolled up and the OLB in the box. A "Loop" Call is an answer. The On Tackle goes through the breast of the DE to the ILB. The Slot blocks the Strong Safety. The QB would treat the OLB as his read.

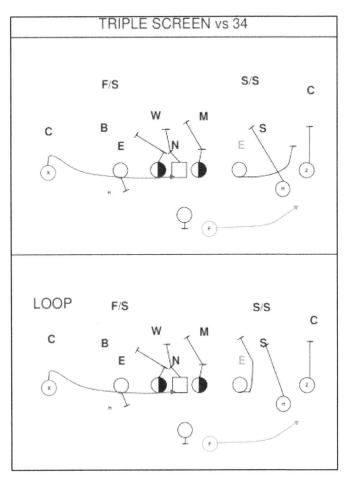

299

Using Other Formations. The most common formation used is a Slot Formation that you've seen in the previous diagrams but we also use Pro Formation and Trips Formation.

- Pro Formation puts a Tight End in the Game to seal the Onside LB. It's just a bigger guy making the block. Everything else stays the same.

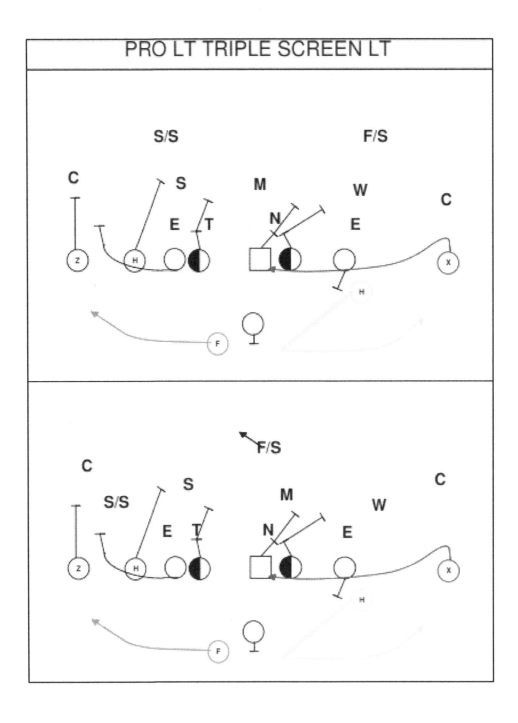

PRO LT TRIPLE SCREEN LT

- Trips – Triple Screen Away. On this Screen, The call side is into the boundary. The Flare to the Tailback is still his first read and the Slot to the Field makes the ball call. So the Call would be Trips right, Screen Left.

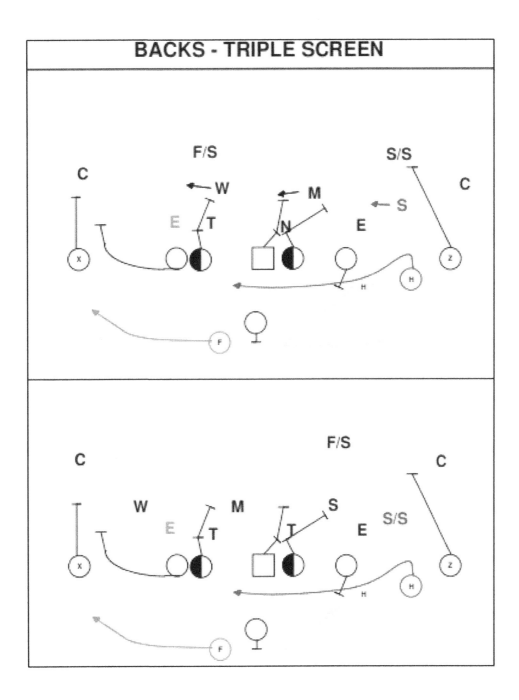

- Trips Flip Screen – All the assignments are the same *except* the Tailback and Slot "Flip" assignments. So the Flare to the Slot is the first choice and the Tailback makes the "Ball call.

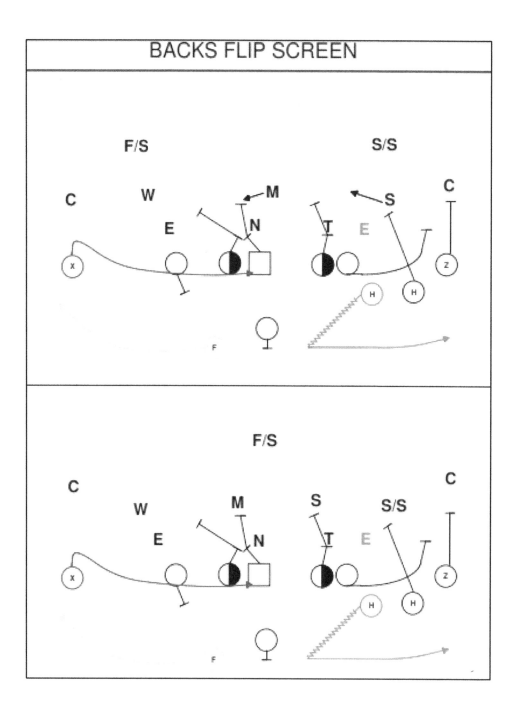

- Empty Double Screen. This is the exact same play as the Slot Triple Screen except the Off Slot doesn't make a ball call but blocks anyone trailing the Wide Receiver. If no one is trailing, he gets downfield and finds work.

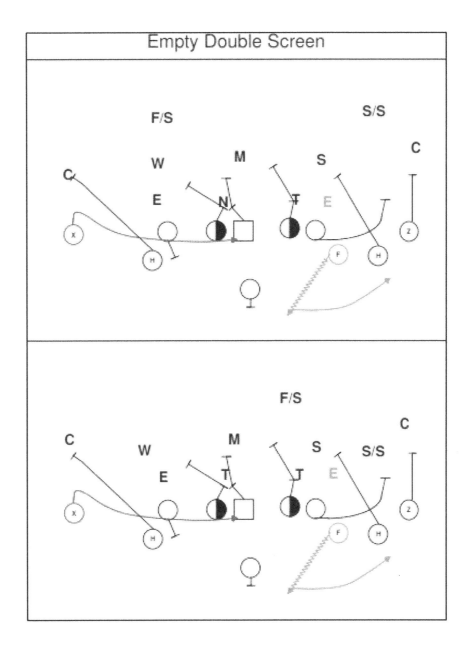

By using multiple formations and reads, it's very easy to disguise the Triple Screen so it can be called more frequently.

The Triple Gun Crack Screen

The Crack Screen is a great compliment to the Triple Screen. Our OC, Ralph Isernia, convinced me to add this screen and it was a great addition. It's a slower screen but it's more deceptive. It also can be used as a \Play Action Screen off the Jet Sweep. The key is the crack block by the Wide Receiver. We always run it away from a 3 X 1 set or away from Jet Motion.

Blocking for the Crack Screen.

- The Onside Wide Receiver has the key block. He releases up field as though he's running a route but eyeballs the OLB. After 3 quick steps up field, he executes a high. repeat high crack block on the OLB. He must keep his head out of the block and make sure the OLB is turning to the Wide Receiver before he blocks him.
- The Onside Tackle deep sets and lets the DE beat him inside, then he washes him down the line of scrimmage.
- The Onside Guard punches the nose, and protects for 2 counts and then releases flat down the line of scrimmage looking for anyone in the alley. Similar to his block on Half Reverse.
- The Center punches and protects for 2 counts and then pulls flat down the Line of scrimmage and looking to kick out the force defender, usually a Cornerback. The Wide Receiver's Crack and the Center's kick out creates the alley for the ball carrier.
- The Offside Guard blocks the protection for 2 counts and releases down the line of scrimmage looking for the MLB.
- The Offside Tackle blocks the protection for 2 counts, then shot puts his man up field and goes downfield to find work.
- The Number One and Number Two receiver to the field block for the Bubble. The Number Three receiver runs the Bubble

Quarterback and Tailback Play. The timing by the Quarterback and Tailback is critical to the success of this play.

- The Tailback dives into the line of scrimmage to the side of the screen hides behind the center. He only releases when the center releases. Then he stays behind the line of scrimmage and catches the ball on the run outside of the tackles alignment.

- The Quarterback checks bubble against a loaded box, if there is no pressure, he drops back 2 more steps, flips his hips to the Tailback and gets a high release off his back foot with a soft toss to the Tailback so he can catch it on the run. If the Tailback is covered drill the ball at his feet.

The Crack Screen is another high percentage, low risk pass that not only moves the chains but also produces big plays because it puts speed in space.

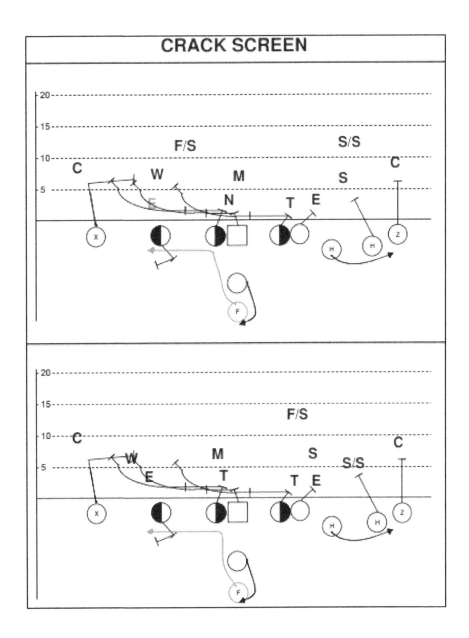

The Crack Screen off The Jet Sweep. We line up in Slot formation and fake the Jet Sweep away from Crack Screen. The Tailback dives away from the screen and the slips to his position behind the center. The QB fakes the Jet Sweep and the drops back and executes the screen. Everyone else just runs The Crack Screen. A great little wrinkle with almost no new teaching.

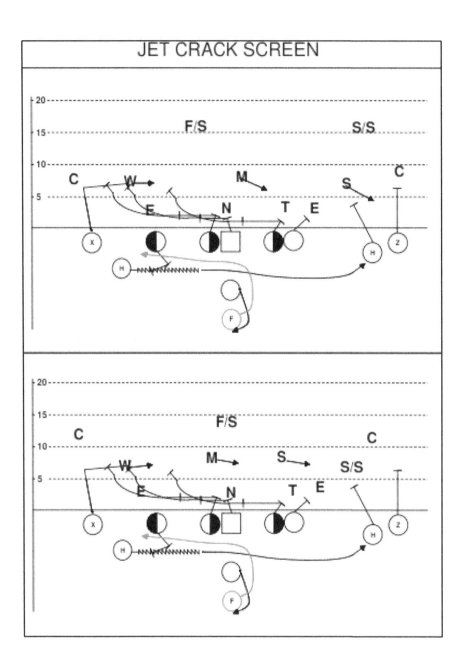

The Triple Gun Draws and RPOs

The Triple Gun Draws are all RPOs because they are all paired with a screen pass. The Triple Gun employs both Tailback Draws and Quarterback Draws. These draws are effective because of the amount of times we throw the ball. Most option teams do not use draws because they rarely pass the ball. The key is to make the draws as simple as possible. So we use as many crossover techniques as possible.

The Tailback Draw is basically a misdirection draw because we use it with "Whirley" Motion or Flip Motion. This gets the Linebackers moving the wrong way. The Slot become the lead blocker. Slot Formation is the only formation we run this play from. The Quarterback can throw the Bubble vs an overloaded box.

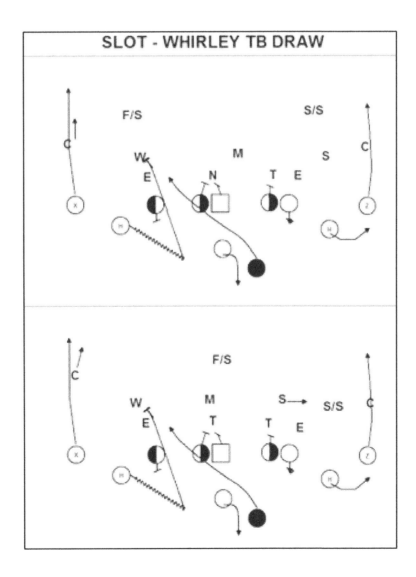

307

- The Line Blocking is ISO blocking, the same blocking we used for QB ISO. *Except* the Line shows pass prior to ISO blocking. Show pass then kick ass. So there is little teaching and little learning anything new for the Offensive Line.
- The Onside Slot and Wide Receiver run the Bubble Screen.
- The Backside Wide Receiver Stalks the DB on him. Or he could run a Fade Route
- The Whirley Slot blocks the Playside OLB. Or he could run a Stick Route
- The Tailback is offset to the Twins side and takes a little jab step and then runs over the ball and runs to daylight.
- The Quarterback can throw the bubble against an overloaded box but if no overload, he pumps the bubble to cause the LBs to move, the pulls the ball down and hands to the Tailback.
- If we want it to be a Quick Tailback Draw, the onside Slot and Wide Receiver execute the Fade/Stick Quick Game Pattern. The QB reads the OLB, he's giving the ball unless the OLB stays, then he throws the Stick Route. Obviously there is no Whirley Motion on the Quick TB Draw.

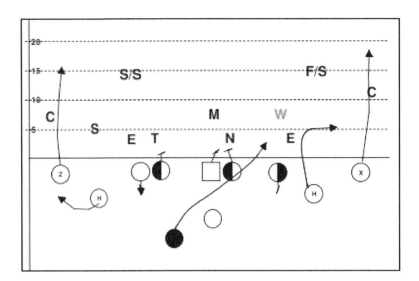

Quick TB Draw Fade Stick

The Tailback Shovel. This the exact same play as Tailback draw except the QB pitches it to the Tailback. This adds a little more deception to the play. The Shovel can also be turned into The Quick Tailback Shovel and the WR and Slot then runs the Fade/Stick and the QB pitches to the TB or throws the Stick depending on what the OLB does.

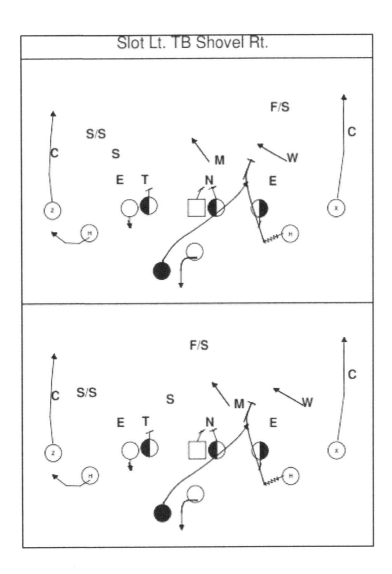

The Quarterback Draw. The Quarterback Draw is run exactly like the Tailback Draw, the same blocking, the same bubble opportunity except now the Tailback is the Lead Blocker and the Quarterback is the runner. Trips and Empty are the most common formations.

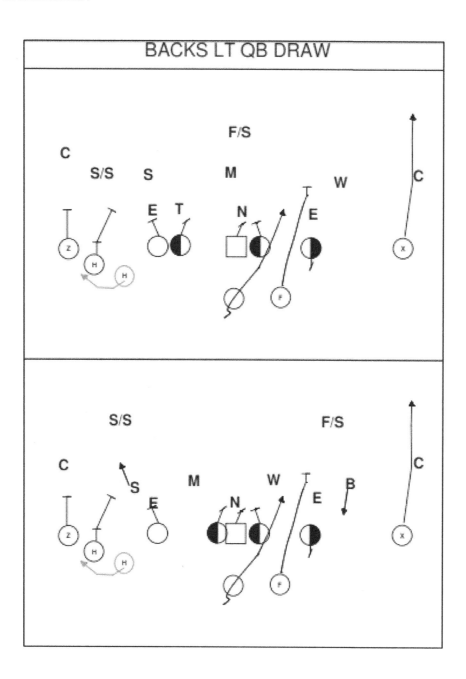

In Empty Formation the QB also has a Flash possibility as well.

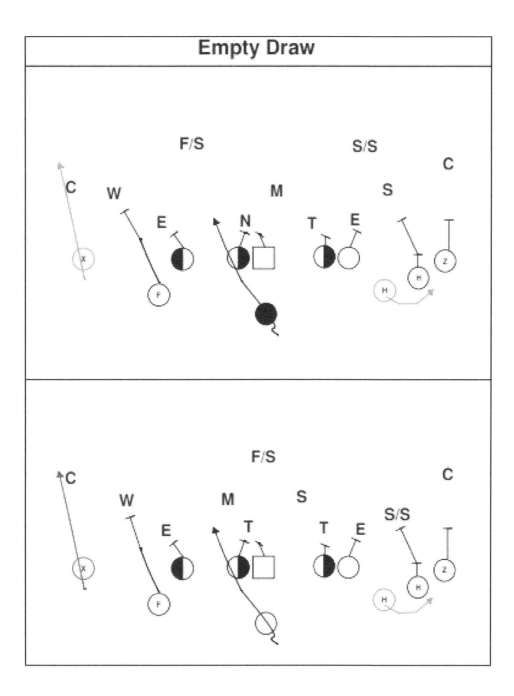

Enter the Dragon. The Dragon was the evolution of the Quarterback Draw into a Triple Option of sorts. It all starts with Empty QB Draw. The Offensive Line Blocks Quarterback Draw but the Quarterback has Bubble to the field and Flash to the Boundary. But this is easily expanded.

- **Dragon Pop.** Adding "Pop" has Number 3 to the field running a Seam Route. (Way back at Iona we called Hot Draw) and the QB reads the Onside Linebacker. His read is "If he drops, I go, if he comes I throw" A very simple RPO.

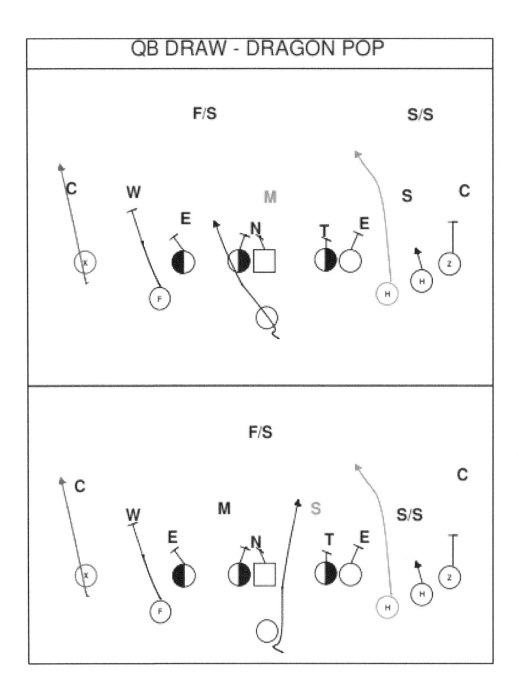

- **Dragon Quick Fade.** This Dragon to the boundary. The boundary receivers run the Fade/Stick Pattern and the QB has the same read on the Onside Linebacker. He drops I go, he comes I throw. This pattern could also be a Flash/Seam.

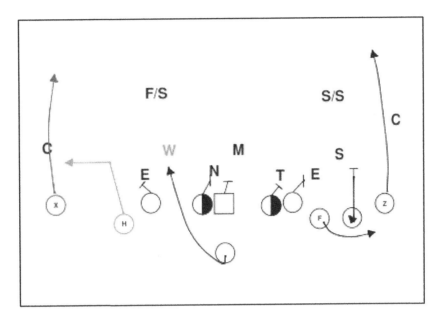

Dragon Fade Stick

These are RPOs that I never called RPOs (not clever enough) but the Empty Quarterback Draw was a great play in the Red Zone or in long yardage situations. It is a very low risk play that was very productive.

Chapter 16
Game Planning
Game Planning – General Tactics

Regardless of the defense we are going to face, there are universal tactics that we employ:

1   **Attack With a Broad Front Early.** The Triple Gun is a unique offense, so scouting reports have a very limited degree of helpfulness. The first quarter is our real scouting report. It's important that we do a great job gathering information on every play.

   - We try to use as many formations as possible and chart the defensive adjustments. Always getting our base Double Slot set, a compressed set, an unbalanced set and a 3 Wide Receiver set.
   - Motions are also charted, both Triple motion and Jet motion. Do they roll their secondary on motion? Do they bounce their Linebackers or slant their front to motion?
   - What about No Motion?
   - Do they substitute based on personnel or down and distance? Or do they play the same personnel regardless?
   - Once you have this info, it's easy to set up the next three quarters.

2. **Always Have Big Mo' on Your Side.** Big Mo' wants to follow up a big play with "No Huddle" fast paced offense. Go for the jugular if given a chance.

   - Take advantage of a "Sudden Change" for a quick strike and The Triple Gun has many Quick strike Plays in its arsenal.
   - Be Bold and audacious as a play caller without being reckless.

3. **A Flexible Attack is best – Sun Tzu.** Sun Tzu felt your attack should be like water adapting as the battle flowed on. The Triple Gun was designed exactly for this style of attack. We might throw for 300 yards in one game while rushing for 150 and completely reverse those numbers in the next game. Remember, a weakness isn't a weakness unless you can exploit it.

4. **Don't Repeat Successful Plays Comeback to them.** But if you want to repeat them, disguise them with a new formation or motion. You can use the same pig just put a mask on him.

5. **Be Unpredictable.** Break tendencies early in the game to weaken the defense's confidence in their game plan. Sun Tzu "Deception is the Art of War" so early use of some misdirection is always good.
   - Vary the tempo early in the game always use some "No-Huddle" early.
   - Stonewall Jackson's Philosophy was: Mystify, Mislead and Confuse. (I found this philosophy helpful to a good marriage as well).
   - Make your Quarterback varies his cadence. Always make the defense think. "If they think, they stink "

6. **Always Have a Second Half Surprise Ready.** It could be anything that they have not seen in the first half. We want the defense to forget the second half adjustments at halftime because we've given them a whole new set of problems. Some examples:
   - Using a high speed ultra-fast tempo.
   - Going to a Empty Formation or even an Empty bunch Set.
   - Using the Hammer Package.
   - Running the Gun Triple with Jet Motion.
   - Using a set of 3 plays on the first sound with no audible (Turn your imagination lose).

7. **Use Time Outs on Big Plays to "set" the defense.** It's always helpful to know what defense you're going to see on a 2 point play or on a big 3rd down. Of course this is an additional use of a time out.

8. **The Clock is your Ally if you use it properly.** Keep the main thing the main thing. The object is to win the game, not anything else. So if you have a good lead (2 TDs+) in the 4th Quarter score slowly, take time between plays. Move the ball, move the chains and move the clock. If you're behind, speed up the tempo to lengthen the game. Remember, like Jimmy Valvano taught me "The only lead that matters is at the end of the game"

Strategic Flexibility Makes Game Planning and Play Calling Simple. The ability of the Triple Gun core plays into another play after the snap makes play calling a snap. The only time you have to check a play is against an overloaded defense.

315

For example: The Gun Triple could become a pass if the defense puts "8 between the Slots" or The Quick Hitch could turn into a Sprint Pass if the Hitch is covered.

This makes scripting your "openers" simple as well because you only have to script formations and motions. (Attack with a broad front early) Your answer plays are called *only* when the defense is unsound against that particular play.

Down and Distance Considerations. The simple guide to play calling for 1st downs is "Get Half of what you need on 1st and 2nd downs and get the 1st down on 3rd down. The ability to convert 3rd downs is one of the strengths of The Triple Gun Offense. Naturally in 4 down territory, you have potentially an extra down to pick up the 1st down. That's why you should know prior to the start of the series whether you are going to kick a field goal or go for it on 4th down. If the field goal will add a possession (7 point lead to 10 point lead) kick it. If it doesn't (10 point to 13 point lead) go for it.

Attacking the 43 Defense

The 43 Defense was the most common defense we saw. The 43 that Jimmy Johnson ran at The University of Miami popularized this defense. Of course, The 'Canes had numerous All Americans on that defense. Jimmy Johnson gave his old College teammate at The University of Arkansas, Batty Switzer, fits shutting down the vaunted Oklahoma Wishbone Offense. Switzer's guards couldn't single block The U's Two Techniques and that was one of the keys to The Cane's dominance in Bowl Games.

The entire Triple Gun Offense is great against this defense.

The Traits of the 43 Defense

It's a 7 Man Front, 4 Shell Defense. They may roll a Safety Down to give an 8 Man Front, 3 Shell defense look.

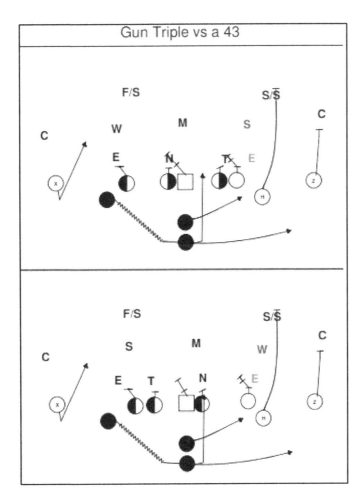

- The Guards are usually covered with a 1 Technique to one side and a 3 Technique to the other. But they might play a 2I and a 3 Tech.
- They will try to get a secondary player to add to run support. Be alert for a Corner Blitz from the boundary.
- They will use the Echo Stunt to confuse the Quarterback's reads where the OLB take Dive and the DE takes QB. The Leverage Pitch discussed in Chapter 6 destroys that stunt.

The entire Triple Gun Offense is great against this defense but there are certain things that you must be prepared for so these stunts can be exploited.

It Always Starts With Gun Triple. It's good to both the 1technique and the 3 technique. It's also easier to "Stack Read" a 43 from the Gun and opens up leverage pitch opportunities. (See Gun Triple against a 43 Defense.

- Using Formations to "Unstack the Stack" Twins is an easy way to get 1 Linebacker to leave the front. If they don't want to do that they have play a 3 Shell which leaves them vulnerable to the Vertical Game.
- Using Formations to widen the Hand Off Key or be vulnerable to a down block by the 6th Lineman.

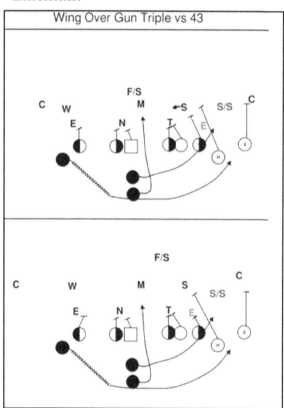

Wing Over Gun Triple vs 43

- Using Whirley and Flip Motion to move the Secondary

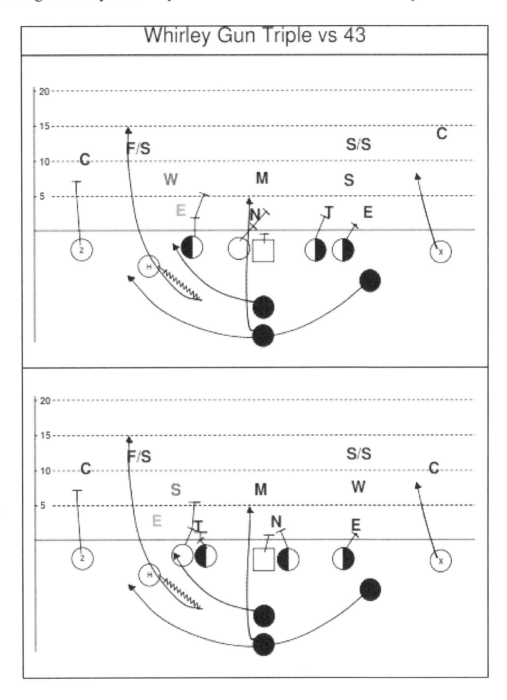

Whirley Gun Triple vs 43

- The Whirley Motion is our Counter Triple Option from Gun formation and Flip Motion from a 3 Wide Receiver set.

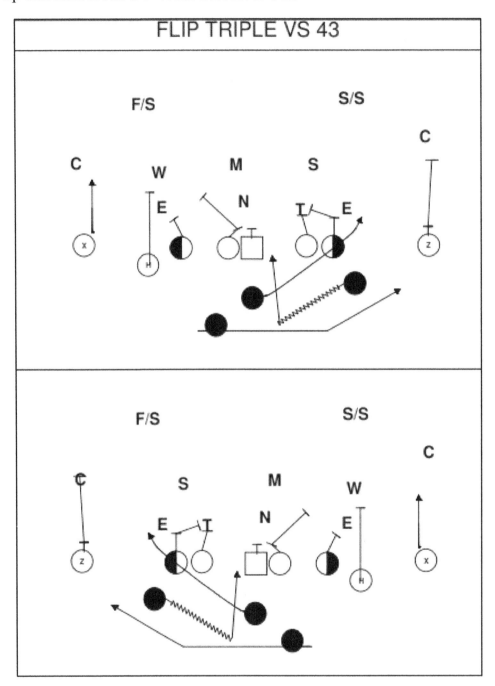

FLIP TRIPLE VS 43

- Empty Formation really spreads out the Defense and always has a misdirection feel.

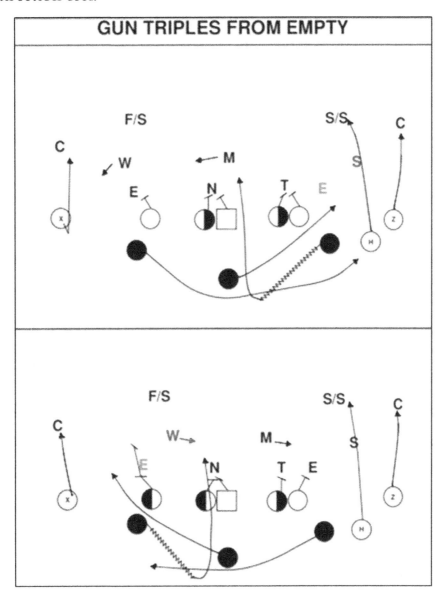

GUN TRIPLES FROM EMPTY

The Gun Triple will always be tough on a 43 Defense as long as you can handle the "Echo Stunt" with the "Stack Read" and Leverage Pitch. These are some tactics to be prepared for by a 43 Defense.

- The 43 will become a 61 to try to pressure the QB but The Gun Triple is very good against this pressure.

- The 43 Defense will try to run their MLB to the perimeter to try to stop the Gun Triple. The easiest answer is just the simple Zone Dive

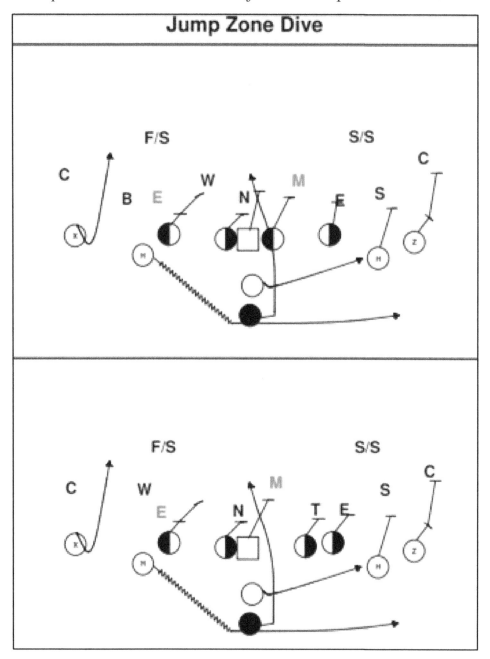

- The Defense will try to squeeze the backside DE and OLB & the answer is The Half Reverse

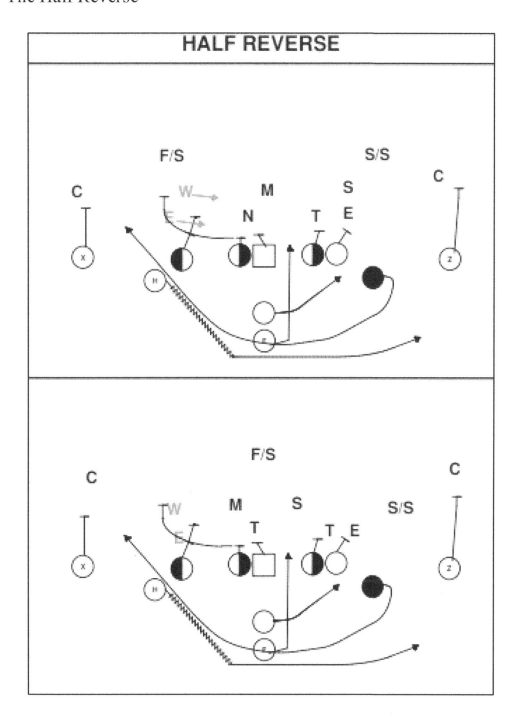

- The Defense will also pinch the Defensive Line to take away the Dive and run the MLB to the perimeter but The Gun Triple's HOK block rule scuttles that ship.

- We can always get the ball pitched by running Speed Option from Gun formation. Empty Speed is also very effective.

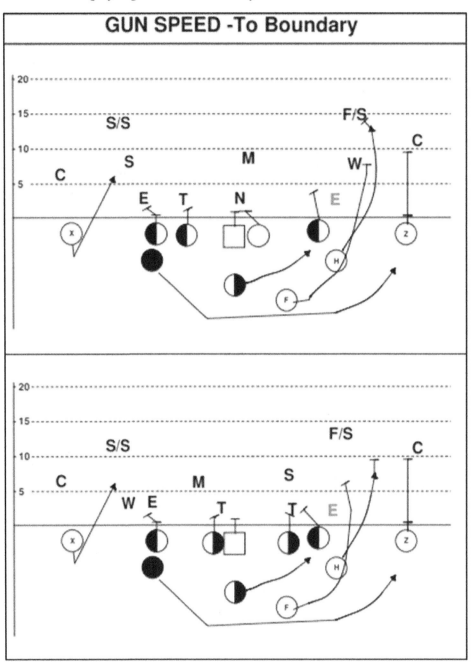

EMPTY SPEED

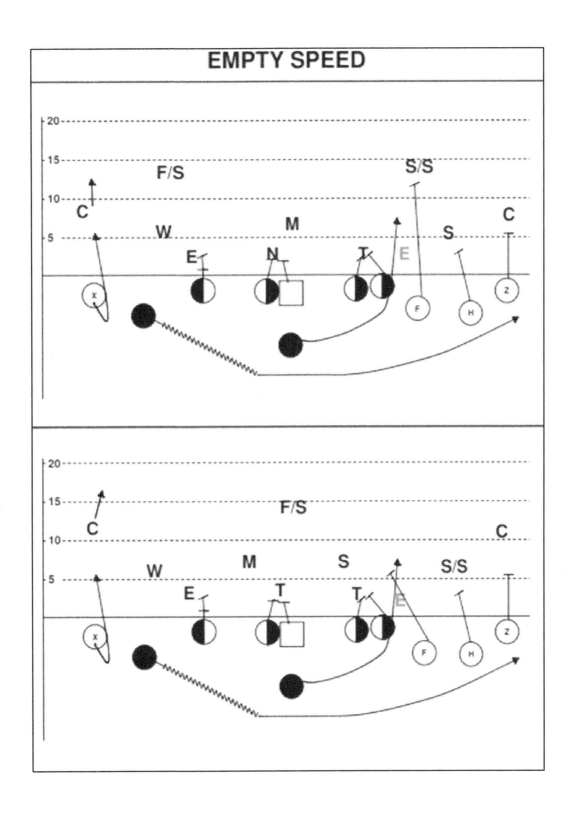

The Quick Game is always effective. Regardless of whether it's a 2 Deep look or a 4 across Quarters look, the Hitch is always good and so is the Fade/Stick. Using motion to throw the Quick Game vs a rolling secondary is like stealing.

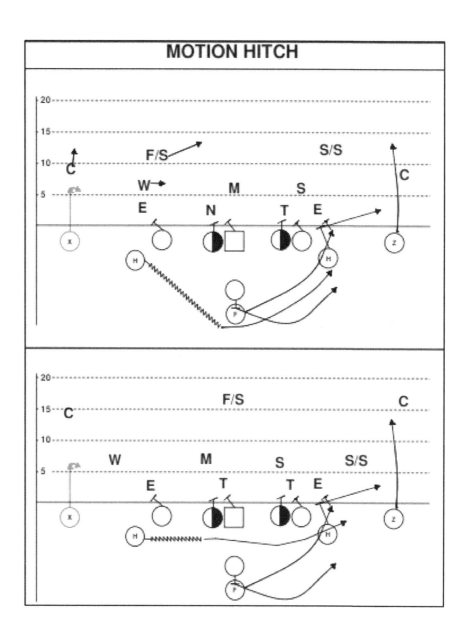

The Play Action Pass Provides the Home Runs. The normal Triple Gun Stretch Pass and Crossers Pass are great against a 43 Defense but by using Whirley Motion on the Stretch and the Post Wheel and it gives the defense a whole set of problems to deal with if they are keying on motion.

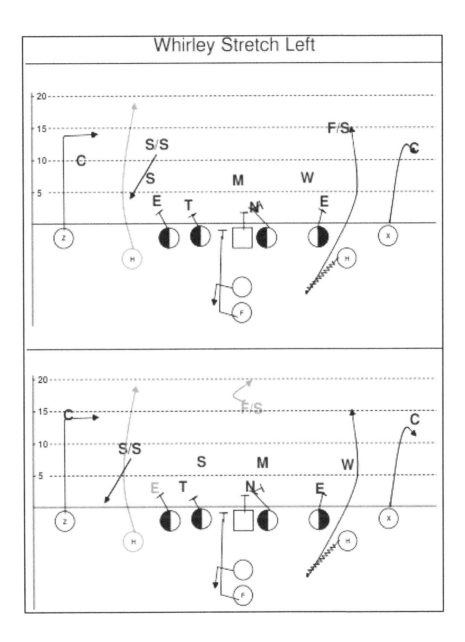

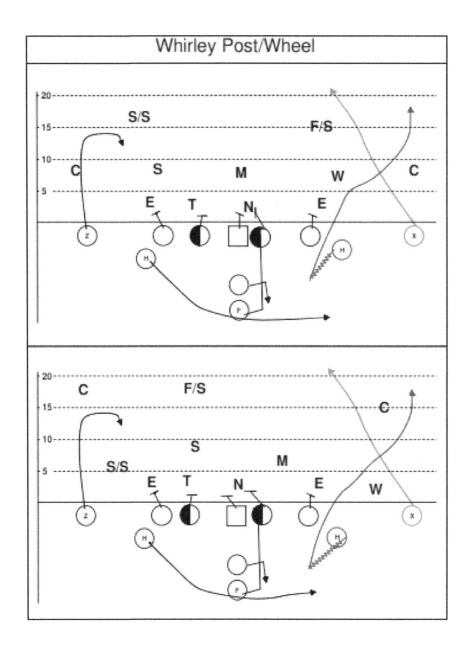

The Empty Dragon Series. The Empty Dragon series opens the door to some simple RPOs and gives the Triple Gun a great alternative style of offense to sprinkle in with Option Attack.

Gun Read Fade/Stick (RPO) The "Echo Stunt" is a big stunt the 43 Defense uses against option teams. But the Stick Route off the Quick Game is very difficult for the OLB to cover especially with a dive back heading at him. So it's an easy RPO. The Quarterback reads the OLB, he will give the ball to the Tailback unless the OLB takes Dive. If the OLB takes Dive, the QB reads the Cornerback just as he would in the Quick Game and the Fade unless the CB runs then the Stick. Note: the Offensive Line Blocks like QB ISO. If the DE pinches down the OT washes the HOK down and the Tailback follow his normal HOK Blocked Rule.

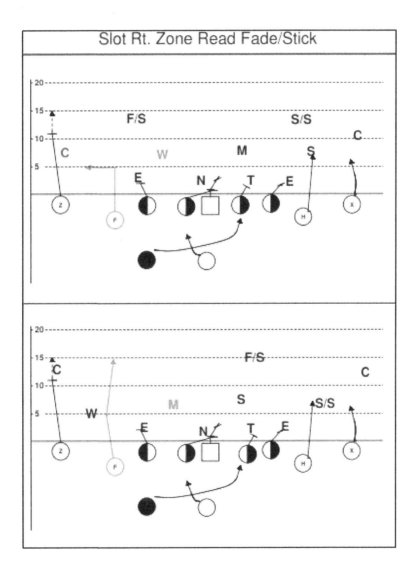

Slot Rt. Zone Read Fade/Stick

Having an offense whose basic plays contain all the answers you'll need against any defense makes game planning a cinch.

Attacking the 44 Defense

The 44 Defense is the second most popular defense played against The Triple Gun Offense. There are a lot of similarities between the 43 and the 44. Both defenses use 4 linemen and they cover both guards. Usually, a 1 technique to one side and a 3 technique to the other side. But there are some significant things that the 44 Defense does that must be prepared for

The Secondary is a 3 Shell which is very vulnerable against the Vertical Game and the Quick Game.

- The Free Safety is going to try to be the 9th run defender by running the Alley. We are going to block that FS with an unbalanced receiver. We're also going to burn Free Safety with Play Action.
- You always must be prepared for the Defense to put 8 between the Slots and pack the front. The Rule is "8 Between the Slots, throw quicks and hots" We can also use "Max Protection and go to war with our Wide Receivers on their Cornerbacks 1 on 1.
- You must get outside on the perimeter so Double Options are a must. "Put Speed in Space and let the big guys chase" Take away the legs of those Defensive Tackles. Never let the defense dictate just give reads because the 44 will make your Quarterback give all day so the ball is going into the strength of the defense.

It all starts with The Gun Triple. Like every game plan, this one starts with the Gun Triple. There are some slight tweaks to the Gun Triple that are built-in the play.

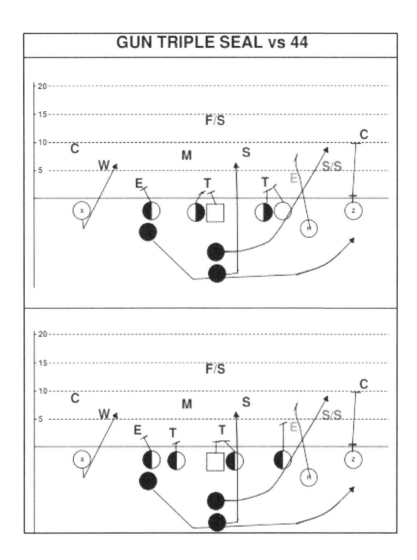

- The first difference for the Gun Triple against the 44 defense is the onside Slot. Against a 3 Shell (1 High Safety) the Slot *seals* first Linebacker head up or inside.
- The Veer Tackle to the 1 technique side should "Square Release" so the defense can't squeeze and scrape.
- The Quarterback and Wide Receiver must always be alert for the offside OLB sneaking into the box. Flash is the built in answer.

- Because it's a level 2 Pitch Key, No Motion and Whirley Motion are very effective in freezing the Linebackers.

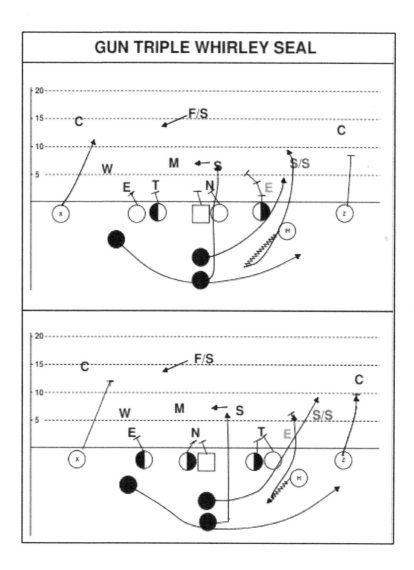

GUN TRIPLE WHIRLEY SEAL

- We like to use Wingover (With a 6th Offensive Lineman) to stretch the HOK to simplify the Quarterback's read.

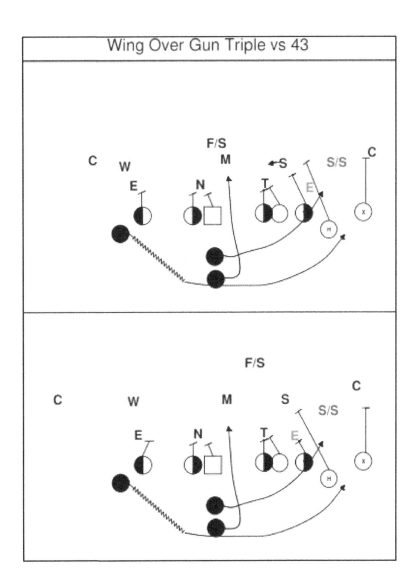

Wing Over Gun Triple vs 43

WING OVER GUN TRIPLE VS 44

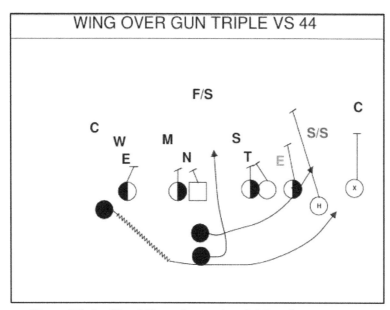

- Using a Two Tight End Set gives the 44 Defense an extra gap to defend.

TIGHT PRO TRIPLE SEAL

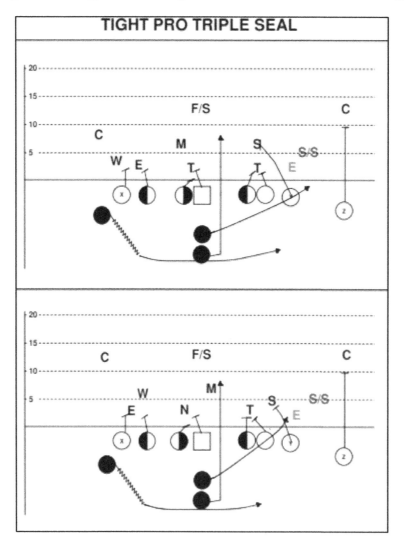

- **Double Options Get Speed in Space.** The key to moving the ball against a 44 Defense is confuse the Hand Off Key. We read him, we pitch off him, we base block him and we double team him. This prevents from playing a sit and read style of defense.

- *The Speed Option – Pitching off The Hand Off Key.* The 2 formations we use the most for The Speed Option are Twins and Empty. Empty puts in position to seal the Inside Linebacker. The #2 Receiver stalks the Strong Safety in either set.

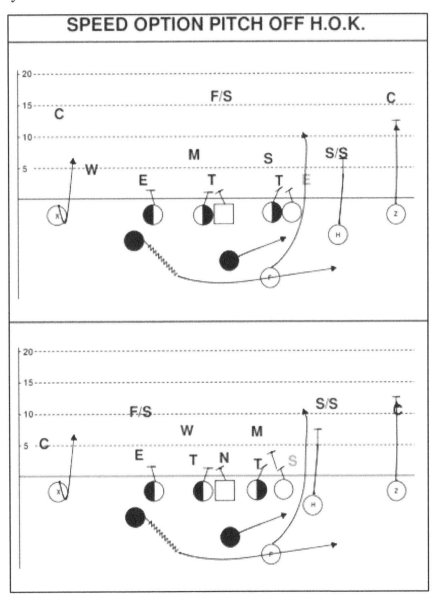

- *The Stud Option – Double Teaming the Hand Off Key.* Double Slot is the first formation for the Stud Option. But Ends and Receivers Formations have a blocker to block the Free Safety. The Tailback is responsible for the Inside Linebacker and the Quarterback pitches off the Strong Safety.

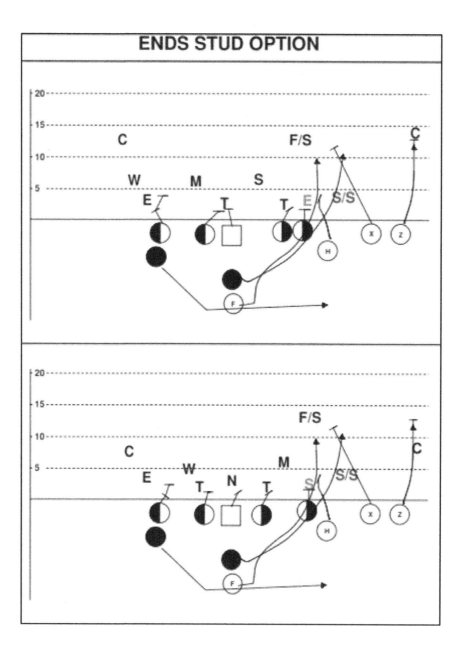

- *The Stud Option from a Compressed Set.* Running the Stud Option from a compressed set gives us the opportunity to "Make a Cover Guy Tackle" because the Wide Receiver cracks the Strong Safety and the Cornerback becomes the pitch key.

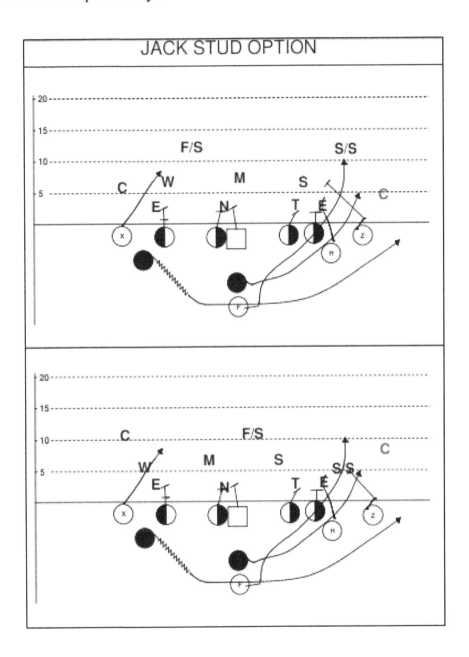

- *Adding a Simple RPO off Stud Option.* Besides always having Flash available on every play, the Dump Pass from Receivers can create problems for the Defense. QB's read "He comes, I throw, he drops I go"

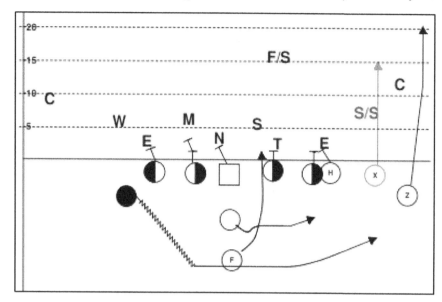

Receivers Dump vs 44 Defense

Hard to Read, Easy to Block. To combat a soft Hand Off Key (that folds back in on the Tailback on give reads) we block him with the Tackle. And the Tailback leads on the Inside Linebacker. The bonus is the Quarterback's ability to cut back if the Linebackers flow to the perimeter.

The Quick Game is a great chain-mover with a vertical threat. The Hitch/Seam is a favorite vs the 44 Defense because the Hitch makes a "Cover Guy Tackle" and the Seam makes a "Tackle Guy Cover" Of course, the boot aspect also creates problems for the 44.

The Play Action Stretch Pass gets a wrinkle by running it into the boundary. Actually we're calling it away from the Free Safety. Again, this makes a "Tackle Guy" have the job of covering the Stretch – advantage to the offense.

The Post/Wheel Play Action to Attack the Outside Linebacker. A little move by the Slot is guaranteed to get him open against a 44 Defense. He moves inside as though he was going to seal the Inside Linebacker, the releases *behind* the Outside Linebacker to run his Wheel Route.

Crossers Pattern is an Excellent Deep Shot. Using Wide Jack Formation and faking The Jet Sweep is a great way to free up the Post Route because the Cornerback can't undercut the post route.

The Dropback Pass is a must but must attack away from the Free Safety. The Dropback game is an excellent weapon against a 3 shell as long as you keep it away from the Free Safety. The Vertical Game produces TNTs and The Stretch Pattern moves the chains.

The overall approach to our attack on a 44 defense is to control the Hand Off Key, get to the perimeter and put speed in space. Control the Free Safety with run and pass. Attack the area between the Linebackers and the Free Safety with the pass.

Attacking the 34 Defense

One of the key positions in the 34 defense is the Nose Guard, the guy over the Center. Our center must not only block but snap the football so it's important we control the nose. This is the key position in an Odd Defense. But the 34 Defense presents other problems as well, let's take a look.

Problems the 34 Defense Presents to an Offense

- The first problem is an active Nose Guard. The Triple Gun's base scheme is Veer Blocking which double teams the Nose Guard. Also the Tailback's tight path lets the Tailback cut behind the Nose.

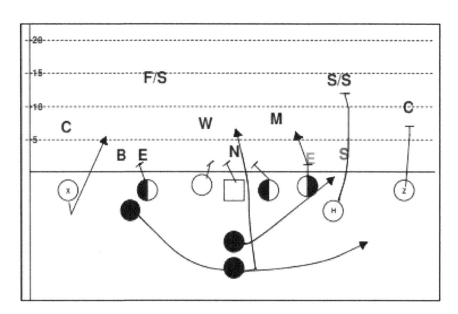

Gun Triple vs 34

- Squeeze and Scrape is a prime stunt of a 34 Defense. The Smart Splits and square release by the Tackle are great weapons to handle this stunt.

- Putting the Defensive Ends in 4I techniques to take away the dive. The Triple Gun answer is the "Hand Off Key Blocked Rule" which turns the Triple Option into Double Option with no audible. Also the "Down Call" turns The Gun Triple into the Wide Veer.

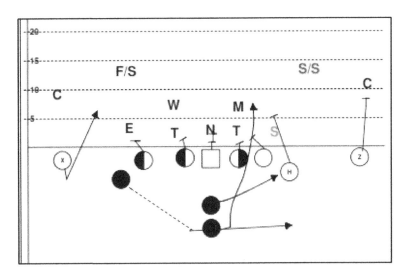

Down Call

- Slanting the front on motion. The Triple Gun has 3 answers: #1 No Motion, #2 Whirley Motion #3 Flip Motion. Plus Veer Blocking handles a Slanting front.

- Walking the ILBs up on the guards. The Triple Gun uses an "Ace Call" which has the Guards treat the ILBs as linemen. So the Guard and Tackle will Double Team the walked up LB

- Edge pressure by the OLBs. The HOK Blocked rule helps because the defense will probably pinch the Defensive Ends. Using a Slot formation is helpful because it forces the Defense to show the blitz. Using a Wingover set gives the offense a guy to block the OLB.

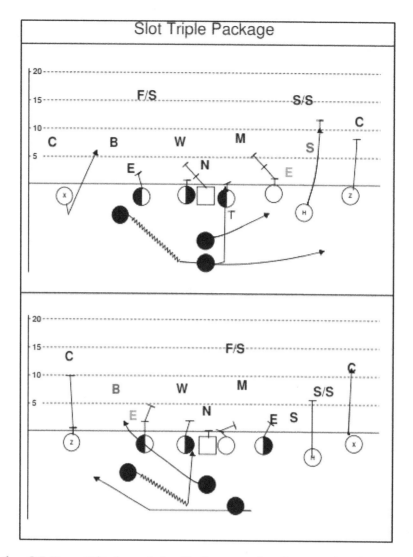

Slot Triple Package

- Inverting the OLB on Pitch and the Safety on the Quarterback. The Gun Triple easily handles this because the Slot will still arc the safety and the Quarterback will keep the ball.
- Rolling the Secondary on Motion. Flash, Motion Hitch, Whirley Motion are very simple answers. The Crossers Pass Pattern is special against this defensive ploy.

These are some Defensive tactics that The Triple gun must be prepared for.

It all starts with Gun Triple. Regardless of the defense, we always start the attack with Gun Triple. It has so many built-in answers that it's always the place to start. Whirley Motion exploits Defensive movement on motion No Motion is also effective. Changing up formations is great especially unbalanced Wingover both to the strength and the Nub if they adjust. Using Slot Triple. Flip Triple is very effective if the defense rolls to Cover 3. Slot forces the OLB out of the box.

Supplemental Runs. Quarterback ISO is very effective vs a sit and read HOK.

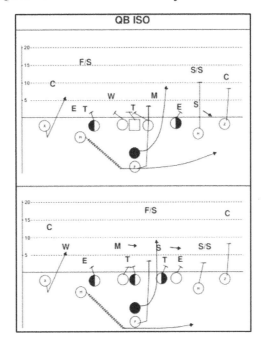

Half Reverse is devastating if the OLBs are chasing the play.

The Zone Dive with a "Fake Half Reverse" really causes confusion in the backside of the defense.. The Zone Dive is very effective vs an active Nose Guard.

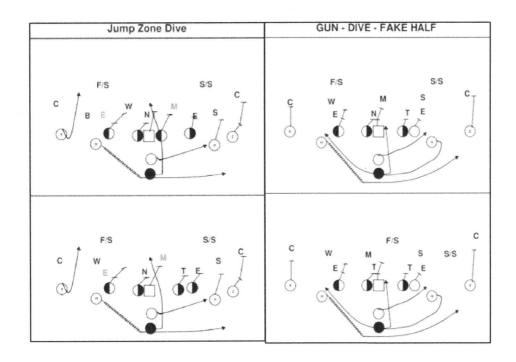

The Passing Game is basically the same as any 4 Shell secondary. We'll use the same thinking we used vs a 43 Defense with a 4 shell. The Quick Game. The Play Action Stretch to the Field and Boundary

- If the Defense plays a Bears or two 4Is the Stick Route is a gimme

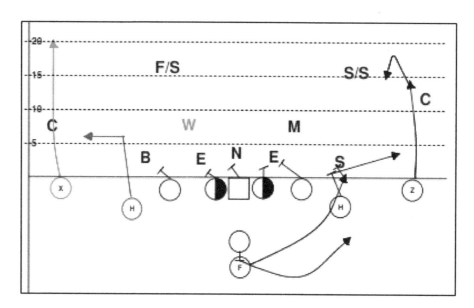

Fade Stick vs Bears

- The 34 Defense will tip which OLB is coming to pressure the Quarterback. Line up in Slot Formation if the Defense Widens the Field OLB, the boundary OLB is coming but if the Defense goes to Cover 3, the Field OLB is coming.

Attacking the 33 Defense

The 33 Defense is a Stacked Odd Defense designed to confuse blocking schemes and pass protections. But remember, attack complexity with simplicity. The 33 Defense puts more speed on the field so it's important to have some misdirection.

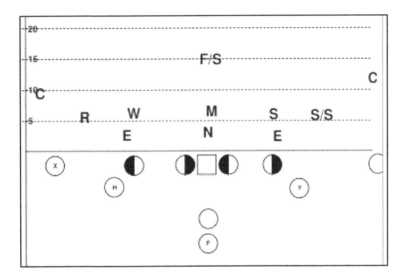

The 33 Stack

Traits of The 33 Stack Defense. Here are some things you must be prepared for when you're facing a 33 Defense:

- The 33 is an 8 man front defense with a 3 Shell Secondary. But they can drop the Strong Safety or the Rover deep to get into a 4 shell.
- The 33 Covers the Nose with a Stack which necessitates teaching the Center and Guards "Squeeze" Technique.
- The 33 has 5 potential Blitzers in the front, so awareness is critical. We must always be aware of the Free Safety's location. He will tip the blitz. It's also important that you change the cadence to also get a tip on a potential blitz.
- The key question is: How are the going to get a 9th man into run support?

It all starts with Gun Triple. This is the play the 33 Stack Defense must stop to slow down the Triple Gun Offense. And that starts with technique. The Guard and Center have the 2 A Gaps. But because of the Stack on the Nose, the Center and

Guard must "Squeeze" the Nose to the MLB. so regardless of how the Stack unfolds both the Nose and MLB are blocked. The Tackle and the Slot use a similar technique on the Stack on the Tackle. On the Tackle's release, he is expecting a "Plug" by the OLB. But if he doesn't Plug the Tackle blocks the MLB. The Slot expects the OLB to Scrape and Seals him. But if the OLB Plugs, the Slot blocks MLB to the Free Safety These techniques are the key to the Gun Triple's success against a 33 Stack. Here are some other ways to use the Gun Triple against a 33 Stack:

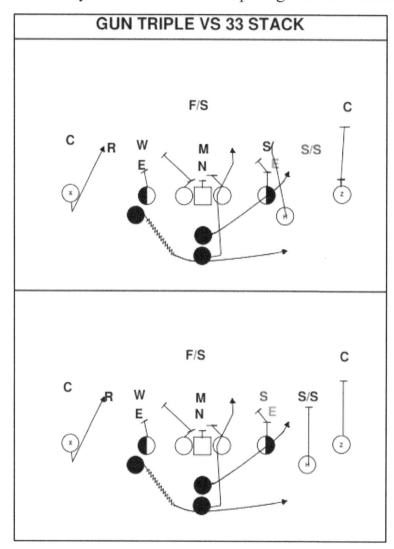

Using a Slot Formation gives the QB a Stack Read

- Using a Slot Formation and "Stack Reading" the Stack. The Slot blocks the Strong Safety and the QB could leverage pitch the ball. Empty Formation is also a great way to Stack Read and Leverage Pitch.
- Whirley Motion gives a little Misdirection to freeze the MLB.

COUNTER TRIPLE VS 33

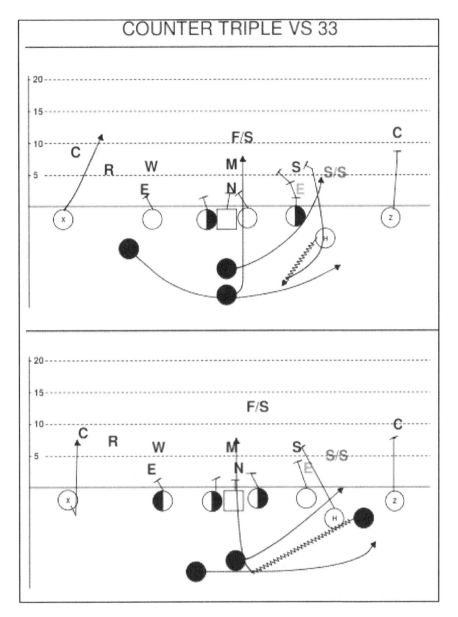

Backs Rt. WEB Motion Flip Triple Rt.

- Wingover presents another set of problems for the 33 Defense. If they don't adjust it's a TED Call but if they do adjust it's a Toad Call

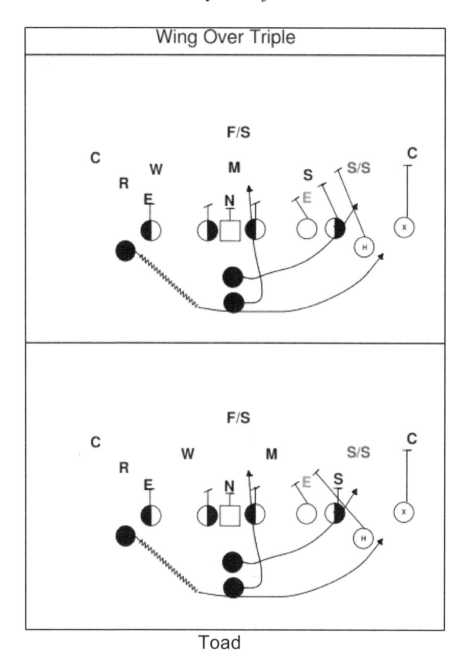

Toad

- Either way the advantage goes to the good guys. Of course, Wingover with Whirley Motion gives some misdirection.

- Empty causes the Defense to unstack and spread out which opens up the Gun Triple and creates blocking angles.

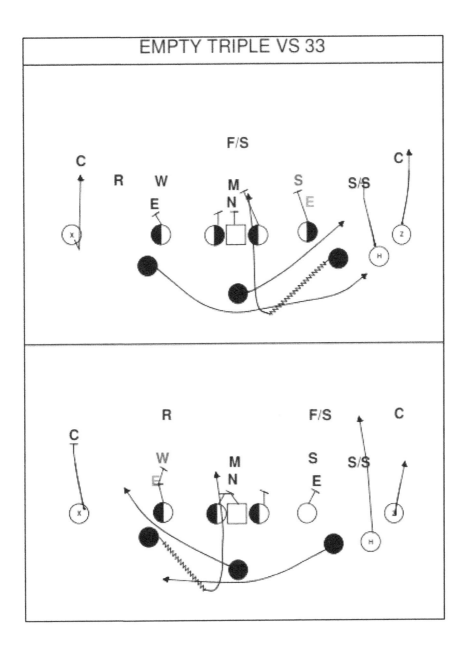

EMPTY TRIPLE VS 33

Double Options against a 33 Defense. It's always important to get "Speed in Space" so having ways to stretch the defense sideline to sideline is critical. Here are some ways we do it:

- *Speed Option* is the way we get the ball pitched. Using Receivers Formation keeps the Wide Receivers eligible and gives us an extra blocker. If the Stack unfolds Stud looks great.

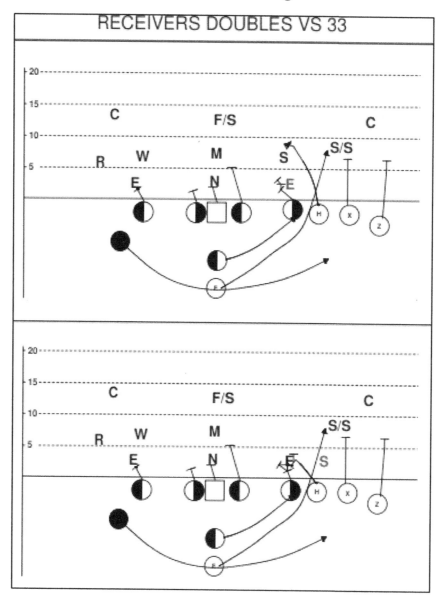

- An RPO is available with the Dump Pass to the Wide Receiver if blocking the Strong Safety is a problem. We can also use Ends to get the extra blocker and could attack the Nub.

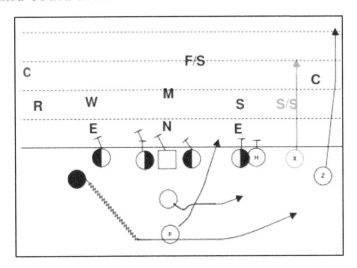

Receivers Dump RPO

- Running Speed Option from an Empty Formation gives our blockers angles and opens an RPO possibility.

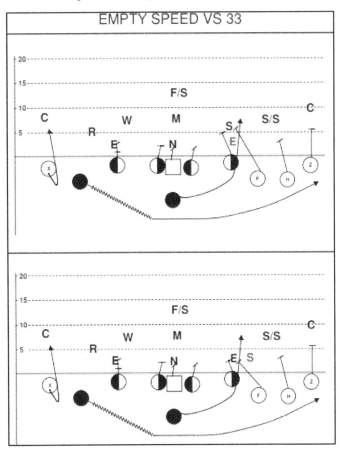

- *Stud Option* is another Double Option that puts Speed in Space. Using Wingover causes the defense a problem similar as Receivers except that we are pitching off the Strong Safety not blocking him. If the Defense adjusts we still "Stud" the end man on the line of Scrimmage. If the Defense over-shifts, the Nub is open for Stud

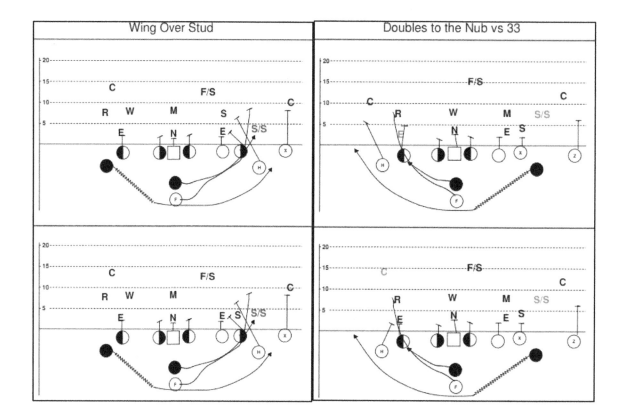

Supplemental Runs against a 33 Defense. Our supplemental runs are answer plays for a specific defensive adjustment. For example Half Reverse is always an answer to over pursuit. The Gun Triple & Gun Double is so good that there is not much need for other runs but there are 2 that we use.

- *Quarterback ISO* is a great inside counter against a fast-flowing MLB. It is also great against a soft HOK. Also, a nice complement to Jet Sweep.

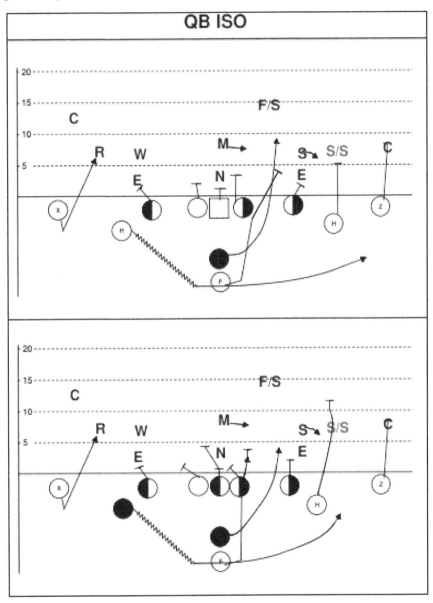

- *Jet Sweep* is great when we run it from an unbalanced set either Ends or Wingover. Those sets cause an adjustment which sets up Gun Triple to the nub.

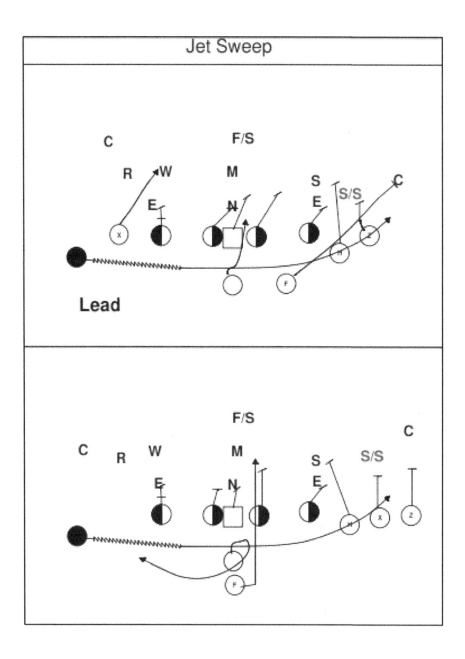

The Pass Attack is basically the same as any 3 Shell Defense but there are a couple of wrinkles that cause the 33 front some problems. The Triple Gun will its entire passing arsenal against this defense but it starts with the Quick Game.

The Quick Game against the 33 Defense with a 3 Shell Secondary.

- *The Hitch* is our "go-to" pass. It's a pass we're going to throw multiple times. However, against a 3 Shell the *Hitch/Seam* is the one to really put pressure on the Free Safety. The other variation is the *Hitch away from Trips*. This gives the QB a 3 level read to Boot to. The Hitch away from Jet Motion give the QB an easy completion if the defense adjusts to motion.

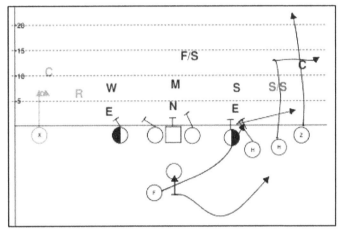

Backs Hitch vs 33

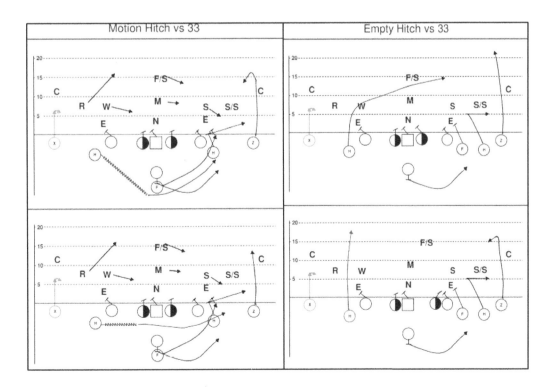

- *The Slice/Seam is* a great Quick Game Combo that forces the Stack OLB to cover the Slot on the Seam Route. The Slice comes under the LB creating a coverage conflict.

The Play Action Plays deliver the Knockout Punches.

- *The Stretch Pass is our number one play action pass.* The Stretch is great against every coverage. Against this defense the backside Out will probably be wide open. Using a Slot Formation forces the Free Safety to make an adjustment, or the Slot will be covered by the Strong Safety who must also play pitch.

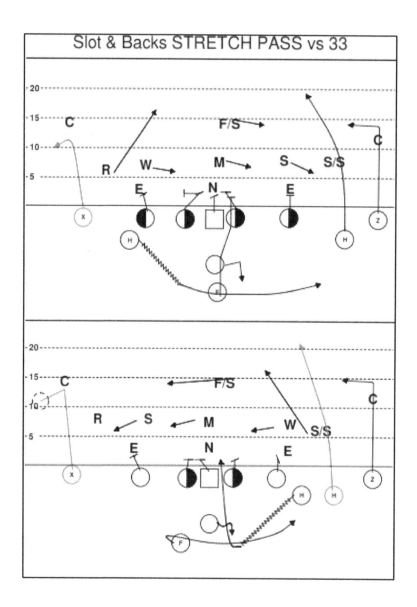

- *The Crossers Pattern* is very effective vs a 4 or 3 Shell Secondary so this is a great weapon vs the 33 defense. It is our go to play action off the Jet Sweep from Wide Jack formation to free up the Post but we also use it off Option Action.

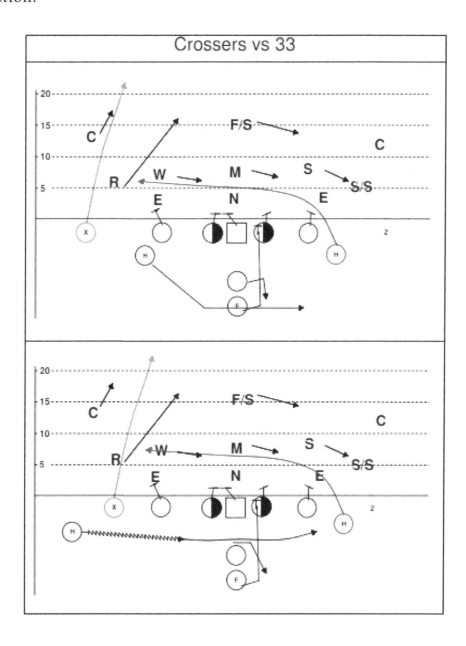

- *The Post/Wheel* is a standard play action pass against a 3 Shell Secondary and so is the Post/Out Combo. We like the Post Wheel to the boundary and The Post/Out to the field.

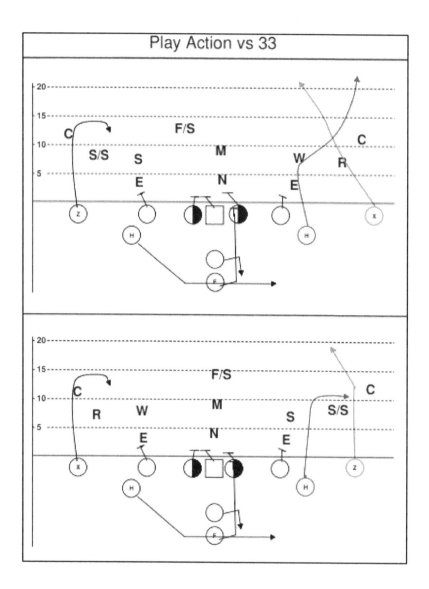

- *The Verticals off the Zone Read* will always cause 3 Shell secondary problems and it gives us another home run opportunity.

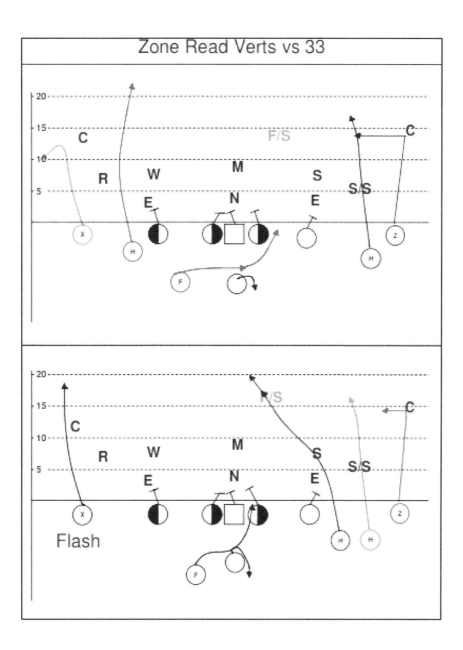

Zone Read Verts vs 33

The Dragon Package provides some effective and simple RPOs.

- *Empty Right Dragon Pop Right.* The Tailback or Number 3 to the field runs his stretch route and looks for the ball. The MLB will have a tough time getting there but if he does it's QB Draw. If the LBs slide to the 3 receiver side, the QB goes "Opposite" and throws it to the 2 receiver side. The number 2 to the boundary just runs his Seam Route.

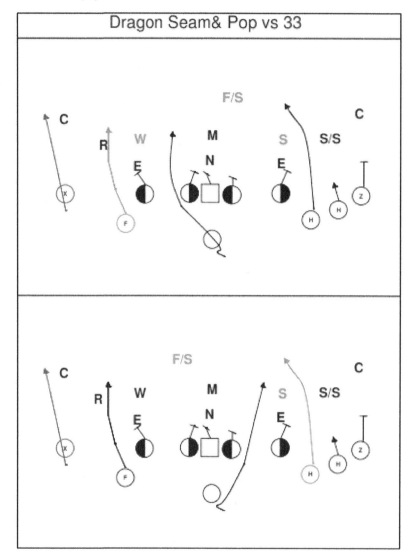

Attacking the 33 Stack Defense with high percentage pass game while throwing in a few deep shots will give the defense nightmares because they can't defend both an effective run game AND an effective pass game.

Attacking Goal Line Defenses

The Triple Gun is a goal line to goal line offense. There is no need fpr a special goal line package. The Triple Gun doesn't need s special Red Zone Package either but there are certain Red Zone considerations that should be covered.

Thoughts on The Red Zone Attack.

- Make a determination of whether it's 4 Down Territory or 3 Down Territory. In other words, will you kick a Field Goal on 4th and short or go for it. So we decide prior to calling the first play in the Red Zone what we will do on 4th down. This is a rule of thumb not etched in stone but a good guideline. If the Field Goal will add a possession to your lead, then kick it. So a 7 point lead can go to 10 kick it. But if it does not, go for it. You have a 3 point lead, go for it (unless it's late in the game). It's the same if you're behind. If a Field Goal reduces the number of possessions to get the lead kick it as long as you have the time to have those possessions.

- The Post/Out Play Action Pass from Wingover is especially good because Wingover is a great Red Zone run formation. The 6th lineman gives you extra pass protection as well and you have a 3 level read for the Quarterback.

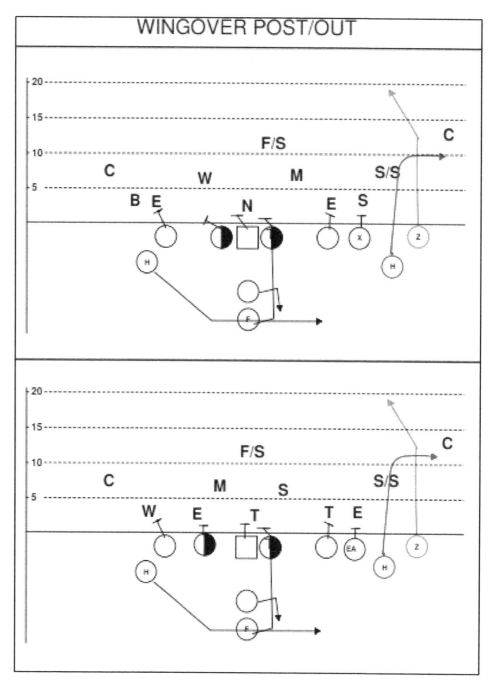

- The Stretch Pass is good in the Red Zone but not on the Goal Line.

- The Empty Dragon Package is an excellent Red Zone RPO. The Empty Set Spreads the Defense out so the QB Draw has a great chance BUT if Defense has left Flash or the Bubble open, the QB has an easy throw.

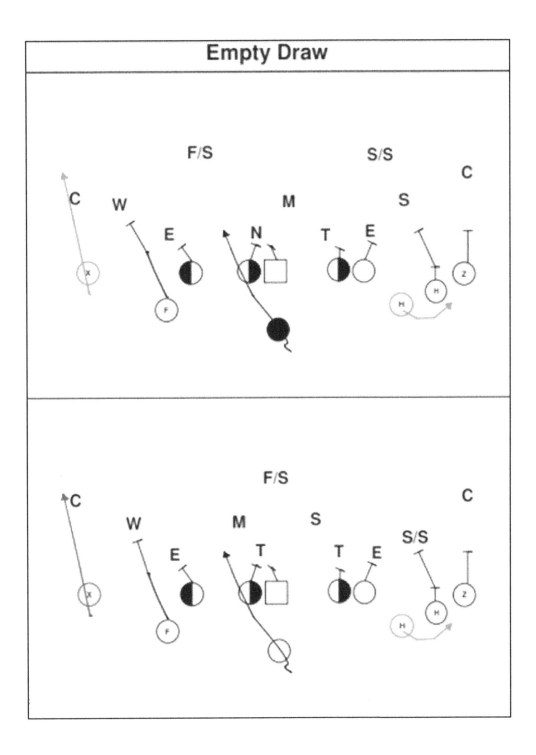

- The Quarterback Draw from Trips is also good with a Bubble Screen against a loaded box.

These are some special thoughts on the Red Zone but all our base offense is great starting with Gun Triple and Wingover gives us a more physical front.

The Triple Screen is also effective in the Red Zone effective.

Now let's talk Goal Line Offense.

Triple Gun Offense on the Goal Line. There is no better offense on the Goal Line than The Triple Gun Offense. It is very effective, and it is 4 down territory because it produces TOUCHDOWNS! It's so effective because it has such a diverse cache of weapons that are effective in a goal line situation.

- *It all Starts with Gun Triple.* The Gun Triple with the Hand Off Key Blocked Rule is very good because it's a built-in answer to edge pressure. But we also like it from Wingover because it stretches the HOK and adds another physical player to the offense .
- *The Quarterback ISO is also effective because we're blocking the HOK.* The Tailback becomes the lead blocker and the QB can just run to daylight. Plus the cutback is available.
- *The Jet Sweep Lead from Wingover.* Using Wingover and tagging the Jet Sweep "Lead" adds 2 extra blockers to the play which makes the Jet Sweep an effective Goal Line Play
- *The Half Reverse has a Place.* The Half Reverse can be an effective play because it's not something a goal line defense prepares for. I've heard coaches say if that's the way they have to score, I'll give them that one. I say, thanks I'll take it.
- *The Hammer Package is an effective change up.* The key is to have the personnel to man the Hammer Formation, it requires 7 Offensive Linemen and 2 H Back or Tight End types. The plays are Double Tailback ISO at the point of attack.

The Triple Gun Pass Game is very effective on the Goal line. Many Goal line Defenses forget about the pass game and just focus on the running game. Here are some of our favorite passes.

- *Jet Naked is a simple RPO.* We like this out of the Wide Jack Formation. The Quarterback has a RPO on the corner with the Wide Receivers Corner Route. If the CB runs with the Jet motion, the corner route by the Wide Receiver will be wide open because the WR has leverage on the CB but if the CB stays, the QB attacks the perimeter.

- *The Quick Game Fade is great against a overmatched Cornerback.* The key is to isolate the CB to make it a one-on-one match up. It's also great in The Red Zone.
- *The Quick Game Slice/Corner is a great Goal Line pass.* This gives the QB an easy read onside while giving a Boot Option backside.

The Triple Gun Goal Line Attack is very simple but also very effective. The key is always being able to execute a handful of diverse plays very well.

Coming Out Offense

Coming out offense is a very important offensive series. Every offensive coordinator would love to direct a 99-yard drive but the reality is the first objective is to get a 1st down.

Our plan for Coming Out Offense is:

- Draw the Defense offsides to make it 1st and 5. This means using a deceptive cadence. We liked using a long count which meant we didn't use motion. So, 1st could be "No Mo QB ISO"
- Other plays we could run with "No Mo" are Gun Triple, Stud Option, Hammer TB Double ISO. and the Quick Game vs a loaded box.
- A formation I like in this situation is Wingover because it stretches the defensive front.
- On 4th Down if we're not at least at the 7 yard line, I give thought to taking a Safety. Why? Because inside the 7 the defense has a shorter distance to block the kick and get a touchdown. Even with a decent punt, our opponent is in Field Goal range and 3 points. Plus, we'll be in tight punt formation which has a tougher time covering the punt and gives the defense a greater chance of a good return. But if you give up 2 points, you get a free kick from the 20 with no chance of a punt block.

We practiced "Coming Out Offense" every Thursday and Friday for a 5 minute period (not counting the punt and taking a safety).

Clutch Offense

Clutch Offense is used at the end of the half when you have to score to win the game. The plays that make up Clutch Offense are just those used to stop the clock. Once the clock is stopped, you can use the entire playbook.

Here are some key factors to consider running Clutch Offense:

- Do you need a touchdown or a field goal?
- How far do you have to go? If you only need a field goal subtract the number of yards that your kicker is a safe bet. So if a 37 yard field goal is automatic then subtract 20 yards from the total yards needed for a TD.
- How much time is left in the half?
- How many timeouts do you have?

Procedures for The Triple Gun Clutch Offense:

- The Clutch Formation is Gun (Double Slot) – the offense lines up in this during a "Clutch Clutch Clutch" call.
- The ball will be snapped on the first send unless "On the Whistle"
- The "Numbers Rule" – If the ball carrier is inside the numbers, then get a 1st Down but if the ball carrier is outside the numbers, then get out of bounds.
- If "Spike Spike Spike" is called – everyone lines up where they are on the Line of Scrimmage.
- Note: First Downs only PAUSE the clock so stay in Clutch Offense.

Plays used to Stop the Clock:

- The Fade/Stick Combo – The Fade will provide a downfield throw and will get out of bounds and the Stick is a good out of bounds play.
- The Hitch/Seam Combo – The Hitch to get out of bounds and the Seam to get a first down and get the ball downfield.
- The Gun Triple into the boundary – will get a first down and a pitch may get the ball out of bounds.
- Slot Right or Left Stretch Pass – the out to the boundary will get the Clock stopped.
- The Spike will stop the clock. Only use on 1st or 2nd down or on 3rd down if you if you want to stop the clock for a field goal attempt

- Plays to use once the Clock is stopped. Basically the whole playbook is available as long as you keep in mind to stay with the base personnel and to adhere to the formula for the need for chunk plays.

The Formula for Chunk Plays:

- Time remaining divided by 15 (time to run a play) equals number of plays you can run
- Add 1 play for every time out you have.
- The yards to go divided by the number of plays you can run equals the number of yards per play.
- Example: 60 yards to go with 90 seconds left and 3 timeouts so you can run 9 plays and average 7 yards per play.

Some key Chunk Plays are:

- The Houston Pass from a 3 X 1 set. This pass gives you a shot downfield with the Stretch Route but also an out route to get the ball out of bounds
- Spread Verticals gives you a Fade and a Seam to the boundary which provides 2 downfield throws and a get out of bounds pass.
- Slot Stretch with a Fade/Stick or another Quick Combo to the boundary is also a great choice.

The Triple Gun is the only Option System that gives you a good chance in a 2-minute situation.

Victory Offense

You have the lead, the clock is winding down and all you have to do is finish it off. But how? The Triple has a built-in Victory Offense in its option attack and in its supplemental runs. But the first thing to figure out is when you can just take a knee.

Formula for Taking a Knee.

- If there is 1:30 left and your opponent has no time outs left – Take a knee.
- If there is 2:00 left and your opponent has no time outs left – run Stud Option with no pitch from unbalanced. Don't get tackled, just slide and stay in bounds. or Stud from Double Slot but no pitches and stay in bounds

If you need a first down. Approach this situation like "Coming Out Offense". Always use a long count to try to draw the defense offsides. We would really like a 1st and 5 situation. Quarterback ISO is a great play in this situation

- The Hammer Package is very useful in this situation. Especially in a 1st & 5 situation. Any time is good to give to your Tailback behind a big O. Line is sound.
- Third and Long. This is a tough call. We're talking 3rd & 7. We like a high percentage pass or a Screen or a QB Draw.

Key Coaching Points:

- Hold the ball with 2 hands – ball security is the most important thing.
- Use all the clock on every snap.
- Stay in Bounds.
- O. Line hold your water.
- Always get up slowly and unpile slowly.
- Celebrate with class

Chapter 17
Some Final Thoughts

Now that you've read this book, studied the many diagrams, and viewed the video, you're ready to be a "True Triple Gunner". Now you know the origins of the Triple Gun and how my interaction with so many great coaches contributed to the building of the Triple Gun Offense. The Triple Gun Offense was the blending of numerous ideas and concepts that I discovered on my football journey into one simple form of offense.

Of course, the key element of this offense was the principle of "Strategic Flexibility" or the ability of one play to morph into another play after the snap of the ball into another play based on the defensive reaction. The Triple Gun is an entire offense built on this principle.

Football is moving further and further in that direction. The number of plays will shrink but their ability to change post snap will grow. The future success in football will be to play fast because of the simplicity of the play sheet. The use of formations and motions will grow and add to Defensive Coordinator nightmares.

Thank You for your interest in the Triple Gun Offense and have great success.

APPENDIX
Always Have a Second Half Surprise

The question of how to game plan or how to prepare your call sheet always comes up. Everyone has their own method and there no right or wrong way to do it.

Bill Walsh & his West Coast disciples always script the first 20 to 25 plays. That certainly worked for Coach Walsh.

Paul Johnson, on the other hand, doesn't even use any play sheet. He knows his Spread Option Attack so well he doesn't need one.

I had the privilege of working for a genius, Tubby Raymond, who knew the Delaware Wing T so well he never used a play sheet either.

The Triple Gun is based on "Strategic Flexibility" so the plays change *after* the snap based on defensive reaction so having an intricate multi-colored play sheet is a necessity. (I also never covered my mouth when I called a play). What I did carry was a card with unusual formations (ie: Bunch Empty) so I would remember to use them. The basic plays never changed from game to game just the wrapping paper.

So what is the correct way? Whatever way works for you. But here are some ideas that fit any play calling system:

1. Attack with a lot of formations early so you know how they are going to line up.
2. Only do what you can execute.
3. Play to your strengths - "If you have a cannon shoot it" Never let a defense take your cannon away.
4. Be prepared for everything – how a team played vs one team doesn't guarantee that's how they'll play you.

The Second Half Surprise

A simple stratagem that I've always had in my bag tricks is "the second half surprise" In other words, I always saved something a little different for the start of the second half. This was effective because our opponents had to figure out a solution and communicate an adjustment amid the heat of the game on the sideline rather during the calm of the halftime locker room.

Examples of Halftime Surprises:

1. A unique formation or formations on offense.
2. A defense blitz that they haven't seen in the first half.
3. A change in Tempo either speeding up or slowing down.
4. A change in style going to more power or more option. On defense coming out with a heavy blitz game.

Now because you have this surprise available doesn't mean you have to use it. If you have the game under control, you can keep the surprise for another day but one of the keys is to always control the first 6 minutes of the second half regardless of the score. The Second Half Surprise can help you ignite your team in the second half & finish the game strong.

Analytics vs Common Sense

The big Buzz Word in sports today is "Analytics" – percentage & probabilities. Every call a coach makes is backed up by analytics. In other words if I go for a 4th & 1 – analytics say that is a good call. However, analytics don't tell the whole story, especially in football. Good old common sense deserves a place in play calling as well as analytics. Here are a couple of examples of analytics backfiring.

Early in the season LSU was playing Texas in a close game. The Longhorns drove deep into LSU territory inside the Tiger 5 yard line. UT's coach, Tom Herman decided to go for it on 4th down even though they hadn't gained a foot on 3 downs. LSU rose up & stuffed the Horns & no points for UT. Later in the game. The exact same scenario came up & Coach Herman did the exact same thing with exactly the same result. No points for UT. The final score was 45-38. If UT had kicked 2 FGs, they would only have needed a FG at the end of the game to win not a TD to tie.

Navy was playing Memphis & leading 20-14 in the 3rd quarter. The ball was on the Navy 29 yard line. It was 4th & 1. Navy loves to go for it on 4th down but Memphis was undefeated at the time & their defense was playing Navy tough especially in short yardage situations. Navy goes for it & gets stuffed giving Memphis the ball on the Navy 29 yard line! Memphis capitalizes on the short field & takes the lead 21-20. The final score Memphis 32 – Navy 23.

Now, I'm not second guessing Coach Herman or Coach Ken, there are many other similar decisions that go wrong but I am criticizing the criteria for the decisions.

Football is a game of people & matchups not percentages & averages. You may make 4th & goal 90% of the time vs Texas Tech, Rice & North Texas but NOT vs LSU! Analytics doesn't know the guys you're playing against. On 4th & 1, Coach Ken may make it 92% of the time vs Holy Cross but not vs Memphis who has been playing them tough all day. It's about people.

Also analytics doesn't take into account the weather. Would you make the same decision in a hurricane as you would on a sunny day.

Usually your gut tells you if you're moving the ball well enough o go for it or are you struggling. For example, Navy was struggling on offense vs Memphis so even if the got the first down, they were only on their 29 yard line. The more experience a coach has the more likely he will sense this is a time to punt. Navy only scored 3 more points the rest of the game.

The numbers that I go by are the Four Meaningful Stats:

1. Score 25 points – Win 88% of your games
2. Hold Opponent to less than 16 points & win 92% of your games
3. Score a Non-Offensive TD & win 90% of your games
4. Have a +2 Turnover Margin & Win 98% of your games

These Stats are the most significant numbers. These Stats matter and so does Common Sense.

Take a listen to the weekly Podcast we did on this topic:

https://compusportsmedia.com/new-podcast-series-from-tony-demeo/

Aristotle and Coaching Football

What does an ancient Greek Philosopher know about coaching football? How can studying Aristotle help us get a first down? Was he an offensive guy or defensive?

Aristotle said "The purpose of education is to pass on values" There is no doubt in my mind football is a big part of a young man's education. It is a *part* of a young man's education not apart from his education.

A coach's job is to pass on values to his players. No sport involves more values than football:

1. The value of hard work. If a player works hard in football, there will be a place for him on the football team. It may "just" be a special team's player but every spot is important. He may not be a great athlete but his heart & determination will get him on the field. This is not the case in other sports. Hard Work Works.

2. The value of courage. The physicality of football requires courage. Golf takes great skill but not a lot of physical courage. I'm a big proponent of safety but the collisions in football is almost a "rite of passage" to a young man. Overcoming fear of contact is a lesson unique to football.

3. The value of perseverance. The ability to keep giving all you have when all seems lost. If you want to know who the competitors are, watch film of a team when they are behind. One of our mottoes was "The Fourth Quarter is Ours" We were always 60 minute men.

4. The value of preparation. Football is a sport that takes a tremendous commitment to off-season conditioning. The strength & conditioning programs are grueling both physically & mentally. The great Vince Lombardi said "Fatigue makes cowards of us all" The job of a coach is to make sure the team never gets fatigued through proper preparation.

5. The value of Teamwork. No value is more important to learn in today's "Me, Me, Me" society. The sacrifice of individual goals for the good of the team is one of the greatest lessons that a player can learn. Players must develop the "WE not Me" attitude for their team to be successful.

These values create the foundation for success throughout a player's life.

Aristotle also said "We are what we repeatedly do. **Excellence** is not an act, but a habit." If a player can learn that excellence can't be turned on & off like a faucet. Excellence must become a way of life. Regardless if he's in the classroom, the weight room, the practice field or in a championship game, he is about excellence. Excellence is about what you become not what you receive. Teaching excellence is big part of a players' education. Maybe the biggest part.

So studying a little Aristotle & passing it along to your team might just get you that edge you're looking for.

Blueprint to a Dynasty

With the New England Patriot victory in Super Bowl LI, there has been a lot of talk about dynasties. There have been some great dynasties in all sports not just football. The Red Auerbach Boston Celtics was a great NBA dynasty. The NY Yankees had a couple of dynasties in the early 50s & the late 90s. The Lombardi led Packers were a dynasty in the NFL as was the Bill Walsh coached 49ers. Of course the Jordan/Jackson Bulls in the NBA has to be included. In college sports the epitome of a dynasty would be John Wooden's UCLA Bruins & Geno Auriammo's UCONN's women's basketball program.

There seems to be some commonality to each of these dynasties and a specific blueprint to the building of a dynasty regardless of the sport. Let's take a look at the commonality: **CONTINUITY IN THE COACHING STAFF.** All of these dynasties held on to their head coach. The Celtics Red Auerbach left as the coach but stayed on as the General Manager after turning over the coaching to his protégé' Bill Russell who kept the Auerbach Philosophy & System intact. The Yankees were led by Casey Stengel in the 50s & Joe Torre in the 90s. The Packers had the inVinceble Lombardi at the helm & Bill Walsh was the Head Coach for the 49ers & then passed the torch to George Seifert but stayed involved helping his successor with the West coast Offense. And of course most recently The Patriots have the great Bill Belichick leading the to 5 Super Bowl victories. So the **Leadership** factor was a big part of the dynasty creation.

What about the other factors in the Building of a Dynasty. What are some of the key ingredients & steps to put this together? Let's take a look:

1. **The System** – Each **of the** dynasties had a specific system in place that magnified the ability of their players. The Packers had -the Green Bay Sweep that led the potent ground game that not only led the attack but kept their defense off the field by controlling the clock. Bill Belichick has a system in place that he plugs in players that immediately become productive. Let's look at the Super Bowl this past year. Tom Brady's receivers were Julian Edlemann, a QB in college, Chris Hogan, a lacrosse player who played only one year of college football, an undrafted Danny Ammendola and the guy who set the Super Bowl record for the most receptions in a game (14) & scored 3 TDs James White their 3rd string Tailback! This crew led by a former 6th round Tom Terrific Brady set a Super Bowl record of 466 yards passing while

coming back from a 28-3 deficit. A great system kept in place gets better & better as the years roll on because of BANKED REPS. The more experience the team gains using the system the greater the team performs in critical situations. So in Super Bowl LI when the Patriots had to execute coming from 25 points down they could. The 49ers had Bill Walsh's West Coast Offense led by Joe Montana who was 3-0 in Super Bowls. Montana a 3rd round draft pick & Brady a 6th round pick both benefitted from great coaches & great systems. The Bulls & Michael Jordan were the benefitted from Phil Jackson's Triangle Offense. The great Michael Jordan was in the league for 6 years with no rings until Zen Master Phil introduced Mike to the Triangle Offense. So having a great SYSTEM is a critical step.

2. **THE PLAYERS-** Getting players that fit the system is the next critical part of the equation. Like Red Auerbach said "I don't want to have the 5 best players on the court, I want the best *five* on the court" So for example if you're a Flex-Bone team it would be silly to recruit a great passing QB who came in 3rd racing a pregnant women.

Casey Stengel always had players that could play numerous positions. For example, Gil McDougal would routinely play every infield position in the same series.
Vince Lombardi wanted running backs that weren't the fastest or the strongest. Lombardi wanted backs who would block for each other and run the ball with vision and could "Run to Daylight" which was the essence of The Lombardi Sweep.
Bill Walsh was looking for a QB with a quick release and leader under pressure and Joe Montana was the perfect fit winning 3 Super Bowls.
Bill Belichick was 5-11 in his first year with Patriots and in his second year his star QB Drew Bledsoe went down BUT along came Tom Brady and The Pats were off on the path to a dynasty and Drew Bledsoe was on his way to Buffalo.

The players must also be "We guys not me guys" In team sports, team players win. Guys who care about individual stats don't win championships. Larry Bird said "Some guys put up numbers and some guys win championships" Red Auerbach developed the 6th man concept and used one of his best players to play it. All Star John Havlicek was the Celtics 6th man & gave up a starting position despite being the team's top scorer. Bill Russell a top scorer in college became a defensive ace for the Celts.

The Patriots never feature just one receiver in their attack but rather spread the ball around to all their skill thus making them more effective.

The Yankees platooned guys like Hank Bauer & Gene Woodling which reduced their individual stats but the Yankees won 5 straight World Series. Stengel had a system and it worked as long as his players were willing to give up numbers for championships.

Great systems magnify the ability of players & improves the performances of those players. Two of the greatest QBs ever to play in the NFL, Joe Montana & Tom Brady, were not big college stars benefitted from great systems crafted by great coaches: Bill Walsh & Bill Belichick. Also neither of Montana's top 2 receivers, Jerry Rice & John Taylor, even played at DI college football. But were perfect for Bill Walsh's West Coast Offense. Likewise 3 of Tom Brady's record setting Super Bowl receivers were undrafted free agents.

Vince Lombardi won Super Bowl II with a fullback that was cut by the last place team in the league. Chuck Mercein came to the Packers because of a rash of injuries to their running backs & he stepped up to play a major role in The Packers Championship run & Super Bowl victory.

3. **Patience-** The last piece of the puzzle is patience by the administration. It takes time to put a system in place and get the right players in place. Bill Belichick was fired in Cleveland with basically the same system that propelled the Patriots into dynasty status. He never had a chance to get a QB in place to run   the   system.

Casey Stengel was fired by the Brooklyn Dodgers & Boston Braves before finding the Bombers from The Bronx.

John Wooden went 14 years before he won a National Championship with The UCLA Bruins and the proceeded to define dynasty by winning 10 yes 10 National championships in 12 years!

Bill Walsh didn't show his genius until his 3rd year in his great run with the 49ers. Walsh was only 8-24 in his first 2 seasons and then had the breakthrough year winning the Super Bowl in year 3.

So these three ingredients are essential if your goal is to build a dynasty. Oh and by the way you also have to have a little luck on your side.

How the Triple Gun Offense Increases Depth

Every football is painfully aware of how devastating an injury to a key player can destroy a team's potential for success. The Triple Gun Offense doesn't provide a miracle cure for a sprained ankle it just provides more ankles.

One of the great advantages of a simple offense is that the players can master multiple positions so you can always have your best healthy eleven on the field. The Triple Gun playlist is very comprehensive but also very small. Our first year at the University of Charleston we were picked last in our conference and had a small group of experienced players so the simplicity of the Triple Gun saved the day. Freshmen learned the system faster and the vets mastered more than one spot. The result was the single-biggest turnaround in conference history.

The offensive line is completely interchangeable. The Wing T requires distinct guards and tackles but the Triple Gun guards and tackles use exactly the same techniques so if an OT goes down in the middle of the 2nd quarter and your next best linemen is a guard – no problem – just slide him in. We also train multiple snappers just in case our center gets nicked.

Though the skill spots aren't as interchangeable – it's close. Here are some of our "Hybrids":

1. OT/TE - Because of scholarship limitations it's difficult to carry many Tight Ends on a DII roster. So any time we went unbalanced (wing over etc.) with a TE we just used a 6th offensive lineman. He is ineligible anyway so why not use a bigger body and better blocker?
2. WR/TE – A big wide receiver can be used as a backside TE in a 2 TE set just to stretch the flank. We usually did this vs an 8 man front.
3. TE/WR – Conversely you could take a talented TE who has some speed and use him as a WR.
4. TE/Slot – A more natural hybrid is a TE/Slot. The TE's blocking would be the same as a Slot but you would have a bigger player doing it. We like this when running our Stud Option when we double team the end man on the LOS. My first year at UC we used our TE a lot in this role.
5. WR/Slot – We also did this the entire first year at UC. We took talented WRs and used them as slots. They only had to learn a couple of blocks and if they were struggling we could go to our TE. The upside was the great speed and

receiving ability they brought to the dance. Again we always had our best on the field.

6. Slots/WRs – Later in the program we had some slots that had great receiving ability and used that ability by splitting them out as WRs. It took little teaching to widen a slot & throw him the hitch.

7. Slots/TBs – Using a talented slot as a TB is also extremely simple. In our last game in 2005 our outstanding TB was sick & our only backup was a slot. We got by with him rushing for 143 yards. As we evolved over the years and our use of Empty formation increased the slot and tailback position were interchangeable.

8. TB/Slot – This was something my OC Ralph Isernia really liked because we had an outstanding blocking TB so if we were having an issue blocking we moved the TB to slot. If you have more than one good TB this is a way to get them both in the game. Again the evolution to Empty really blurred the lines between these positions unlike the Flex-Bone where the fullback & slots are very different.

So as you prepare for your upcoming season, plan who you need to cross train to always be able to have your best on the field.

It All Starts With Discipline

Over the years I've given many clinics on offensive football. From The Multi-Bone to The Triple Gun, Xs & Os were always a significant part of our success because we were always unique in our approach. Teams only had a few days to prepare for us. So I'm aware of the difference Xs & Os can make.

I'm also aware of the importance of the Jimmys & the Joes. Having talented players is an absolute necessity to building a winning program. We always recruited talented players but players that were also team oriented. All you had to do is watch our skill guys block & you could see: The Team Comes First.

But there is a foundation that isn't as sexy as Xs & Os or as cool as recruiting but even MORE essential to building a program: **DISCIPLINE.** For some reason coaches don't like to discuss discipline. For some reason some school boards don't like to enforce discipline. Parents LOVE discipline except for their child. Every successful coach or administrator knows: **Discipline is the Foundation for Success.**

Then why is there such a reluctance to teach discipline? Here are a few reasons:

1. Everyone wants to be liked. Everyone wants to be the cool guy. So some coaches are reluctant to teach something that might upset someone. The **need** to be liked is one of the greatest weaknesses any leader can have.
2. Coaches don't realize or don't communicate that "Discipline is something done **for** the player not **to** the player. Discipline is not harassment. It's teaching young to do the right thing at the right time every time.
3. Lack of school board backing. People on the school board want to be liked as well and they have zero skin in the game. But regardless of the school board, the coach always has the power of The Bench.

When you look at the successful coaches, regardless of the level, high school to the Pros, they are all teachers of discipline. Their teaching styles may differ but the subject was the same. Vince Lombardi & Tom Landry when it came to style. Lombardi was bombastic while Landry rarely raised his voice but both were teachers of discipline.

Last season, James Franklin chased down one of his players for walking off the field without shaking his opponents hand after a frustrating loss. Franklin took a loss & made it a teachable moment that will hatch many wins in the future. James Franklin also benched 2 key players prior to the 2016 Rose Bowl for breaking team rules.

Obviously James Franklin knows the importance of discipline & has restored a culture of discipline at Penn St. & restored it to a Top 10 program.

Soft spoken John Wooden had some of the most disciplined teams in the history of College Basketball. A winner of 10 National Championships in 12 years, Wooden began each basketball season by teaching his players how to put on their sweat socks & sneakers so they wouldn't get blisters. Doing things the right way every time starts with little things.

You can tell when a team is not disciplined. When things go wrong, how do they react? There is an old saying "If you want to find out what's in an orange, squeeze it" If you want to see what team is made of, watch react when things are not going their way. Do they bow up? Or do they unravel? Do they come together of fall apart? I saw a team that was 4-0 going into Saturday. They got in a dogfight & completely unraveled. They got 4, count them 4, unsportsmanlike conduct penalties. They could not focus & wound up getting blown out & their high-powered offense held to only 7 points. Their problem was not Xs & Os nor Jimmys & Joes — it was lack of discipline that was exposed when the kitchen got hot.

So before you worry about an RPO or a Zone Blitz, build your team's discipline & you'll have the foundation to build everything else. Remember, teaching the importance of daily discipline is one of the greatest gifts you can give a player.

Sometimes Talent Can Kill a Team

Every coach wishes he had more talent. "If we just had more speed" or "if we just had more size" I have heard those groans before and even uttered a few myself. But be careful what you wish for because you just might get it.

I have witnessed winning programs be destroyed by a talented malcontent. Sure he had great speed & could catch anything in the air but his ego was so off the charts that the team concept went down the drain and a winning program become mediocre overnight. The disease of me is powerful indeed.

There are countless examples of the Me First Club. One glaring example is The NY Knicks. In their Golden Era 1969 – 1973 they were the model of teamwork & won two Championships led by Willis Reid & Walt Frazier. They had a great cast around them and were coached by a team first guy Red Holtzman. On that team was a back-up forward named Phil Jackson who was absorbing the formula Red was teaching.

Fast forward to 2012, the Knicks had redefined mediocrity for decades but now things finally seemed to be turned around. They had a bright young coach, Mike D'Antoni and some talented players they had a surprising catalyst named Jeremy Lin that led them to 7 straight wins & created a buzz called "Linsanity". With Lin in the lineup the Knicks were 9-3 but Lin & D;Antoni's style didn't sit well with their talented star Carmelo Anthony. D'Antoni believed in team play & the pick & roll offense. Melo believed in isolating himself one on one. The Knicks sided with Melo & fired D'Antoni. They went with Melo's style & back to mediocrity.

When Phil Jackson took over the Bulls, they had the talented Michael Jordan but in the 6 years with arguably the best player in the NBA, they had zero championships. Jackson sold Jordan on the Triangle Offense which got his teammates involved in scoring and the Bulls became a dynasty. So when talent is directed & incorporated in a team concept; great things happen. When talent has the "Me first" attitude it's off to Palookaville.

I was always about using talent with a team concept. We called it "We Not Me" – it was "the team comes first" attitude. We were always complimented on how well our skill players blocked for one another. I believe that was a manifestation of the "We Not Me" attitude. We developed an offensive system where all the skill players shared the rock. This was a great way to develop morale while making us more difficult to defend. The result was a team that functioned at a high level of performance and won more games over our 6 years at the University of Charleston than any 6 years in the school's history. In our first season at UC we had the greatest single season turnaround in the history of the conference. How did this happen? Simple – TEAMWORK.

Never, ever underestimate the value of synergy. The 1+1=3 model. The total is greater than the sum of the individual parts. To achieve this model you must reward team play. You must recruit team players and weed out divas & selfish players because no matter how talented, divas will bring you down. How many championships did Ocho Cinco win with the Bengals? How many coaches did strong-armed QB Jeff George get fired?

A great example of teamwork in college football are the service academies. Watching those teams play is watching synergy in action. Army's great turnaround in 2017 was just an outstanding coaching job by Jeff Monken & his staff. They did it with a QB that couldn't pass. Impossible in the era of The Spread Offense & RPOs but no one told the Cadets that. They finished 10-3 & won the Commander & Chief Trophy.

The guys that win championships are the guys that are willing to put their egos on a shelf, roll up their sleeves and get after it every day. I have a saying:

To Be #1 You Must Be One

You can take that saying to the bank.

The Key to a Successful System

I believe in having a "System" of offense. Whether it's the Wing T, The Run & Shoot, The Flexbone, The Air Raid or of course The Triple Gun. Systems are always more effective than a goody bag full of non-related or loosely related plays. However systems can go bad if you are not careful. Here are a few maintenance tips to keep your system sharp:

1. Don't let your system get fat by continuously adding new plays. The fewer the plays, the more reps your players will get. The more reps, the better the execution. Execution wins games. I always say "I'd rather run a lousy play great than a great play lousy" There is a tendency that as you get comfortable with your system, you look to add new concepts that are radically different from your core scheme. This will snowball into more plays & sure disaster. Remember a good system is the solution.

2. Adapt your system to your personnel. Don't change the menu just feature the part of the menu that showcases your talent. For example, my first year at The University of Charleston, we had a dropback QB who had never run the option. We did not abandon The Triple Gun, we just used more of the passing game and had our QB use a "Pitch unless…" thought process on the option.

3. Your "answer plays" should get the ball to your playmaker. If you are running the triple option & your dive back is your stud, you can NEVER let the defense take him out of the game merely by giving your QB pull reads. Instead use some predetermined Give reads by blocking the HOK with a Slot or Tight End. Also use him as a Pitchman like we do with our Flip Triple. The key is to **GET HIM THE BALL.** The same is true with a great wide out or slot.

4. Keep techniques to a minimum. Make sure you can use these techniques in as many of your schemes as possible. For cxample, in the Triple Gun Offense, we use the same techniques on The Gun Triple, Flip Triple, Whirley Triple, Speed Option, & Stud Option. That is a lot of plays with the same techniques. We also use almost the same techniques on QB ISO. When you minimize the amount of techniques to master & maximize their use, your practice time grows more productive.

5. Make as many positions as possible interchangeable. In the Triple Gun, the Slots & the tailback are interchangeable. Up front the entire offensive line spots are interchangeable as well. So if one of our linemen goes down, our

6th best can jump in. It's the same in the backfield. This really increases the depth of the team & always puts the best players on the field.

6. Always have Clock Control ability. To win games, your offense must be capable of slowing the game down vs a superior team and speeding it up vs a less talented team. Your offense must also have a way of finishing a game when you have the lead & coming from behind when you are trailing. A good System can do both.

7. Create reactions not decisions. Use unless rules to eliminate doubt. As I always say "If you think, you stink" The team that plays fast with more certainty usually wins. Treat the game as martial arts not chess. Choices should be intuitive.

Concluding, a successful system can score 25+ against the best on your schedule without turning the ball over. That's the real measure of the system.

Winning the Six Minute Games

Everybody has a system of Game-planning. Some coaches script the first 15 or 20 plays, some coaches like Paul Johnson wing it based on his experience. Coaches color code & highlighters became their life-blood. But how about time-management?

Well of course everyone has their 2 minute drill ready or their 4 minute victory offense and the word "Tempo" is a popular buzzword used hundreds of times per game by the "experts". But as someone once said is that all there is?

I had the great fortune of working with a strategic genius, who could have also been a stand-up comic, Jim Valvano. Jimmy used the clock like Picasso used a pastel. He used up-tempo or slow down stall ball based on opponent or situation. His adage that I took to heart was: "He who controls the pace, wins the race" – basically when facing a superior opponent – shorten the game BUT if you had the superior team then put your foot on the gas & make them play. I soaked up everything I could in the 4 years I worked with him. I've spoken often about idea of Tempo-Control & even had a chapter about it in my book: Commonsense Rules for Everyday Leaders. (See "Tempo is not a philosophy, it's a tool to use" earlier in this book).

Another great piece of Valvano Wisdom that I used throughout my career was: "The Six Minute Games". Even though "V" was a Hoops Coach, there were many of his ideas that were very applicable to football.

The Six Minute Games

In every game there are 4 key Six Minute Periods that your team must control. They are:

1. The first 6 minutes of the game.
2. The 6 minutes prior to the end of the half
3. The first 6 minutes of the second half
4. The last 6 minutes of the game

Those were the 4 areas that Jim thought you had to control.

This was my approach to a game using these 4 Six Minute periods:

1. The first 6 minutes of the game was really our real scouting report. We were always unique on offense so how a team defensed a previous opponent didn't

tell us too much about how they were going to defend us. So we always attacked with a broad front, showing a wide variety of formations & motions. Once we knew how they were going to line up, the fun began & we attacked based on their adjustments.

2. The last 6 minutes of the half was designed to go into the locker room with Big Mo going with us. But as Harry Gamble used to warn me when I worked for him at Penn: "Don't lose the game at the half" Great advice. In other words, don't be careless with the ball. However, if we could get in position for a score, we'd go for it. But if we were struggling on "O" we were not going to let them get the ball back.

3. The first 6 minutes of the second half. Time for "The Second Half Surprise" – I've done an entire article on this tactic (See "Always have a Second Half Surprise" earlier in the Appendix). The idea is to use something that our opponent did not discuss at half-time. The longer you can use your "Surprise" the more likely your opponent's players will forget their half-time adjustments. The key is to gain control of the second half during this period. If you have the lead, the goal is to use the clock while adding a possession lead. For example if you're up 7, a field goal adds a possession to your lead. Conversely if you are trailing, you must get the lead or at least make it a one possession closer to the lead. This period will set the tone for the second half.

4. The final 6 minutes is the period you either get the lead while killing the clock or maintain the lead or add a possession to your lead while killing the clock. The most important part of this period is killing the clock regardless of your situation UNLESS you are behind by 2 possessions. Then it's high tempo to cut it to one possession as quickly as possible. But the entire game-plan should get your team in position to win the game with 6 minutes to go. So ideally, at this point in the game, your team either has the lead or is in one possession from the lead.

This was a very helpful blueprint for me, as a head coach, to break a game down into more manageable segments. Using this along with use of Meaningful Stats help us with four College turnarounds.

Epilogue

I retired after the 2010 season at The University of Charleston. We had a nice run there going 43 – 23 in our 6 years there which was very satisfying after taking over a program literally in shambles.

I finished my career of 25 years as a head college football coach at 137 – 108 – 4 record and was honored to be inducted in the Iona College Hall of Fame and The Mercyhurst University Hall of Fame. But more importantly, I really love seeing the successful lives that my players have enjoyed. Their accomplishments are amazing and I am always thankful that I was so fortunate to be surrounded by so many winners.

Since retiring I have been doing Triple Gun camps and installing the Triple Gun at high schools across the country. I've done 77 camps and 66 of those teams went to the playoffs.

My last bit of advice is this: football is a vehicle to teach excellence. Once your players develop the craving for excellence, everything else falls into place.

Video QR Codes
Gun Triple

Triple - HOK blocked.WMV - YouTube

m.youtube.com

GUN TRIPLE VS 3-4 - YouTube

m.youtube.com

GUN TRIPLE VS EVEN DEFENSE - YouTube

m.youtube.com

June 19, 2020 - YouTube

m.youtube.com

Counter Triples

EMPTY TRIPLE PITCH - YouTube

m.youtube.com

Gun Flip Triple on Vimeo

vimeo.com

SLOT FLIP TRIPLE - YouTube

m.youtube.com

Whirley Option Pitch.WMV - YouTube

m.youtube.com

Double Options

June 18, 2020 - YouTube

www.youtube.com

ZONE READ FROM EMPTY - YouTube

m.youtube.com

Empty Zone Read - YouTube

www.youtube.com

DOUBLE OPTION TO ENDS - YouTube

m.youtube.com

Flip Zone Read.WMV - YouTube

www.youtube.com

Triple - HOK blocked.WMV - YouTube

m.youtube.com

SPEED OPTION VS WEAK EAGLE
DEFENSE - YouTube

m.youtube.com

Slot Lt Midline Lead - Give on Vimeo

vimeo.com

Slot Over Zone Read Lead - YouTube

www.youtube.com

Flip Zone Read.WMV - YouTube

m.youtube.com

Double Options (continued)

SPEED OPTION WITH COUNTER LEAD MOTION - YouTube

m.youtube.com

SPEED OPTION AWAY FROM UNBALANCED - YouTube

www.youtube.com

Slot Over Zone Read Lead - YouTube

m.youtube.com

ZONE READ - YouTube

m.youtube.com

ZONE READ - YouTube

www.youtube.com

SPEED OPTION - YouTube

m.youtube.com

Supplemental Runs

INSIDE ZONE WITH FAKE REVERSE - YouTube

www.youtube.com

JET SWEEP FROM EMPTY - YouTube

www.youtube.com

Ends Jet Sweep.WMV - YouTube

www.youtube.com

TD QB ISO 1 - YouTube

m.youtube.com

TD GUN QB ISO 5 - YouTube

m.youtube.com

Half reverse - 2009 season - YouTube

www.youtube.com

HAMMER PACKAGE - ISO AWAY FROM MOTION - YouTube

www.youtube.com

QB iso off jet motion - YouTube

www.youtube.com

Supplemental Runs (continued)

**9 - 6 WIDE JACK JET SWEEP RT
on Vimeo**

vimeo.com

TD QB ISO 1 - YouTube

www.youtube.com

QB ISO - YouTube

www.youtube.com

QB ISO WITH TRIPLE ACTION - YouTube

m.youtube.com

QB iso off jet motion - YouTube

m.youtube.com

Quick Game

**QUICK GAME - BOOT TO TRIPS
- YouTube**

www.youtube.com

TD GUN FADE SEAM - YouTube

www.youtube.com

Fade Stick - YouTube

www.youtube.com

**QUICK GAME - COVER 2 FADE
- YouTube**

www.youtube.com

June 18, 2020 - YouTube

www.youtube.com

August 24, 2020 - YouTube

www.youtube.com

Motion Hitch.WMV - YouTube

www.youtube.com

Quick Game (continued)

**Quick Game Slice/Corner - sBoot
on Vimeo**

vimeo.com

11 - 11Gun Quick Slice Corner on Vimeo

vimeo.com

**QUICK GAME-SLICE/CORNER
- YouTube**

www.youtube.com

Play Action Passes

12 - 5 Gun Crossers Pass on Vimeo

vimeo.com

Jet Crossers Pass - YouTube

www.youtube.com

Jet Naked on the Goal Line.WMV
- YouTube

www.youtube.com

Wide Jack Jet Naked Keep - YouTube

www.youtube.com

JET PA DRAG - YouTube

www.youtube.com

PLAY ACTION CHOICE ROUTE.WMV
- YouTube

www.youtube.com

Play Action Stretch Pass Rt. on Vimeo

vimeo.com

PLAYACTION - FRONTSIDE STRETCH
- YouTube

www.youtube.com

PLAYACTION-STRETCH ROUTE OFF
COUNTER MOTION - You...

www.youtube.com

Play Action Verts vs 4.WMV - YouTube

www.youtube.com

Play Action Passes (continued)

PLAYACTION - FRONTSIDE POST OUT - YouTube

www.youtube.com

PLAYACTION - FRONTSIDE POST WHEEL - YouTube

www.youtube.com

PLAYACTION - FRONTSIDE POST/ WHEEL - YouTube

www.youtube.com

PLAYACTION - STRETCH ROUTE WITH TRIPLE ACTION - Y...

www.youtube.com

PLAYACTION - BACKSIDE POST/WHEEL - YouTube

www.youtube.com

PLAYACTION - BOOT FROM TRIPS - YouTube

www.youtube.com

Playaction off Zone Read - YouTube

www.youtube.com

July 11, 2020 - YouTube

www.youtube.com

PLAYACTION - SWITCH ROUTE WITH ZONE READ ACTION I...

www.youtube.com

Dropback Passes

TD WH STRETCH - YouTube

www.youtube.com

Slot Rt Stretch Pass vs 4 Shell - YouTube

www.youtube.com

13 - 3 Slot RT Stretch Pass Vs 3 Shell Stop on Vi...

vimeo.com

FLASH SCREEN - YouTube

www.youtube.com

13 - 6 Slot Rt Dropback Stretch w Fade Stick Stic...

vimeo.com

July 11, 2020 - YouTube

www.youtube.com

13 - 9 TWINS LT VERTS SLICE vs 44 on Vimeo

vimeo.com

TD Slot Dropback Stretch vs 3 Shell - YouTube

www.youtube.com

Dropback Passes (continued)

July 11, 2020 - YouTube

www.youtube.com

Trips Houston vs 4 Shell - YouTube

www.youtube.com

July 11, 2020 - YouTube

www.youtube.com

July 28, 2020 - YouTube

www.youtube.com

Screens And Draws

TD BACKS LT QB DRAW vs 44 - YouTube

www.youtube.com

BUBBLE SCREEN - YouTube

www.youtube.com

TB Crack Screen away Trips.WMV - YouTube

www.youtube.com

Empty Draw.WMV - YouTube

www.youtube.com

FLIP ICE DRAW - YouTube

www.youtube.com

Gun Triple Flash - YouTube

www.youtube.com

13 Slot Lt Shovel Pass Rt on Vimeo

vimeo.com

14 - 5 Slot Rt Triple Screen Rt Flare on Vimeo

vimeo.com

Screens And Draws (continued)

TB SCREEN.WMV - YouTube

www.youtube.com

TRIPLE SCREEN- TB TO FIELD - YouTube

www.youtube.com

14 - 2 Trips Bubble on Vimeo

vimeo.com

14 - 7 Trips Triple Screen on Vimeo

vimeo.com

Uncovered Pass.WMV - YouTube

www.youtube.com

Game Planning and Attacking Defenses
Clutch Offense

QUICK GAME - STICK ROUTE - YouTube

www.youtube.com

TD Slot Dropback Stretch vs 3 Shell - YouTube

www.youtube.com

13 - 6 Slot Rt Dropback Stretch w Fade Stick Stic...

vimeo.com

TD SPREAD FADE SEAM - YouTube

www.youtube.com

Coming Out Offense

Coming Out Pass - Crossers - Go on Vimeo

vimeo.com

no mo iso.WMV - YouTube

www.youtube.com

15 - 14 TACKLES OVER GUN TRIPLE _ HOK BLK on Vimeo

vimeo.com

15 - 46 WO RT GT Keep on Vimeo

vimeo.com

Game Plan vs 3-4

GUN TRIPLE VS ODD 2009 - YouTube

www.youtube.com

15 - 27 SLOT LT TRIPLE LT vs 34 - Give #2 on Vimeo

vimeo.com

PLAYACTION - STRETCH ROUTE WITH TRIPLE ACTION - Y...

www.youtube.com

PLAYACTION - FRONTSIDE POST OUT - YouTube

www.youtube.com

Game Plan vs 4-3

TD WH STRETCH - YouTube

www.youtube.com

EMPTY TRIPLE PITCH - YouTube

m.youtube.com

DoubleOption.WMV - YouTube

www.youtube.com

Triple - HOK blocked.WMV - YouTube

m.youtube.com

GUN TRIPLE VS EVEN DEFENSE - YouTube

m.youtube.com

Half reverse - 2009 season - YouTube

www.youtube.com

Motion Hitch.WMV - YouTube

www.youtube.com

Game Plan vs 4-3 (continued)

SLOT FLIP TRIPLE - YouTube

m.youtube.com

15 - 12 Whirley Post Wheel on Vimeo

vimeo.com

Game Plan vs 4-4

DOUBLE OPTION TO ENDS - YouTube

m.youtube.com

15 - 20 Seam Hitch vs 44 on Vimeo

vimeo.com

June 18, 2020 - YouTube

www.youtube.com

TD GUN QB ISO 5 - YouTube

www.youtube.com

15 - 17 GUN STUD OPT. VS 44 Pitch on Vimeo

vimeo.com

Gun Triple - Pitch on Vimeo

vimeo.com

12 - 7 JET CROSSERS VS 44 on Vimeo

vimeo.com

PLAYACTION - FRONTSIDE POST WHEEL - YouTube

www.youtube.com

Game Plan vs 4-4 (continued)

GUN TRIPLE FROM PRO - YouTube

www.youtube.com

TD Slot Dropback Stretch vs 3 Shell - YouTube

www.youtube.com

15 - 14 TACKLES OVER GUN TRIPLE _ HOK BLK on Vimeo

vimeo.com

15 - 16 TWINS LT SPEED on Vimeo

vimeo.com

Playaction off Zone Read - YouTube

www.youtube.com

QB iso off jet motion - YouTube

www.youtube.com

Goal Line and Red Zone

TD BACKS LT QB DRAW vs 44 - YouTube

www.youtube.com

Empty Draw.WMV - YouTube

www.youtube.com

15 - 31 Empty Draw on Vimeo

vimeo.com

August 24, 2020 - YouTube

www.youtube.com

YouTube

www.youtube.com

11 - 8 GUN FADE vs Press on Vimeo

vimeo.com

15 - 36 Gun Triple vs Goalline - HOK BLOCKED on V...

vimeo.com

HAMMER PACKAGE- DOUBLE ISO - YouTube

www.youtube.com

Wide Jack Jet Naked Keep - YouTube

www.youtube.com

Jet Naked on the Goal Line.WMV - YouTube

www.youtube.com

Goal Line and Red Zone (continued)

Play Action Stretch Pass Rt. on Vimeo

vimeo.com

QB ISO - YouTube

www.youtube.com

15 - 43 Red zone Fade on Vimeo

vimeo.com

QUICK GAME-SLICE/CORNER - YouTube

www.youtube.com

TRIPLE SCREEN (Boundary) - YouTube

www.youtube.com

15 - 33 Whirley Gun Triple on Vimeo

vimeo.com

15 - 34 WO Gun Triple Give GIVE on Vimeo

vimeo.com

PLAYACTION - FRONTSIDE POST OUT - YouTube

www.youtube.com

Victory Offense

15 - 53 GUN STUD OPTION VS 44 on Vimeo

vimeo.com

Gun Triple - HOK blocked.WMV - YouTube

www.youtube.com

Made in the USA
Monee, IL
21 November 2024

70747092R00227